A NEW APPROACH TO STUDYING

THE COVENANTS *of* OUR FATHERS

A HARMONY OF GENESIS, MOSES AND ABRAHAM

• • •

ORGANIZED BY EVENTS
EMPHASIZING NARRATORS, SPEAKERS,
LOCATIONS, QUOTED PASSAGES AND
JOSEPH SMITH TRANSLATIONS

• • •

LYNN A. ROSENVALL
DAVID L. ROSENVALL

Published by
THE OLIVE LEAF FOUNDATION
*An Organization Dedicated to the
Development of Innovative Scripture Study Resources*

Annotations and Formatting
© 2017 by The Olive Leaf Foundation.
All rights reserved.

The Pearl of Great Price, The Old Testament
© 1981, 2013 by Intellectual Reserve, Inc.
All rights reserved. Used by Permission.

ISBN 978-0-9987178-1-4
Printed in China
2017

www.StudyTheScriptures.com

BEHOLD, I will reveal unto you the Priesthood, by the hand of Elijah the prophet, before the coming of the great and dreadful day of the Lord. And he shall plant in the hearts of the children the promises [covenants] made to the fathers, and the hearts of the children shall turn to their fathers. If it were not so, the whole earth would be utterly wasted at his coming.

DOCTRINE AND COVENANTS 2:1-3

AN EXPLANATION OF THE
FORMATTING AND ANNOTATIONS

This work is a harmony or merging of the text of the books of Genesis, Moses and Abraham. The scriptural accounts in these three books often parallel or overlap each other, allowing for such an harmonization. The book's central purpose, however, is to emphasize the covenants of God the Father and His Son, Jesus Christ, to the Old Testament prophets and their followers within the time span from Adam to Moses.

JOSEPH SMITH TRANSLATION

In his inspired translation of the Bible, the prophet Joseph Smith made many corrections, additions and deletions to the text of Genesis—more than in all the other books of the Old Testament combined. These changes add substantial information to our understanding of these sacred covenants to the ancient prophets (see the Prologue and the Epilogue). The Joseph Smith Translation, unlike other translations, restores the words of the original author—the equivalent of many pages—to Genesis. For more information, see "Joseph Smith Translation (JST)" in the LDS Bible Dictionary. This study edition would not be complete without the obvious contributions and insights of this inspired translation.

In the LDS scriptures shorter Joseph Smith Translation (JST) changes are provided in the chapter footnotes. Longer passages are placed in the Appendix at the end of the Bible. Because the JST changes in the first six chapters of Genesis (Genesis 1:1 to 6:13) are so numerous and complex, they are published separately in the Pearl of Great Price of the LDS scriptures as the Book of Moses. Thus the chapters of the Book of Moses are the inspired textual replacement for the first six chapters of Genesis with the addition of Moses' face to face encounter with God and the visions that followed (Moses, chapter 1). In this harmony, all the JST text changes, including the complete Book of Moses, are integrated directly within Genesis where they textually belong.

In some chapters or events, the verse numbers of the Joseph Smith Translation do not match the verse numbers of the corresponding text in the King James version. Thus unavoidable versification anomalies may appear in some events. To minimize confusion, longer JST passages are shown with no verse numbers. These missing verse numbers are available within the JST entries in the Appendix of the LDS scriptures. Except in the eight chapters of the Book of Moses, which consist solely of Joseph Smith Translation text, translation changes are indicated with *italicized text*. This allows the reader to readily spot these changes within the text of the standard King James version of Genesis.

ORGANIZED BY EVENTS

To create this work, the text of the books of Genesis, Moses and Abraham was first harmonized chronologically and then divided into events (episodes) rather than chapters. An event-based approach provides an alternate way to read the scripture text without the obvious intrusion of verse and chapter breaks which can obscure the narrative as it was originally written or even the continuity of doctrinal discourses and historic accounts. These events, almost without exception, follow the order of the original chapters they replace.

TEXT FORMATTING AND ANNOTATIONS

To assist the reader, an innovative formatting structure has been applied to the scripture text. After experimenting with several formats, the current structure was selected as best for the desired goal. It was resolved that not one word, letter or even a punctuation mark of the actual verses should be deleted or altered in the process, except as dictated by the Joseph Smith translation changes. Only the formatting has been enhanced by adding margin indents, two type sizes and spaces between textual subdivisions to help the reader more readily follow the scripture narrative. It was further concluded that the names of speakers, locations of events and reference sources by chapter and verse would be beneficial annotations in the margins. These formatting enhancements are designed to help the reader visualize the context, speaker, history and doctrine of the scripture narrative within "space" and "time."

The formatting enhancements are of two types:

1. *Regular Text Size* to indicate an event's prime narration.

Determining the "narrator" of the Book of Moses and Genesis (The First Book of Moses) presents somewhat of a dilemma. One could presuppose that Moses served as the prime narrator. But it should be noted that the narrator, in several places employs the name, "I, the Lord God" (see Moses 4:1, 28-29; 5:1, 40). Thus it appears that the words of the prime narration in the Book of Moses and Genesis are those of the Lord God, and Moses' only role was as a scribe, and indeed the Lord God instructed Moses to "write" the things he shall speak (Moses 1:40). To avoid an unnecessary doctrinal quandary as to whether Moses or a member of the Godhead is the narrator, it was determined to simply call the one providing the narration the "Narrator," rather than attempting to indicate the person by name. In the Book of Abraham, however, Abraham is clearly the narrator. In all events, the text of the prime narration is shown in regular size type and unindented.

2. *Indented and Reduced Text Size* to indicate quoted passages.

The books of Genesis, Moses and Abraham contain substantial material that is quoted directly from others, often the words of God the Father or His son Jesus Christ. In all events the cited text is shown in a smaller type size and slightly indented on the left margin. Moreover, the text often contains quotations within quotations. For example, in Moses 6:53 the narrator quotes Enoch who in turn quotes Adam and the Lord (event 32). All such nested quotations are simply indicated by spaces between the excerpts to set them apart, a wider indentation and the placement of the quoted person's name in the left margin.

The annotations are of three types:

1. *Speaker Names in the Left Margin*

The text in the books of Genesis, Moses and Abraham is remarkably specific in identifying for the reader the actual author or speaker of any given event, verse or quotation. There are only a few instances where one may not be reasonably certain of the speaker's correct identification. This speaker information has been added as a short text heading in the left margin at the beginning of each event and next to every break or verse where a change of speaker occurs. For consistency in event titles and speaker names, we have used the names Abraham and Jacob rather than their alternate names of Abram and Israel. For an explanation of the use of "God," as well as "The Lord God" and "The Lord" as speaker names, see the Prologue.

2. *Scriptural References in the Right Margin*

The reference citation for each scripture segment within a given event has been placed in the right margin. This is essential, especially when an event consists of text from more than one scripture source. To assist the reader, all the scriptural references comprising a given event are shown at the bottom of the event.

3. *Place Names in the Right Margin*

The record keepers provide place names or locational information for nearly all events described in their accounts. In most instances, the location is a specific place, city or land. For some events, however, the location can only be indicated by a less definitive name such as "Egypt" or "Canaan." Where possible we have favored the more common names, such as Haran, Shechem, Bethel and Hebron rather than the little-known regional names of these locations. All these locations, as recorded in the text, have been replicated in the right margin alongside the applicable verses. Each recorded location is carried forward at the top of the right margin of each page until the next location appears in the text. A map showing significant locations has been placed in the Appendix.

ALTERNATE TRANSLATIONS AND MEANINGS

In recent editions of the LDS scriptures, numerous explanations as well as alternate translations and meanings of key words and phrases are provided in the footnotes. It was felt that this information was too important to not be included in this harmony. This information is integrated within the scripture text where it can be readily seen. Longer passages are placed at the end of events and visually linked to the text by an asterisk (*). When placed within the text, these explanations, alternate translations and meanings are shown within [square brackets]. In a few instances, we have placed our own note at the end of a event to clarify anomalies in the text narrative.

HEB An alternate translation from the Hebrew.
IE An explanation of idioms and difficult wording.
OR Alternate words that clarify the meaning of an archaic expression.

Acknowledgements—We express appreciation to The Church of Jesus Christ of Latter-day Saints for providing a license to publish the text of the 2013 edition of the scriptures. Our intention has been to follow the text of the books of Genesis, Moses and Abraham as accurately as possible, but, understandably, the formatting and annotations, in some instances, are based on our best judgment.

We gratefully acknowledge the assistance of all who have helped with verifying the final text.

NAMES AND ORDER OF EVENTS

NOAH

ABRAHAM

ISAAC

JACOB

JOSEPH

MOSES

EPILOGUE

APPENDIX

HARMONY OF EVENTS

THE CREATION

EVENT	ABRAHAM	MOSES	GENESIS	EXODUS
1 Abraham Learns about the Heavens	3:1-21			
2 The Council in Heaven	3:22-28	4:1-4		
3 The First Day of Creation	4:1-5	2:1-5	1:1-5	
4 The Second Day of Creation	4:6-8	2:6-8	1:6-8	
5 The Third Day of Creation	4:9-13	2:9-13	1:9-13	
6 The Fourth Day of Creation	4:14-19	2:14-19	1:14-19	
7 The Fifth Day of Creation	4:20-23	2:20-23	1:20-23	
8 The Sixth Day of Creation	4:24-31	2:24-31	1:24-31	
9 The Seventh Day of Creation	5:1-3	3:1-3	2:1-3	
10 Spiritual Creation Explained	5:4-5	3:4-5	2:4-5	
11 A Mist Waters the Face of the Ground	5:6	3:6	2:6	

ADAM

EVENT	ABRAHAM	MOSES	GENESIS	EXODUS
12 Man Formed from Dust of Earth	5:7	3:7	2:7	
13 A Garden Planted in Eden	5:8-10	3:8-14	2:8-14	
14 Adam and Animals Placed in Garden	5:11-13 5:20-21	3:15-20	2:15-17	
15 The Gods Form a Help Meet for Adam	5:14-19, 21	3:21-25	2:18-25	
16 Satan's Temptations Lead to Fall		4:5-13	3:1-7	
17 The Earth Cursed for Transgression		4:14-25	3:8-22	
18 Adam and Eve Sent Forth from Eden		4:26-32 5:1	3:23-24	
19 Descendants of Adam and Eve Multiply		5:2-3		
20 Adam to Sacrifice Firstlings of Flocks		5:4-12		
21 All Men Commanded to Repent		5:13-15		
22 Cain and Abel Born to Adam and Eve		5:16-27	4:1-7	
23 Satan Persuades Cain to Kill Abel		5:28-41	4:8-15	
24 Cain's Descendants Named		5:42-50	4:16-24	
25 Secret Combinations Prevail		5:51-55		
26 Gospel Preached from the Beginning		5:56-59		
27 Seth Born to Adam and Eve		6:1-4	4:25-26	
28 Book of Remembrance Kept by Adam		6:5-12	5:1-2	
29 Seth's Posterity Down to Enoch Named		6:13-25	5:3-20	

ENOCH

EVENT	ABRAHAM	MOSES	GENESIS	EXODUS
30 Enoch Called to Preach the Gospel		6:26-36		
31 Enoch Explains His Ministry		6:37-46		
32 Enoch Teaches Plan of Salvation		6:47-68 7:1		
33 Enoch Prophesies to the People		7:2-11		
34 Enoch Calls on People to Repent		7:12-17		
35 Enoch's Followers Called Zion		7:18-27		
36 Enoch Shown Wickedness of Man		7:28-40		
37 Enoch Shown Mission of Noah		7:41-46		
38 Enoch Shown Mortal Ministry of Christ		7:47-58		

EVENT	ABRAHAM	MOSES	GENESIS	EXODUS
39 Enoch Shown Second Coming of Christ		7:59-69 8:1		
40 Enoch Begets Methuselah		8:2-7	5:21-27	

NOAH

EVENT	ABRAHAM	MOSES	GENESIS	EXODUS
41 Lemech Begets Noah		8:8-14	5:28-32	
42 Noah Called to Preach Repentance		8:15-24	6:1-10	
43 The Lord Vows to Destroy All Flesh		8:25-27	6:11-13	
44 Noah Commanded to Build Ark		8:28-30	6:14-22	
45 Noah's Family and Animals Enter Ark			7:1-16	
46 Flood Destroys Many Forms of Life			7:17-24	
47 Waters Recede off Face of Earth			8:1-14	
48 Noah's Family and Animals Leave Ark			8:15-22	
49 Noah's Family Commanded to Multiply			9:1-7	
50 God Covenants with Noah's Seed			9:8-17	
51 Noah's Descendants Multiply			9:18-29	
52 Descendants of Noah's Sons Named			10:1-32	
53 The Lord Confounds the Language			11:1-9	

ABRAHAM

EVENT	ABRAHAM	MOSES	GENESIS	EXODUS
54 Abraham's Lineage from Shem Named			11:10-27	
55 Abraham Seeks Blessings of the Fathers	1:1-7			
56 Pharaoh's Priests Try to Slay Abraham	1:8-14			
57 The Lord Saves Abraham from Priests	1:15-19			
58 Records Preserved by Abraham	1:20-31			
59 Abraham Leaves Ur to Settle in Canaan	2:1-5		11:28-32 12:1	
60 The Lord Blesses Abraham's Posterity	2:6-13		12:2-3	
61 The Lord Appears to Abraham at Bethel	2:14-20		12:4-8	
62 Abraham Journeys Down to Egypt	2:21-25		12:9-13	
63 Abraham Encounters Pharaoh in Egypt			12:14-20	
64 Abraham Returns to Land of Bethel			13:1-4	
65 Abraham and Lot Go Separate Ways			13:5-13	
66 Abraham Dwells in Land of Hebron			13:14-18	
67 Abraham Rescues Lot from Captivity			14:1-17	
68 Abraham Pays Tithes to Melchizedek			14:18-24	
69 Abraham Promised Numerous Posterity			15:1-11	
70 Abraham's Seed Promised a Vast Land			15:12-21	
71 Sarai Gives Hagar to Abraham as a Wife			16:1-9	
72 Hagar Bares Ishmael, Abraham's Son			16:10-16	
73 Abram's Name Changed to Abraham			17:1-8	
74 Circumcision, Token of God's Covenant			17:9-14	
75 Sarai Promised a Son			17:15-22	
76 Men of Abraham's House Circumcised			17:23-27	
77 The Lord and Angels Visit Abraham			18:1-22	
78 Fate of Sodom and Gomorrah Declared			18:23-33	
79 Angels Warn Lot to Flee Sodom			19:1-22	
80 Fire Rains upon Sodom and Gomorrah			19:23-29	
81 Lot's Daughters Preserve Their Seed			19:30-38	
82 Abraham Prays for Abimelech			20:1-18	
83 Sarah Bares Isaac, Abraham's Son			21:1-8	
84 Hagar's Son Ishmael Saved From Death			21:9-21	
85 Abraham and Abimelech Reconcile			21:22-34	
86 Abraham Commanded to Sacrifice Isaac			22:1-19	

Event	Abraham	Moses	Genesis	Exodus
87 Rebekah Born to Nahor's Daughter			22:20-24	
88 Sarah Buried in Cave of Machpelah			23:1-20	

ISAAC

Event	Abraham	Moses	Genesis	Exodus
89 Servant Seeks Wife for Isaac			24:1-9	
90 Servant Guided to Rebekah			24:10-28	
91 Servant Relates His Errand to Family			24:29-52	
92 Rebekah Agrees to Return with Servant			24:53-61	
93 Rebekah Becomes Isaac's Wife			24:62-67	
94 Abraham Buried in Cave of Machpelah			25:1-11	
95 Ishmael's Descendants Named			25:12-18	
96 Rebekah Bares Twins, Esau and Jacob			25:19-26	
97 Esau Sells His Birthright to Jacob			25:27-34	
98 The Lord Prospers Isaac			26:1-25	
99 Isaac and Abimelech Make Covenant			26:26-33	
100 Esau Takes Judith, a Hittite, to Wife			26:34-35	

JACOB

Event	Abraham	Moses	Genesis	Exodus
101 Rebekah Leads Isaac in Jacob's Blessing			27:1-29	
102 As Firstborn, Esau Desires a Blessing			27:30-40	
103 Esau Purposes to Slay Jacob			27:41-45	
104 Jacob Seeks Wife of Laban's Daughters			27:46	
			28:1-5	
105 Esau Marries a Daughter of Ishmael			28:6-9	
106 The Lord Blesses Jacob			28:10-15	
107 Jacob Vows to Give Tenth of his Goods			28:16-22	
108 Jacob Meets Rachel in Haran			29:1-14	
109 Jacob Serves Laban Seven Years			29:15-20	
110 Jacob Required to First Marry Leah			29:21-24	
111 Jacob Serves More Years for Rachel			29:25-30	
112 Leah Bares Four Sons			29:31-35	
113 Jacob Marries Bilhah and Zilpah			30:1-13	
114 Leah Bares More Sons and a Daughter			30:14-21	
115 Rachel Bares a Son Named Joseph			30:22-24	
116 Jacob and Laban Divide Their Flocks			30:25-43	
117 Jacob Returns to Canaan			31:1-16	
118 Laban Accuses Jacob of Stealing Images			31:17-42	
119 Jacob and Laban Make Covenant			31:43-55	
120 Jacob Fears Meeting Esau			32:1-23	
121 Jacob's Name to Be Changed to Israel			32:24-32	
122 Jacob and Esau Reconcile			33:1-15	
123 Jacob Settles at Shechem in Canaan			33:16-20	
124 Shechem, a Hivite, Defiles Dinah			34:1-24	
125 Simeon and Levi Revenge Defilement			34:25-31	
126 God Directs Jacob to Bethel			35:1-8	
127 God Gives Jacob the Name of Israel			35:9-15	
128 Rachel Travails and Bares Benjamin			35:16-18	
129 Rachel Buried Near Bethlehem			35:19-20	
130 Jacob's Twelve Sons Named			35:21-26	
131 Isaac Dies and Buried in Hebron			35:27-29	
132 Descendants of Esau Named			36:1-43	

JOSEPH

EVENT	ABRAHAM	MOSES	GENESIS	EXODUS
133 Jacob Favors Joseph			37:1-4	
134 Joseph Dreams Family Will Obey Him			37:5-11	
135 Joseph Sold to Ishmeelite Merchants			37:12-28	
136 Jacob Told Joseph Was Killed by Beasts			37:29-36	
137 Shuah Bares Judah Three Sons			38:1-5	
138 Tamar Bares Judah Twin Sons			38:6-30	
139 Joseph Becomes Potiphar's Overseer			39:1-6	
140 Joseph Resists Potiphar's Wife			39:7-19	
141 Joseph Placed in Prison			39:20-23	
142 Joseph Interprets Two Dreams			40:1-19	
143 Pharaoh's Chief Baker Hanged			40:20-23	
144 Pharaoh Dreams of Kine and Corn			41:1-13	
145 Pharaoh Calls Joseph to Interpret Dream			41:14-24	
146 Joseph Interprets Pharaoh's Dream			41:25-36	
147 Joseph Placed Over Land of Egypt			41:37-44	
148 Joseph Marries Asenath and Stores Food			41:45-49	
149 Asenath Bares Manasseh and Ephraim			41:50-52	
150 During Famine, Joseph Provides Food			41:53-57	
151 Jacob Sends Sons to Buy Grain in Egypt			42:1-13	
152 Brothers to Prove They Are Not Spies			42:14-20	
153 Joseph Sends Grain to Jacob			42:21-28	
154 Brothers to Return With Benjamin			42:29-38	
155 Jacob Allows Benjamin Go to Egypt			43:1-14	
156 Brothers Dine With Joseph			43:15-34	
157 Joseph Hinders Return to Hebron			44:1-13	
158 Judah Offered as Benjamin's Bondsman			44:14-34	
159 Joseph Reveals Himself to His Brothers			45:1-15	
160 Pharaoh Invites Jacob's Family to Egypt			45:16-28	
161 God Sends Jacob's Family to Egypt			46:1-7	
162 Jacob's Descendants in Egypt Named			46:8-27	
163 Joseph Meets His Father and Weeps			46:28-34	
164 Jacob's Family Settles in Goshen			47:1-6	
165 Jacob Meets Pharaoh and Blesses Him			47:7-12	
166 Joseph Challenged by Famine			47:13-26	
167 Jacob Requests Burial in Canaan			47:27-31	
168 Jacob Claims Joseph's Two Sons as His			48:1-7	
169 Jacob Sets Ephraim Before Manasseh			48:8-22	
170 Jacob Blesses Sons and Predicts Future			49:1-28	
171 Jacob Dies In Egypt			49:29-33	
172 Many Return to Canaan to Bury Jacob			50:1-13	
173 Joseph Forgives His Brothers			50:14-21	
174 Joseph Foresees Moses and Joseph Smith			50:22-26	

MOSES

EVENT	ABRAHAM	MOSES	GENESIS	EXODUS
175 Children of Israel Multiply in Egypt				1:1-7
176 Taskmasters Afflict Israelites				1:8-14
177 Pharaoh Seeks to Destroy Israelite Sons				1:15-22
178 Moses Born to Levite Family				2:1-10
179 Moses Marries Zipporah				2:11-22
180 Israelites Pray for Relief				2:23-25
181 Moses Sees and Talks with God				3:1-6
182 Moses Shown Works of God		1:1-8		
183 Satan Appears and Tempts Moses		1:9-23		

Event	Abraham	Moses	Genesis	Exodus
184 Moses to Deliver Israel from Bondage		1:24-26		
185 Moses Shown in Vision Many Earths		1:27-35		
186 Moses Shown in Vision This Earth		1:36-42		

KEY TO TEXT ADDITIONS AND CHANGES

The Joseph Smith Translation (JST) additions and changes are indicated with *italicized text*, with the exception of the Book of Moses where the entire text is from the Joseph Smith Translation.

The following explanations from the footnotes of the books of Genesis, Moses and Abraham are placed in the text with [square brackets].

> Alternate translations from the Hebrew.
> Explanations of idioms and difficult wording.
> Alternate words that clarify the meaning of archaic expressions.

Longer explanations are placed at the end of events and visually linked to the text by an asterisk (*).

PROLOGUE
THE COVENANTS OF OUR FATHERS

A gospel covenant is an agreement between God the Father and His children. God sets the terms of the agreement and His children can accept or reject them. From the time of Adam until now God has covenanted with the prophets and followers of righteousness that they may inherit all that He has and "be made partakers of the glories" by gaining exaltation and eternal life. This comprehensive covenant is called the New and Everlasting Covenant. It is everlasting because it began with Adam and it is new because it has been renewed in our day as part of the restoration of the gospel. This covenant includes individual covenants such as those associated with baptism, the receiving of the Melchizedek priesthood, temple ordinances and eternal marriage. The Lord declared this everlasting covenant as the "fulness of [His] gospel," or the sum of all gospel covenants:

> Verily I say unto you, blessed are you for receiving mine everlasting covenant, even the fulness of my gospel, sent forth unto the children of men, that they might have life and be made partakers of the glories which are to be revealed in the last days, as it was written by the prophets and apostles in days of old. (Doctrine and Covenants 66:2)

God also confirmed other individual covenants with the early prophets, known as "the fathers" (Doctrine and Covenants 2:2). For example, when Abraham was promised exaltation and eternal life, he was also promised these blessings would be offered to his numerous posterity (or children), along with the inheritance of certain lands (Abraham 2:6-11; event 60). These covenants and promises are among those referred to as the Abrahamic Covenant. Likewise, Enoch and Noah were promised that the earth would never again be cursed with a flood (Genesis 9:8-17; see also JST Genesis 9:21-25; event 50). God provides tokens (or reminders) to help those who have entered into a covenant to remember the promises of the covenant. The rainbow was a token of the covenant that the earth would never again be destroyed by a flood (Genesis 9:13; event 50).

JOSEPH SMITH TRANSLATION

Unfortunately, much of the text describing these covenants between God and the prophets has been deleted from the Bible, including the King James version. This contemptible act was described by an angel of the Lord to the prophet Nephi:

> And after they [the books of the Bible] go forth by the hand of the twelve apostles of the Lamb, from the Jews unto the Gentiles, thou seest the formation of that great and abominable church, which is most abominable above all other churches; for behold, they have taken away from the gospel of the Lamb many parts which are plain and most precious; and also many covenants of the Lord have they taken away. (1 Nephi 13:26)

Thankfully these deleted biblical passages, including several additional accounts of the covenants, were restored in the Joseph Smith Translation (JST). To assist the reader in understanding these essential covenants, this harmony includes these JST changes and additions.

CHRONOLOGICAL ORDER OF THE HARMONY

The books of Genesis, Moses and Abraham contain accounts of God's everlasting covenant with Adam, Enoch, Noah, Abraham, Isaac, Jacob, Joseph and Moses. This covenant is the common theme throughout the scriptural text of these three books. To highlight this covenant, the harmony is organized in chronological order with a separate section for each of the eight prophets (or patriarchal fathers). We note the visions of Moses are recorded in the first chapter of the Book of Moses. These visions were received by Moses—the last of the eight prophets—later in his life and are out of chronological order with the events that follow in the Book of Moses such as the earlier historical accounts of the dispensations of Adam, Enoch and Noah. In this harmony, the visions of Moses are placed chronologically at the end, within the section that pertains to his life.

SPEAKER NAMES

The text of the books of Genesis, Moses and Abraham is remarkably specific in providing names of the authors or speakers of quoted passages or verses. One special case, however, concerns the names of Deity as represented by the term "God," as well as the phrases "The Lord" and "The Lord God." When Deity is speaking in the text one could assume these words refer to the same person of the Godhead, namely Jesus Christ, the God of the Old Testament. A careful reading of the text, however, leads us to suggest that both God the Father and His Son, Jesus Christ, were the speakers of many quoted passages, often within the same event. This is not unlike Joseph Smith's first vision when both members of the Godhead spoke to him. In this harmony, the speaker names of Deity shown in the left margin are the same as the names recorded within the associated text. We suggest the identification of these names consistently follows a pattern—a pattern that is confirmed in the names selected by the narrators:

> The term "God" refers to God the Father.
> The phrase "The Lord God" also refers to God the Father.
> The phrase "The Lord" refers to His Son, The Lord Jesus Christ.

These suggested meanings of the words for Deity match well with the context of all events, except event two, which contains two minor variations from this naming pattern (see Abraham 3:27). We note with interest that within the events that occurred before the time when Adam and Eve were sent forth out of the garden of Eden (event 18), the narration uses such phrases as "and I the Lord God said" or "I God said" (see Moses 4:26-32; 5:1). After Adam and Eve leave the garden (event 19), the narration changes grammatically from first person to third person by using such phrases as "and God said" or "the Lord said."

For additional information on the structure of the harmony, see the section, "An Explanation of the Formatting and Annotations."

THE CREATION

WE will go down, for there is space there, and we will take of these materials, and we will make an earth whereon these may dwell; And we will prove them herewith, to see if they will do all things whatsoever the Lord their God shall command them; And they who keep their first estate shall be added upon; and they who keep not their first estate shall not have glory in the same kingdom with those who keep their first estate; and they who keep their second estate shall have glory added upon their heads for ever and ever.

ABRAHAM 3:24-26

ABRAHAM LEARNS ABOUT THE HEAVENS
[1]

Abraham   AND I, Abraham, had the Urim and Thummim, which the   Abr. 3:1-21
Lord my God had given unto me, in Ur of the Chaldees;
2 And I saw the stars, that they were very great, and that one
of them was nearest unto the throne of God; and there were
many great ones which were near unto it; 3 And the Lord
said unto me:

The Lord   These are the governing ones; and the name of the great one is
Kolob, because it is near unto me, for I am the Lord thy God: I
have set this one to govern all those which belong to the same
order as that upon which thou standest.

Abraham   4 And the Lord said unto me, by the Urim and Thummim,
that Kolob was after the manner of the Lord, according to its
times and seasons in the revolutions thereof; that one
revolution was a day unto the Lord, after his manner of
reckoning, it being one thousand years according to the time
appointed unto that whereon thou standest. This is the
reckoning of the Lord's time, according to the reckoning of
Kolob. 5 And the Lord said unto me:

The Lord   The planet which is the lesser light, lesser than that which is to rule
the day, even the night, is above or greater* than that upon which
thou standest in point of reckoning, for it moveth in order more
slow; this is in order because it standeth above the earth upon
which thou standest, therefore the reckoning of its time is not so
many as to its number of days, and of months, and of years.

Abraham   6 And the Lord said unto me:

The Lord   Now, Abraham, these two facts exist, behold thine eyes see it; it is
given unto thee to know the times of reckoning, and the set time,
yea, the set time of the earth upon which thou standest, and the set
time of the greater light which is set to rule the day, and the set
time of the lesser light which is set to rule the night. 7 Now the set
time of the lesser light is a longer time as to its reckoning than the
reckoning of the time of the earth upon which thou standest. 8 And
where these two facts exist, there shall be another fact above them,
that is, there shall be another planet whose reckoning of time shall
be longer still; 9 And thus there shall be the reckoning of the time
of one planet above another, until thou come nigh unto Kolob,
which Kolob is after the reckoning of the Lord's time; which
Kolob is set nigh unto the throne of God, to govern all those
planets which belong to the same order as that upon which thou
standest. 10 And it is given unto thee to know the set time of all the
stars that are set to give light, until thou come near unto the throne
of God.

Abraham   11 Thus I, Abraham, talked with the Lord, face to face, as
one man talketh with another; and he told me of the works
which his hands had made; 12 And he said unto me:

The Lord	My son, my son (and his hand was stretched out), behold I will show you all these.

Abr. 3:1-21

Abraham And he put his hand upon mine eyes, and I saw those things which his hands had made, which were many; and they multiplied before mine eyes, and I could not see the end thereof. 13 And he said unto me:

The Lord   This is Shinehah, which is the sun.

Abraham And he said unto me:

The Lord   Kokob, which is star.

Abraham And he said unto me:

The Lord   Olea, which is the moon.

Abraham And he said unto me:

The Lord   Kokaubeam, which signifies stars, or all the great lights, which were in the firmament of heaven.

Abraham 14 And it was in the night time when the Lord spake these words unto me:

The Lord   I will multiply thee, and thy seed after thee, like unto these; and if thou canst count the number of sands, so shall be the number of thy seeds.

Abraham 15 And the Lord said unto me:

The Lord   Abraham, I show these things unto thee before ye go into Egypt, that ye may declare all these words. 16 If two things exist, and there be one above the other, there shall be greater things above them; therefore Kolob is the greatest of all the Kokaubeam that thou hast seen, because it is nearest unto me. 17 Now, if there be two things, one above the other, and the moon be above the earth, then it may be that a planet or a star may exist above it; and there is nothing that the Lord thy God shall take in his heart to do but what he will do it.

18 Howbeit that he made the greater star; as, also, if there be two spirits, and one shall be more intelligent than the other, yet these two spirits, notwithstanding one is more intelligent than the other, have no beginning; they existed before, they shall have no end, they shall exist after, for they are gnolaum**, or eternal.

Abraham 19 And the Lord said unto me:

The Lord   These two facts do exist, that there are two spirits, one being more intelligent than the other; there shall be another more intelligent than they; I am the Lord thy God, I am more intelligent than they all. 20 The Lord thy God sent his angel to deliver thee from the hands of the priest of Elkenah. 21 I dwell in the midst of them all; I now, therefore, have come down unto thee to declare unto thee the works which my hands have made, wherein my wisdom excelleth them all, for I rule in the heavens above, and in the earth beneath,

The Lord   in all wisdom and prudence, over all the intelligences thine eyes   Abr. 3:1-21
             have seen from the beginning; I came down in the beginning in the
             midst of all the intelligences thou hast seen.

Reference: Abr. 3:1-21

* It rotates on its axis more slowly. See also v. 7.

** *Gnolaum* is a transliteration of a Hebrew word meaning eternal.

THE COUNCIL IN HEAVEN

[2]

Abraham · NOW the Lord had shown unto me, Abraham, the intelligences that were organized before the world was; and among all these there were many of the noble and great ones; 23 And God saw these souls that they were good, and he stood in the midst of them, and he said:

Abr. 3:22-28

God · These I will make my rulers;

Abraham · for he stood among those that were spirits, and he saw that they were good; and he said unto me:

God · Abraham, thou art one of them; thou wast chosen before thou wast born.

Abraham · 24 And there stood one among them that was like unto God, and he said unto those who were with him:

The Lord · We will go down, for there is space there, and we will take of these materials, and we will make an earth whereon these may dwell; 25 And we will prove them herewith, to see if they will do all things whatsoever the Lord their God shall command them; 26 And they who keep their first estate shall be added upon; and they who keep not their first estate shall not have glory in the same kingdom with those who keep their first estate; and they who keep their second estate shall have glory added upon their heads for ever and ever.

Abraham · 27 And the Lord [God] said:

God · Whom shall I send?

Abraham · And one answered like unto the Son of Man:

The Lord · Here am I, send me.

Abraham · And another answered and said:

Satan · Here am I, send me.

Abraham · And the Lord [God] said:

God · I will send the first.

Abraham · 28 And the second was angry, and kept not his first estate; and, at that day, many followed after him.

God · 1 AND I, the Lord God, spake unto Moses, saying:

Moses 4:1-4

That Satan, whom thou hast commanded in the name of mine Only Begotten, is the same which was from the beginning, and he came before me, saying—

Satan · Behold, here am I, send me, I will be thy son, and I will redeem all mankind, that one soul shall not be lost, and surely I will do it; wherefore give me thine honor.

God	2 But, behold, my Beloved Son, which was my Beloved and Chosen from the beginning, said unto me—	Moses 4:1-4

The Lord   Father, thy will be done, and the glory be thine forever.

God   3 Wherefore, because that Satan rebelled against me, and sought to destroy the agency of man, which I, the Lord God, had given him, and also, that I should give unto him mine own power; by the power of mine Only Begotten, I caused that he should be cast down; 4 And he became Satan, yea, even the devil, the father of all lies, to deceive and to blind men, and to lead them captive at his will, even as many as would not hearken unto my voice.

———————

References: Abr. 3:22-28; Moses 4:1-4

Note: The context of Abraham 3:27 implies that God the Father is the speaker. See Prologue for an explanation of the various names of Diety that appear in the text.

THE FIRST DAY OF CREATION
[3]

Moses Account

Narrator   AND it came to pass that the Lord spake unto Moses, saying: Moses 2:1-5

The Lord   Behold, I reveal unto you concerning this heaven, and this earth; write the words which I speak.

God   I am the Beginning and the End, the Almighty God; by mine Only Begotten I created these things; yea, in the beginning I created the heaven, and the earth upon which thou standest.

2 And the earth was without form, and void; and I caused darkness to come up upon the face of the deep; and my Spirit moved upon the face of the water; for I am God. 3 And I, God, said:

Let there be light;

and there was light. 4 And I, God, saw the light; and that light was good. And I, God, divided the light from the darkness. 5 And I, God, called the light Day; and the darkness, I called Night; and this I did by the word of my power, and it was done as I spake; and the evening and the morning were the first day*.

Abraham Account

Abraham   1 And then the Lord said: Abr. 4:1-4

The Lord   Let us go down.

Abraham   And they went down at the beginning, and they, that is the Gods, organized and formed the heavens and the earth.

2 And the earth, after it was formed, was empty and desolate, because they had not formed anything but the earth; and darkness reigned upon the face of the deep, and the Spirit of the Gods was brooding upon the face of the waters. 3 And they (the Gods) said:

The Gods   Let there be light;

Abraham   and there was light. 4 And they (the Gods) comprehended the light, for it was bright; and they divided the light, or caused it to be divided, from the darkness. 5 And the Gods called the light Day, and the darkness they called Night.

Abraham   And it came to pass that from the evening until morning   Abr. 4:1-4
they called night; and from the morning until the evening
they called day; and this was the first, or the beginning, of
that which they called day and night.

References: Moses 2:1-5; Abr. 4:1-5; Gen. 1:1-5

* The Abraham account of the creation periods uses the term "time"
rather than "day" (see, for example, Abr. 4:8).

THE SECOND DAY OF CREATION
[4]

Moses Account

God   AND again, I, God, said: Moses 2:6-8

Let there be a firmament in the midst of the water,

and it was so, even as I spake; and I said:

Let it divide the waters from the waters;

and it was done; 7 And I, God, made the firmament and divided the waters, yea, the great waters under the firmament from the waters which were above the firmament, and it was so even as I spake. 8 And I, God, called the firmament Heaven*; and the evening and the morning were the second day.

Abraham Account

Abraham   6 And the Gods also said: Abr. 4:6-8

The Gods   Let there be an expanse in the midst of the waters, and it shall divide the waters from the waters.

Abraham   7 And the Gods ordered the expanse, so that it divided the waters which were under the expanse from the waters which were above the expanse; and it was so, even as they ordered. 8 And the Gods called the expanse, Heaven.

And it came to pass that it was from evening until morning that they called night; and it came to pass that it was from morning until evening that they called day; and this was the second time that they called night and day.

References: Moses 2:6-8; Abr. 4:6-8; Gen. 1:6-8

* The whole expanse around about the earth, its atmosphere, and beyond are generically here called "Heaven." The same word is also used sometimes to refer to paradise, to the dwelling place of God, and to the kingdoms of glory.

THE THIRD DAY OF CREATION
[5]

Moses Account

God   AND I, God, said: Moses 2:9-13

> Let the waters under the heaven be gathered together unto one place,

and it was so; and I, God, said:

> Let there be dry land;

and it was so. 10 And I, God, called the dry land Earth*; and the gathering together of the waters, called I the Sea; and I, God, saw that all things which I had made were good. 11 And I, God, said:

> Let the earth bring forth grass, the herb yielding seed, the fruit tree yielding fruit, after his kind, and the tree yielding fruit, whose seed should be in itself upon the earth,

and it was so even as I spake. 12 And the earth brought forth grass, every herb yielding seed after his kind, and the tree yielding fruit, whose seed should be in itself, after his kind; and I, God, saw that all things which I had made were good; 13 And the evening and the morning were the third day.

Abraham Account

Abraham   9 And the Gods ordered, saying: Abr. 4:9-13

The Gods
> Let the waters under the heaven be gathered together unto one place, and let the earth come up dry;

Abraham   and it was so as they ordered; 10 And the Gods pronounced the dry land, Earth; and the gathering together of the waters, pronounced they, Great Waters; and the Gods saw that they were obeyed. 11 And the Gods said:

The Gods
> Let us prepare the earth to bring forth grass; the herb yielding seed; the fruit tree yielding fruit, after his kind, whose seed in itself yieldeth its own likeness upon the earth;

Abraham   and it was so, even as they ordered. 12 And the Gods organized the earth to bring forth grass from its own seed, and the herb to bring forth herb from its own seed, yielding seed after his kind; and the earth to bring forth the tree from its own seed, yielding fruit, whose seed could only bring forth the same in itself, after his kind; and the Gods saw that they were obeyed.

Abraham   13 And it came to pass that they numbered the days; from the evening until the morning they called night; and it came to pass, from the morning until the evening they called day; and it was the third time.   Abr. 4:9-13

References: Moses 2:9-13; Abr. 4:9-13; Gen. 1:9-13

* The whole sphere or any of its parts above the seas is called "Earth."

THE FOURTH DAY OF CREATION
[6]

Moses Account

God AND I, God, said: Moses 2:14-19

Let there be lights in the firmament of the heaven, to divide the day from the night, and let them be for signs, and for seasons, and for days, and for years; 15 And let them be for lights in the firmament of the heaven to give light upon the earth;

and it was so. 16 And I, God, made two great lights; the greater light to rule the day, and the lesser light to rule the night, and the greater light was the sun, and the lesser light was the moon; and the stars also were made even according to my word. 17 And I, God, set them in the firmament of the heaven to give light upon the earth, 18 And the sun to rule over the day, and the moon to rule over the night, and to divide the light from the darkness; and I, God, saw that all things which I had made were good; 19 And the evening and the morning were the fourth day.

———

Abraham Account

Abraham 14 And the Gods organized the lights in the expanse of the   Abr. 4:14-19
heaven, and caused them to divide the day from the night; and organized them to be for signs and for seasons, and for days and for years; 15 And organized them to be for lights in the expanse of the heaven to give light upon the earth; and it was so.

16 And the Gods organized the two great lights, the greater light to rule the day, and the lesser light to rule the night; with the lesser light they set the stars also; 17 And the Gods set them in the expanse of the heavens, to give light upon the earth, and to rule over the day and over the night, and to cause to divide the light from the darkness. 18 And the Gods watched those things which they had ordered until they obeyed.

19 And it came to pass that it was from evening until morning that it was night; and it came to pass that it was from morning until evening that it was day; and it was the fourth time.

———

References: Moses 2:14-19; Abr. 4:14-19; Gen. 1:14-19

THE FIFTH DAY OF CREATION
[7]

Moses Account

God   AND I, God, said: Moses 2:20-23

> Let the waters bring forth abundantly the moving creature that hath life, and fowl which may fly above the earth in the open firmament of heaven.

21 And I, God, created great whales, and every living creature that moveth, which the waters brought forth abundantly, after their kind, and every winged fowl after his kind; and I, God, saw that all things which I had created were good. 22 And I, God, blessed them, saying:

> Be fruitful, and multiply, and fill the waters in the sea; and let fowl multiply in the earth;

23 And the evening and the morning were the fifth day.

Abraham Account

Abraham   20 And the Gods said: Abr. 4:20-23

The Gods   Let us prepare the waters to bring forth abundantly the moving creatures that have life; and the fowl, that they may fly above the earth in the open expanse of heaven.

Abraham   21 And the Gods prepared the waters that they might bring forth great whales, and every living creature that moveth, which the waters were to bring forth abundantly after their kind; and every winged fowl after their kind. And the Gods saw that they would be obeyed, and that their plan was good. 22 And the Gods said:

The Gods   We will bless them, and cause them to be fruitful and multiply, and fill the waters in the seas or great waters; and cause the fowl to multiply in the earth.

Abraham   23 And it came to pass that it was from evening until morning that they called night; and it came to pass that it was from morning until evening that they called day; and it was the fifth time.

References: Moses 2:20-23; Abr. 4:20-23; Gen. 1:20-23

THE SIXTH DAY OF CREATION
[8]

Moses Account

God   AND I, God, said: Moses 2:24-31

> Let the earth bring forth the living creature after his kind, cattle, and creeping things, and beasts of the earth after their kind,

and it was so; 25 And I, God, made the beasts of the earth after their kind, and cattle after their kind, and everything which creepeth upon the earth after his kind; and I, God, saw that all these things were good. 26 And I, God, said unto mine Only Begotten, which was with me from the beginning:

> Let us make man in our image, after our likeness;

and it was so. And I, God, said:

> Let them have dominion over the fishes of the sea, and over the fowl of the air, and over the cattle, and over all the earth, and over every creeping thing that creepeth upon the earth.

27 And I, God, created man in mine own image, in the image of mine Only Begotten created I him; male and female created I them. 28 And I, God, blessed them, and said unto them:

> Be fruitful, and multiply, and replenish the earth, and subdue it, and have dominion over the fish of the sea, and over the fowl of the air, and over every living thing that moveth upon the earth.

29 And I, God, said unto man:

> Behold, I have given you every herb bearing seed, which is upon the face of all the earth, and every tree in the which shall be the fruit of a tree yielding seed; to you it shall be for meat. 30 And to every beast of the earth, and to every fowl of the air, and to everything that creepeth upon the earth, wherein I grant life, there shall be given every clean herb for meat;

and it was so, even as I spake. 31 And I, God, saw everything that I had made, and, behold, all things which I had made were very good; and the evening and the morning were the sixth day.

Abraham Account

Abraham   24 And the Gods prepared the earth to bring forth the living   Abr. 4:24-31
creature after his kind, cattle and creeping things, and beasts of the earth after their kind; and it was so, as they had said. 25 And the Gods organized the earth to bring forth the beasts

Abraham   after their kind, and cattle after their kind, and every thing   Abr. 4:24-31
that creepeth upon the earth after its kind; and the Gods saw
they would obey. 26 And the Gods took counsel among
themselves and said:

The Gods   Let us go down and form man in our image, after our likeness; and
we will give them dominion over the fish of the sea, and over the
fowl of the air, and over the cattle, and over all the earth, and over
every creeping thing that creepeth upon the earth.

Abraham   27 So the Gods went down to organize man in their own
image, in the image of the Gods to form they him, male and
female to form they them. 28 And the Gods said:

The Gods   We will bless them.

Abraham   And the Gods said:

The Gods   We will cause them to be fruitful and multiply, and replenish the
earth, and subdue it, and to have dominion over the fish of the sea,
and over the fowl of the air, and over every living thing that
moveth upon the earth.

Abraham   29 And the Gods said:

The Gods   Behold, we will give them every herb bearing seed that shall come
upon the face of all the earth, and every tree which shall have fruit
upon it; yea, the fruit of the tree yielding seed to them we will give
it; it shall be for their meat. 30 And to every beast of the earth, and
to every fowl of the air, and to every thing that creepeth upon the
earth, behold, we will give them life, and also we will give to them
every green herb for meat, and all these things shall be thus
organized.

Abraham   31 And the Gods said:

The Gods   We will do everything that we have said, and organize them; and
behold, they shall be very obedient.

Abraham   And it came to pass that it was from evening until morning
they called night; and it came to pass that it was from
morning until evening that they called day; and they
numbered the sixth time.

References: Moses 2:24-31; Abr. 4:24-31; Gen. 1:24-31

THE SEVENTH DAY OF CREATION
[9]

Moses Account

God   THUS the heaven and the earth were finished, and all the host   Moses 3:1-3
of them. 2 And on the seventh day I, God, ended my work,
and all things which I had made; and I rested on the seventh
day from all my work, and all things which I had made were
finished, and I, God, saw that they were good; 3 And I, God,
blessed the seventh day, and sanctified it; because that in it I
had rested from all my work which I, God, had created and
made.

Abraham Account

Abraham   1 And thus we will finish the heavens and the earth, and all   Abr. 5:1-3
the hosts of them. 2 And the Gods said among themselves:

The Gods   On the seventh time we will end our work, which we have
counseled; and we will rest on the seventh time from all our work
which we have counseled.

Abraham   3 And the Gods concluded upon the seventh time, because
that on the seventh time they would rest from all their works
which they (the Gods) counseled among themselves to form;
and sanctified it. And thus were their decisions at the time
that they counseled among themselves to form the heavens
and the earth.

References: Moses 3:1-3; Abr. 5:1-3; Gen. 2:1-3

SPIRITUAL CREATION EXPLAINED
[10]

Moses Account

God   AND now, behold, I say unto you, that these are the   Moses 3:4-5
generations of the heaven and of the earth, when they were
created, in the day that I, the Lord God, made the heaven
and the earth, 5 And every plant of the field before it was in
the earth, and every herb of the field before it grew. For I,
the Lord God, created all things, of which I have spoken,
spiritually, before they were naturally upon the face of the
earth. For I, the Lord God, had not caused it to rain upon the
face of the earth. And I, the Lord God, had created all the
children of men; and not yet a man to till the ground; for in
heaven created I them; and there was not yet flesh upon the
earth, neither in the water, neither in the air;

Abraham Account

Abraham   4 And the Gods came down and formed these the   Abr. 5:4-5
generations of the heavens and of the earth, when they were
formed in the day that the Gods formed the earth and the
heavens, 5 According to all that which they had said
concerning every plant of the field before it was in the earth,
and every herb of the field before it grew; for the Gods had
not caused it to rain upon the earth when they counseled to
do them, and had not formed a man to till the ground.

References: Moses 3:4-5; Abr. 5:4-5; Gen. 2:4-5

A MIST WATERS THE FACE OF THE GROUND
[11]

Moses Account

God   BUT I, the Lord God, spake, and there went up a mist from   Moses 3:6
the earth, and watered the whole face of the ground.

———————

Abraham Account

Abraham   6 But there went up a mist from the earth, and watered the   Abr. 5:6
whole face of the ground.

———————

References: Moses 3:6; Abr. 5:6; Gen. 2:6

ADAM

ADAM ... was carried down into the water, and was laid under the water, and was brought forth out of the water ... and the Spirit of God descended upon him, and thus he was born of the Spirit ... and he heard a voice out of heaven, saying: Thou art baptized with fire, and with the Holy Ghost. This is the record of the Father, and the Son, from henceforth and forever; and thou art after the order of him who was without beginning of days or end of years, from all eternity to all eternity. Behold, thou art one in me, a son of God; and thus may all become my sons.

MOSES 6:64-68

MAN FORMED FROM DUST OF EARTH
[12]

Moses Account

God AND I, the Lord God, formed man from the dust of the   Moses 3:7
ground, and breathed into his nostrils the breath of life; and
man became a living soul, the first flesh upon the earth, the
first man also; nevertheless, all things were before created;
but spiritually were they created and made according to my
word.

Abraham Account

Abraham 7 And the Gods formed man from the dust of the ground,   Abr. 5:7
and took his spirit (that is, the man's spirit), and put it into
him; and breathed into his nostrils the breath of life, and
man became a living soul.

References: Moses 3:7; Abr. 5:7; Gen. 2:7

A GARDEN PLANTED IN EDEN
[13]

Moses Account

God AND I, the Lord God, planted a garden eastward in Eden, and there I put the man whom I had formed. 9 And out of the ground made I, the Lord God, to grow every tree, naturally, that is pleasant to the sight of man; and man could behold it. And it became also a living soul. For it was spiritual in the day that I created it; for it remaineth in the sphere in which I, God, created it, yea, even all things which I prepared for the use of man; and man saw that it was good for food. And I, the Lord God, planted the tree of life also in the midst of the garden, and also the tree of knowledge of good and evil.

Moses 3:8-14
Garden of Eden

10 And I, the Lord God, caused a river to go out of Eden to water the garden; and from thence it was parted, and became into four heads. 11 And I, the Lord God, called the name of the first Pison, and it compasseth the whole land of Havilah, where I, the Lord God, created much gold; 12 And the gold of that land was good, and there was bdellium and the onyx stone. 13 And the name of the second river was called Gihon; the same that compasseth the whole land of Ethiopia*. 14 And the name of the third river was Hiddekel; that which goeth toward the east of Assyria. And the fourth river was the Euphrates.

———————

Abraham Account

Abraham 8 And the Gods planted a garden, eastward in Eden, and there they put the man, whose spirit they had put into the body which they had formed. 9 And out of the ground made the Gods to grow every tree that is pleasant to the sight and good for food; the tree of life, also, in the midst of the garden, and the tree of knowledge of good and evil.

Abr. 5:8-10
Garden of Eden

10 There was a river running out of Eden, to water the garden, and from thence it was parted and became into four heads.

———————

References: Moses 3:8-14; Abr. 5:8-10; Gen. 2:8-14

* In the area of Eden and Adam-ondi-Ahman there were rivers and lands that received names that were later attached to other lands and rivers. As to the location of Eden and its environs, see D&C 117:8-9.

ADAM AND ANIMALS PLACED IN GARDEN
[14]

Moses Account

God   AND I, the Lord God, took the man, and put him into the   Moses 3:15-20
Garden of Eden, to dress it, and to keep it. 16 And I, the Lord   Garden of Eden
God, commanded the man, saying:

> Of every tree of the garden thou mayest freely eat, 17 But of the
> tree of the knowledge of good and evil, thou shalt not eat of it,
> nevertheless, thou mayest choose for thyself, for it is given unto
> thee; but, remember that I forbid it, for in the day thou eatest
> thereof thou shalt surely die.

18 And I, the Lord God, said unto mine Only Begotten,

> that it was not good that the man should be alone; wherefore, I will
> make an help meet for him.

19 And out of the ground I, the Lord God, formed every
beast of the field, and every fowl of the air; and commanded
that they should come unto Adam, to see what he would call
them; and they were also living souls; for I, God, breathed
into them the breath of life, and commanded that whatsoever
Adam called every living creature, that should be the name
thereof. 20 And Adam gave names to all cattle, and to the
fowl of the air, and to every beast of the field; but as for
Adam, there was not found an help meet for him.

Abraham Account

Abraham   11 And the Gods took the man and put him in the Garden of   Abr. 5:11-13
Eden, to dress it and to keep it. 12 And the Gods commanded   Garden of Eden
the man, saying:

The Gods   Of every tree of the garden thou mayest freely eat, 13 But of the
tree of knowledge of good and evil, thou shalt not eat of it; for in
the time that thou eatest thereof, thou shalt surely die.

Abraham   Now I, Abraham, saw that it was after the Lord's time,
which was after the time of Kolob; for as yet the Gods had
not appointed unto Adam his reckoning.

20 And out of the ground the Gods formed every beast of the   Abr. 5:20-21
field, and every fowl of the air, and brought them unto Adam
to see what he would call them; and whatsoever Adam
called every living creature, that should be the name thereof.
21 And Adam gave names to all cattle, to the fowl of the air,
to every beast of the field;

References: Moses 3:15-20; Abr. 5:11-13; Abr. 5:20-21; Gen. 2:15-17

THE GODS FORM A HELP MEET FOR ADAM
[15]

Moses Account

God | AND I, the Lord God, caused a deep sleep to fall upon Adam; and he slept, and I took one of his ribs and closed up the flesh in the stead thereof; 22 And the rib which I, the Lord God, had taken from man, made I a woman, and brought her unto the man. 23 And Adam said:

Moses 3:21-25

Garden of Eden

Adam | This I know now is bone of my bones, and flesh of my flesh; she shall be called Woman, because she was taken out of man.

God | 24 Therefore shall a man leave his father and his mother, and shall cleave unto his wife; and they shall be one flesh. 25 And they were both naked, the man and his wife, and were not ashamed.

Abraham Account

Abraham | 14 And the Gods said:

Abr. 5:14-19

Garden of Eden

The Gods | Let us make an help meet for the man, for it is not good that the man should be alone, therefore we will form an help meet for him.

Abraham | 15 And the Gods caused a deep sleep to fall upon Adam; and he slept, and they took one of his ribs, and closed up the flesh in the stead thereof; 16 And of the rib which the Gods had taken from man, formed they a woman, and brought her unto the man. 17 And Adam said:

Adam | This was bone of my bones, and flesh of my flesh; now she shall be called Woman, because she was taken out of man;

Abraham | 18 Therefore shall a man leave his father and his mother, and shall cleave unto his wife, and they shall be one flesh. 19 And they were both naked, the man and his wife, and were not ashamed.

And for Adam, there was found an help meet for him.

Abr. 5:21

References: Moses 3:21-25; Abr. 5:14-19, 21; Gen. 2:18-25

SATAN'S TEMPTATIONS LEAD TO FALL
[16]

God   AND now the serpent was more subtle than any beast of the   Moses 4:5-13
field which I, the Lord God, had made. 6 And Satan put it   Garden of Eden
into the heart of the serpent, (for he had drawn away many
after him,) and he sought also to beguile Eve, for he knew
not the mind of God, wherefore he sought to destroy the
world. 7 And he said unto the woman:

Satan   Yea, hath God said—

God   Ye shall not eat of every tree of the garden? (And he spake by
the mouth of the serpent.)

8 And the woman said unto the serpent:

Eve   We may eat of the fruit of the trees of the garden; 9 But of the fruit
of the tree which thou beholdest in the midst of the garden, God
hath said—

God   Ye shall not eat of it, neither shall ye touch it, lest ye die.

10 And the serpent said unto the woman:

Satan   Ye shall not surely die; 11 For God doth know that in the day ye eat
thereof, then your eyes shall be opened, and ye shall be as gods,
knowing good and evil.

God   12 And when the woman saw that the tree was good for food,
and that it became pleasant to the eyes, and a tree to be
desired to make her wise, she took of the fruit thereof, and
did eat, and also gave unto her husband with her, and he did
eat. 13 And the eyes of them both were opened, and they
knew that they had been naked. And they sewed fig-leaves
together and made themselves aprons.

References: Moses 4:5-13; Gen. 3:1-7

THE EARTH CURSED FOR TRANSGRESSION
[17]

God AND they heard the voice of the Lord God, as they were walking in the garden, in the cool of the day; and Adam and his wife went to hide themselves from the presence of the Lord God amongst the trees of the garden. 15 And I, the Lord God, called unto Adam, and said unto him:

Moses 4:14-25

Garden of Eden

Where goest thou?

16 And he said:

Adam I heard thy voice in the garden, and I was afraid, because I beheld that I was naked, and I hid myself.

God 17 And I, the Lord God, said unto Adam:

Who told thee thou wast naked? Hast thou eaten of the tree whereof I commanded thee that thou shouldst not eat, if so thou shouldst surely die?

18 And the man said:

Adam The woman thou gavest me, and commandest that she should remain with me, she gave me of the fruit of the tree and I did eat.

God 19 And I, the Lord God, said unto the woman:

What is this thing which thou hast done?

And the woman said:

Eve The serpent beguiled me, and I did eat.

God 20 And I, the Lord God, said unto the serpent:

Because thou hast done this thou shalt be cursed above all cattle, and above every beast of the field; upon thy belly shalt thou go, and dust shalt thou eat all the days of thy life; 21 And I will put enmity between thee and the woman, between thy seed and her seed; and he shall bruise thy head, and thou shalt bruise his heel.

22 Unto the woman, I, the Lord God, said:

I will greatly multiply thy sorrow and thy conception. In sorrow thou shalt bring forth children, and thy desire shall be to thy husband, and he shall rule over thee.

23 And unto Adam, I, the Lord God, said:

Because thou hast hearkened unto the voice of thy wife, and hast eaten of the fruit of the tree of which I commanded thee, saying—

Thou shalt not eat of it,

cursed shall be the ground for thy sake; in sorrow shalt thou eat of it all the days of thy life. 24 Thorns also, and thistles shall it bring

God   forth to thee, and thou shalt eat the herb of the field. 25 By the   Moses 4:14-25

sweat of thy face shalt thou eat bread, until thou shalt return unto   Garden of Eden

the ground—

for thou shalt surely die—

for out of it wast thou taken: for dust thou wast, and unto dust shalt thou return.

References: Moses 4:14-25; Gen. 3:8-22

ADAM AND EVE SENT FORTH FROM EDEN

[18]

God AND Adam called his wife's name Eve, because she was the mother of all living; for thus have I, the Lord God, called the first of all women, which are many. 27 Unto Adam, and also unto his wife, did I, the Lord God, make coats of skins, and clothed them. 28 And I, the Lord God, said unto mine Only Begotten:

Moses 4:26-32
Garden of Eden

> Behold, the man is become as one of us to know good and evil; and now lest he put forth his hand and partake also of the tree of life, and eat and live forever, 29 Therefore I, the Lord God, will send him forth from the Garden of Eden, to till the ground from whence he was taken; 30 For as I, the Lord God, liveth, even so my words cannot return void, for as they go forth out of my mouth they must be fulfilled.

31 So I drove out the man, and I placed at the east of the Garden of Eden, cherubim and a flaming sword, which turned every way to keep the way of the tree of life.

East of Eden

32 (And these are the words which I spake unto my servant Moses, and they are true even as I will; and I have spoken them unto you. See thou show them unto no man, until I command you, except to them that believe. Amen.)

1 AND it came to pass that after I, the Lord God, had driven them out, that Adam began to till the earth, and to have dominion over all the beasts of the field, and to eat his bread by the sweat of his brow, as I the Lord had commanded him. And Eve, also, his wife, did labor with him.

Moses 5:1

———————

References: Moses 4:26-32; Moses 5:1; Gen. 3:23-24

DESCENDANTS OF ADAM AND EVE MULTIPLY
[19]

Narrator   AND Adam knew his wife, and she bare unto him sons and   Moses 5:2-3

daughters, and they began to multiply and to replenish the   East of Eden

earth.

3 And from that time forth, the sons and daughters of Adam began to divide two and two in the land, and to till the land, and to tend flocks, and they also begat sons and daughters.

———————

Reference: Moses 5:2-3

Note: Within the events that occurred before the time when Adam and Eve were sent forth out of the garden of Eden (event 18), the narration uses such phrases as "and I the Lord God said" or "I God said" (see Moses 4:26-32; 5:1). After Adam and Eve leave the garden (event 19), the narration changes grammatically from first person to third person by using such phrases as "and God said" or "the Lord said."

ADAM TO SACRIFICE FIRSTLINGS OF FLOCKS

[20]

Narrator | AND Adam and Eve, his wife, called upon the name of the Lord, and they heard the voice of the Lord from the way toward the Garden of Eden, speaking unto them, and they saw him not; for they were shut out from his presence. 5 And he gave unto them commandments, that they should worship the Lord their God, and should offer the firstlings of their flocks, for an offering unto the Lord. And Adam was obedient unto the commandments of the Lord. 6 And after many days an angel of the Lord appeared unto Adam, saying:

Moses 5:4-12
East of Eden

Angel | Why dost thou offer sacrifices unto the Lord?

Narrator | And Adam said unto him:

Adam | I know not, save the Lord commanded me.

Narrator | 7 And then the angel spake, saying:

Angel | This thing is a similitude of the sacrifice of the Only Begotten of the Father, which is full of grace and truth. 8 Wherefore, thou shalt do all that thou doest in the name of the Son, and thou shalt repent and call upon God in the name of the Son forevermore.

Narrator | 9 And in that day the Holy Ghost fell upon Adam, which beareth record of the Father and the Son, saying:

The Lord | I am the Only Begotten of the Father from the beginning, henceforth and forever, that as thou hast fallen thou mayest be redeemed, and all mankind, even as many as will.

Narrator | 10 And in that day Adam blessed God and was filled, and began to prophesy concerning all the families of the earth, saying:

Adam | Blessed be the name of God, for because of my transgression my eyes are opened, and in this life I shall have joy, and again in the flesh I shall see God.

Narrator | 11 And Eve, his wife, heard all these things and was glad, saying:

Eve | Were it not for our transgression we never should have had seed, and never should have known good and evil, and the joy of our redemption, and the eternal life which God giveth unto all the obedient.

Narrator | 12 And Adam and Eve blessed the name of God, and they made all things known unto their sons and their daughters.

Reference: Moses 5:4-12

ALL MEN COMMANDED TO REPENT
[21]

Narrator	AND Satan came among them, saying:	Moses 5:13-15
Satan	I am also a son of God;	East of Eden
Narrator	and he commanded them, saying:	
Satan	Believe it* not;	

Narrator   and they believed it not, and they loved Satan more than God. And men began from that time forth to be carnal, sensual, and devilish. 14 And the Lord God called upon men by the Holy Ghost everywhere and commanded them that they should repent; 15 And as many as believed in the Son, and repented of their sins, should be saved; and as many as believed not and repented not, should be damned; and the words went forth out of the mouth of God in a firm decree; wherefore they must be fulfilled.

Reference: Moses 5:13-15

* Satan commanded Adam and Eve and their sons and daughters to not believe "it," that is, the words of the angel and the Lord (event 20).

CAIN AND ABEL BORN TO ADAM AND EVE
[22]

Narrator   AND Adam and Eve, his wife, ceased not to call upon God.   Moses 5:16-27
And Adam knew Eve his wife, and she conceived and bare   East of Eden
Cain, and said:

Eve   I have gotten a man from the Lord; wherefore he may not reject his words.

Narrator   But behold, Cain hearkened not, saying:

Cain   Who is the Lord that I should know him?

Narrator   17 And she again conceived and bare his brother Abel. And Abel hearkened unto the voice of the Lord. And Abel was a keeper of sheep, but Cain was a tiller of the ground. 18 And Cain loved Satan more than God. And Satan commanded him, saying:

Satan   Make an offering unto the Lord.

Narrator   19 And in process of time it came to pass that Cain brought of the fruit of the ground an offering unto the Lord. 20 And Abel, he also brought of the firstlings of his flock, and of the fat thereof. And the Lord had respect unto Abel, and to his offering; 21 But unto Cain, and to his offering, he had not respect. Now Satan knew this, and it pleased him. And Cain was very wroth, and his countenance fell. 22 And the Lord said unto Cain:

The Lord   Why art thou wroth? Why is thy countenance fallen? 23 If thou doest well, thou shalt be accepted. And if thou doest not well, sin lieth at the door, and Satan desireth to have thee; and except thou shalt hearken unto my commandments, I will deliver thee up, and it shall be unto thee according to his desire. And thou shalt rule over him; 24 For from this time forth thou shalt be the father of his lies; thou shalt be called Perdition; for thou wast also before the world. 25 And it shall be said in time to come—

That these abominations were had from Cain;

for he rejected the greater counsel which was had from God; and this is a cursing which I will put upon thee, except thou repent.

Narrator   26 And Cain was wroth, and listened not any more to the voice of the Lord, neither to Abel, his brother, who walked in holiness before the Lord. 27 And Adam and his wife mourned before the Lord, because of Cain and his brethren.

References: Moses 5:16-27; Gen. 4:1-7

SATAN PERSUADES CAIN TO KILL ABEL
[23]

Narrator	AND it came to pass that Cain took one of his brothers' daughters to wife, and they loved Satan more than God. 29 And Satan said unto Cain:

Moses 5:28-41

East of Eden

Satan — Swear unto me by thy throat, and if thou tell it thou shalt die; and swear thy brethren by their heads, and by the living God, that they tell it not; for if they tell it, they shall surely die; and this that thy father may not know it; and this day I will deliver thy brother Abel into thine hands. 30 And Satan sware unto Cain that he would do according to his commands. And all these things were done in secret.

Narrator — 31 And Cain said:

Cain — Truly I am Mahan, the master of this great secret, that I may murder and get gain.

Narrator — Wherefore Cain was called Master Mahan*, and he gloried in his wickedness. 32 And Cain went into the field, and Cain talked with Abel, his brother.

And it came to pass that while they were in the field, Cain rose up against Abel, his brother, and slew him. 33 And Cain gloried in that which he had done, saying:

Cain — I am free; surely the flocks of my brother falleth into my hands.

Narrator — 34 And the Lord said unto Cain:

The Lord — Where is Abel, thy brother?

Narrator — And he said:

Cain — I know not. Am I my brother's keeper?

Narrator — 35 And the Lord said:

The Lord — What hast thou done? The voice of thy brother's blood cries unto me from the ground. 36 And now thou shalt be cursed from the earth which hath opened her mouth to receive thy brother's blood from thy hand. 37 When thou tillest the ground it shall not henceforth yield unto thee her strength. A fugitive and a vagabond shalt thou be in the earth.

Narrator — 38 And Cain said unto the Lord:

Cain — Satan tempted me because of my brother's flocks. And I was wroth also; for his offering thou didst accept and not mine; my punishment is greater than I can bear. 39 Behold thou hast driven me out this day from the face of the Lord, and from thy face shall I be hid; and I shall be a fugitive and a vagabond in the earth; and it shall come to pass, that he that findeth me will slay me, because of mine iniquities, for these things are not hid from the Lord.

The Lord — 40 And I the Lord said unto him:

The Lord	Whosoever slayeth thee, vengeance shall be taken on him sevenfold.	Moses 5:28-41 East of Eden

And I the Lord set a mark upon Cain, lest any finding him should kill him.

Narrator	41 And Cain was shut out from the presence of the Lord, and with his wife and many of his brethren dwelt in the land of Nod, on the east of Eden.	Land of Nod

---

References: Moses 5:28-41; Gen. 4:8-15

* "Mind," "destroyer," and "great one" are possible meanings of the roots evident in "Mahan."

CAIN'S DESCENDANTS NAMED
[24]

Narrator   AND Cain knew his wife, and she conceived and bare   Moses 5:42-50
Enoch, and he also begat many sons and daughters. And he   Land of Nod
builded a city, and he called the name of the city* after the
name of his son, Enoch.

43 And unto Enoch was born Irad, and other sons and
daughters.

And Irad begat Mahujael, and other sons and daughters.

And Mahujael begat Methusael, and other sons and
daughters.

And Methusael begat Lamech.

44 And Lamech took unto himself two wives; the name of
one being Adah, and the name of the other, Zillah. 45 And
Adah bare Jabal; he was the father of such as dwell in tents,
and they were keepers of cattle; and his brother's name was
Jubal, who was the father of all such as handle the harp and
organ. 46 And Zillah, she also bare Tubal Cain, an instructor
of every artificer in brass and iron. And the sister of Tubal
Cain was called Naamah.

47 And Lamech said unto his wives, Adah and Zillah:

Lamech   Hear my voice, ye wives of Lamech, hearken unto my speech; for I
have slain a man to my wounding, and a young man to my hurt.

Narrator   48 If Cain shall be avenged sevenfold, truly Lamech shall be
seventy and seven fold**; 49 For Lamech having entered
into a covenant with Satan, after the manner of Cain,
wherein he became Master Mahan, master of that great
secret which was administered unto Cain by Satan; and Irad,
the son of Enoch, having known their secret, began to reveal
it unto the sons of Adam; 50 Wherefore Lamech, being
angry, slew him, not like unto Cain, his brother Abel, for the
sake of getting gain, but he slew him for the oath's sake.

References: Moses 5:42-50; Gen. 4:16-24

* There was a man named Enoch in Cain's lineage, and a city by that
name among his people. Do not confuse these with the Enoch of the
righteous line of Seth and with his city, Zion, also called "City of Enoch."

** Lamech presumptively boasted that far more would be done for him
than for Cain. The reasons for his assumption are given in verses 49
and 50.

SECRET COMBINATIONS PREVAIL
[25]

Narrator   FOR, from the days of Cain, there was a secret combination,   Moses 5:51-55
and their works were in the dark, and they knew every man   Land of Nod
his brother.

52 Wherefore the Lord cursed Lamech, and his house, and all
them that had covenanted with Satan; for they kept not the
commandments of God, and it displeased God, and he
ministered not unto them, and their works were
abominations, and began to spread among all the sons of
men. And it was among the sons of men. 53 And among the
daughters of men these things were not spoken, because that
Lamech had spoken the secret unto his wives, and they
rebelled against him, and declared these things abroad, and
had not compassion;

54 Wherefore Lamech was despised, and cast out, and came
not among the sons of men, lest he should die. 55 And thus
the works of darkness began to prevail among all the sons of
men.

_____

Reference: Moses 5:51-55

GOSPEL PREACHED FROM THE BEGINNING
[26]

Narrator   AND God cursed the earth with a sore curse, and was angry   Moses 5:56-59
with the wicked, with all the sons of men whom he had   Land of Shulon
made; 57 For they would not hearken unto his voice, nor
believe on his Only Begotten Son, even him whom he
declared should come in the meridian of time, who was
prepared from before the foundation of the world.

58 And thus the Gospel began to be preached, from the
beginning, being declared by holy angels sent forth from the
presence of God, and by his own voice, and by the gift of
the Holy Ghost. 59 And thus all things were confirmed unto
Adam, by an holy ordinance, and the Gospel preached, and a
decree sent forth, that it should be in the world, until the end
thereof; and thus it was. Amen.

———————

Reference: Moses 5:56-59

SETH BORN TO ADAM AND EVE
[27]

Narrator AND Adam hearkened unto the voice of God, and called
upon his sons to repent.

Moses 6:1-4
Land of Shulon

2 And Adam knew his wife again, and she bare a son, and he
called his name Seth. And Adam glorified the name of God;
for he said:

Adam   God hath appointed me another seed, instead of Abel, whom Cain
slew.

Narrator 3 And God revealed himself unto Seth, and he rebelled not,
but offered an acceptable sacrifice, like unto his brother
Abel. And to him also was born a son, and he called his
name Enos. 4 And then began these men to call upon the
name of the Lord, and the Lord blessed them;

References: Moses 6:1-4; Gen. 4:25-26

BOOK OF REMEMBRANCE KEPT BY ADAM
[28]

Narrator AND a book of remembrance was kept, in the which was   Moses 6:5-12
recorded, in the language of Adam, for it was given unto as   Land of Shulon
many as called upon God to write by the spirit of
inspiration; 6 And by them their children were taught to read
and write, having a language which was pure and undefiled.

7 Now this same Priesthood, which was in the beginning,
shall be in the end of the world also. 8 Now this prophecy
Adam spake, as he was moved upon by the Holy Ghost, and
a genealogy was kept of the children of God. And this was
the book of the generations of Adam, saying:

Adam In the day that God created man, in the likeness of God made he
him; 9 In the image of his own body, male and female, created he
them, and blessed them, and called their name Adam, in the day
when they were created and became living souls in the land upon
the footstool of God.

Narrator 10 And Adam lived one hundred and thirty years, and begat a
son in his own likeness, after his own image*, and called his
name Seth. 11 And the days of Adam, after he had begotten
Seth, were eight hundred years, and he begat many sons and
daughters; 12 And all the days that Adam lived were nine
hundred and thirty years, and he died.

References: Moses 6:5-12; Gen. 5:1-2

* Seth was in the likeness and image of Adam, as Adam was in the
image of God.

SETH'S POSTERITY DOWN TO ENOCH NAMED
[29]

Narrator   SETH lived one hundred and five years, and begat Enos, and   Moses 6:13-25
prophesied in all his days, and taught his son Enos in the   Land of Shulon
ways of God; wherefore Enos prophesied also. 14 And Seth
lived, after he begat Enos, eight hundred and seven years,
and begat many sons and daughters.

15 And the children of men were numerous upon all the face
of the land. And in those days Satan had great dominion
among men, and raged in their hearts; and from thenceforth
came wars and bloodshed; and a man's hand was against his
own brother, in administering death, because of secret
works, seeking for power. 16 All the days of Seth were nine
hundred and twelve years, and he died.

17 And Enos lived ninety years, and begat Cainan. And Enos   Land of Cainan
and the residue of the people of God came out from the land,
which was called Shulon, and dwelt in a land of promise*,
which he called after his own son, whom he had named
Cainan. 18 And Enos lived, after he begat Cainan, eight
hundred and fifteen years, and begat many sons and
daughters. And all the days of Enos were nine hundred and
five years, and he died.

19 And Cainan lived seventy years, and begat Mahalaleel;
and Cainan lived after he begat Mahalaleel eight hundred
and forty years, and begat sons and daughters. And all the
days of Cainan were nine hundred and ten years, and he
died.

20 And Mahalaleel lived sixty-five years, and begat Jared;
and Mahalaleel lived, after he begat Jared, eight hundred
and thirty years, and begat sons and daughters. And all the
days of Mahalaleel were eight hundred and ninety-five
years, and he died.

21 And Jared lived one hundred and sixty-two years, and
begat Enoch; and Jared lived, after he begat Enoch, eight
hundred years, and begat sons and daughters. And Jared
taught Enoch in all the ways of God.

22 And this is the genealogy of the sons of Adam, who was
the son of God, with whom God, himself, conversed. 23 And
they were preachers of righteousness, and spake and
prophesied, and called upon all men, everywhere, to repent;
and faith was taught unto the children of men.

24 And it came to pass that all the days of Jared were nine
hundred and sixty-two years, and he died.

Narrator   25 And Enoch lived sixty-five years, and begat Methuselah.   Moses 6:13-25

                                                                              Land of Cainan

References: Moses 6:13-25; Gen. 5:3-20

* This land of Cainan is not the same as the land of Canaan at the time
of Enoch nor the land of Canaan which was settled after the time of the
flood and given to the descendants of Abraham as an everlasting
possession.

ENOCH

AND righteousness will I send down out of heaven; and truth
will I send forth out of the earth, to bear testimony of mine
Only Begotten; his resurrection from the dead; yea, and also
the resurrection of all men.

MOSES 7:62

ENOCH CALLED TO PREACH THE GOSPEL
[30]

Narrator   AND it came to pass that Enoch journeyed in the land,   Moses 6:26-36
among the people; and as he journeyed, the Spirit of God   Near the Sea East
descended out of heaven, and abode upon him. 27 And he
heard a voice from heaven, saying:

The Lord   Enoch, my son, prophesy unto this people, and say unto them—

Repent,

for thus saith the Lord:

I am angry with this people, and my fierce anger is kindled
against them; for their hearts have waxed hard, and their ears
are dull of hearing, and their eyes cannot see afar off; 28 And
for these many generations, ever since the day that I created
them, have they gone astray, and have denied me, and have
sought their own counsels in the dark; and in their own
abominations have they devised murder, and have not kept the
commandments, which I gave unto their father, Adam.
29 Wherefore, they have foresworn themselves, and, by their
oaths, they have brought upon themselves death; and a hell I
have prepared for them, if they repent not; 30 And this is a
decree, which I have sent forth in the beginning of the world,
from my own mouth, from the foundation thereof, and by the
mouths of my servants, thy fathers, have I decreed it, even as it
shall be sent forth in the world, unto the ends thereof.

Narrator   31 And when Enoch had heard these words, he bowed
himself to the earth, before the Lord, and spake before the
Lord, saying:

Enoch   Why is it that I have found favor in thy sight, and am but a lad, and
all the people hate me; for I am slow of speech; wherefore am I thy
servant?

Narrator   32 And the Lord said unto Enoch:

The Lord   Go forth and do as I have commanded thee, and no man shall
pierce thee. Open thy mouth, and it shall be filled, and I will give
thee utterance, for all flesh is in my hands, and I will do as seemeth
me good. 33 Say unto this people:

Choose ye this day, to serve the Lord God who made you.

34 Behold my Spirit is upon you, wherefore all thy words will I
justify; and the mountains shall flee before you, and the rivers shall
turn from their course; and thou shalt abide in me, and I in you;
therefore walk with me.

Narrator   35 And the Lord spake unto Enoch, and said unto him:

The Lord   Anoint thine eyes with clay, and wash them, and thou shalt see.

Narrator   And he did so. 36 And he beheld the spirits that God had   Moses 6:26-36
created; and he beheld also things which were not visible to   Near the Sea East
the natural eye; and from thenceforth came the saying
abroad in the land:

A seer hath the Lord raised up unto his people.

———————

Reference: Moses 6:26-36

ENOCH EXPLAINS HIS MINISTRY
[31]

Narrator   AND it came to pass that Enoch went forth in the land,   Moses 6:37-46
among the people, standing upon the hills and the high   Land of Shum
places, and cried with a loud voice, testifying against their
works; and all men were offended because of him. 38 And
they came forth to hear him, upon the high places, saying
unto the tent-keepers:

People   Tarry ye here and keep the tents, while we go yonder to behold the
seer, for he prophesieth, and there is a strange thing in the land; a
wild man hath come among us.

Narrator   39 And it came to pass when they heard him, no man laid
hands on him; for fear came on all them that heard him; for
he walked with God. 40 And there came a man unto him,
whose name was Mahijah, and said unto him:

Mahijah   Tell us plainly who thou art, and from whence thou comest?

Narrator   41 And he said unto them:

Enoch   I came out from the land of Cainan, the land of my fathers, a land
of righteousness unto this day. And my father taught me in all the
ways of God. 42 And it came to pass, as I journeyed from the land
of Cainan, by the sea east, I beheld a vision; and lo, the heavens I
saw, and the Lord spake with me, and gave me commandment;
wherefore, for this cause, to keep the commandment, I speak forth
these words.

Narrator   43 And Enoch continued his speech, saying:

The Lord which spake with me, the same is the God of heaven, and
he is my God, and your God, and ye are my brethren, and why
counsel ye yourselves, and deny the God of heaven? 44 The
heavens he made; the earth is his footstool; and the foundation
thereof is his. Behold, he laid it, an host of men hath he brought in
upon the face thereof. 45 And death hath come upon our fathers;
nevertheless we know them, and cannot deny, and even the first of
all we know, even Adam. 46 For a book of remembrance we have
written among us, according to the pattern given by the finger of
God; and it is given in our own language.

Reference: Moses 6:37-46

ENOCH TEACHES PLAN OF SALVATION
[32]

Narrator	AND as Enoch spake forth the words of God, the people trembled, and could not stand in his presence. 48 And he said unto them:	Moses 6:47-68 Land of Shum
Enoch	Because that Adam fell, we are; and by his fall came death; and we are made partakers of misery and woe. 49 Behold Satan hath come among the children of men, and tempteth them to worship him; and men have become carnal, sensual, and devilish, and are shut out from the presence of God. 50 But God hath made known unto our fathers that all men must repent. 51 And he called upon our father Adam by his own voice, saying:	
God	I am God; I made the world, and men before they were in the flesh.	
Enoch	52 And he also said unto him:	
God	If thou wilt turn unto me, and hearken unto my voice, and believe, and repent of all thy transgressions, and be baptized, even in water, in the name of mine Only Begotten Son, who is full of grace and truth, which is Jesus Christ, the only name which shall be given under heaven, whereby salvation shall come unto the children of men, ye shall receive the gift of the Holy Ghost, asking all things in his name, and whatsoever ye shall ask, it shall be given you.	
Enoch	53 And our father Adam spake unto the Lord, and said:	
Adam	Why is it that men must repent and be baptized in water?	
Enoch	And the Lord said unto Adam:	
The Lord	Behold I have forgiven thee thy transgression in the Garden of Eden.	
Enoch	54 Hence came the saying abroad among the people, that the Son of God hath atoned for original guilt, wherein the sins of the parents cannot be answered upon the heads of the children, for they are whole from the foundation of the world. 55 And the Lord spake unto Adam, saying:	
The Lord	Inasmuch as thy children are conceived in sin, even so when they begin to grow up, sin conceiveth in their hearts, and they taste the bitter, that they may know to prize the good. 56 And it is given unto them to know good from evil; wherefore they are agents unto themselves, and I have given unto you another law and commandment. 57 Wherefore teach it unto your children, that all men, everywhere, must repent, or they can in nowise inherit the kingdom of God, for no unclean thing can dwell there, or dwell in his presence; for, in the language of Adam, Man of Holiness is his name, and the name of his Only Begotten is the Son of Man, even Jesus Christ, a righteous Judge, who shall come in the meridian of time. 58 Therefore I give unto you a commandment, to teach these things freely unto your children, saying:	

| The Lord | 59 That by reason of transgression cometh the fall, which fall bringeth death, and inasmuch as ye were born into the world by water, and blood, and the spirit, which I have made, and so became of dust a living soul, even so ye must be born again into the kingdom of heaven, of water, and of the Spirit, and be cleansed by blood, even the blood of mine Only Begotten; that ye might be sanctified from all sin, and enjoy the words of eternal life in this world, and eternal life in the world to come, even immortal glory; 60 For by the water ye keep the commandment; by the Spirit ye are justified, and by the blood ye are sanctified; | Moses 6:47-68 Land of Shum |

61 Therefore it is given to abide in you; the record of heaven; the Comforter; the peaceable things of immortal glory; the truth of all things; that which quickeneth all things, which maketh alive all things; that which knoweth all things, and hath all power according to wisdom, mercy, truth, justice, and judgment. 62 And now, behold, I say unto you:

This is the plan of salvation unto all men, through the blood of mine Only Begotten, who shall come in the meridian of time.

63 And behold, all things have their likeness, and all things are created and made to bear record of me, both things which are temporal, and things which are spiritual; things which are in the heavens above, and things which are on the earth, and things which are in the earth, and things which are under the earth, both above and beneath: all things bear record of me.

Enoch 64 And it came to pass, when the Lord had spoken with Adam, our father, that Adam cried unto the Lord, and he was caught away by the Spirit of the Lord, and was carried down into the water, and was laid under the water, and was brought forth out of the water. 65 And thus he was baptized, and the Spirit of God descended upon him, and thus he was born of the Spirit, and became quickened in the inner man. 66 And he heard a voice out of heaven, saying:

Voice from Heaven Thou art baptized with fire, and with the Holy Ghost. This is the record of the Father, and the Son, from henceforth and forever; 67 And thou art after the order of him who was without beginning of days or end of years, from all eternity to all eternity. 68 Behold, thou art one in me, a son of God; and thus may all become my sons. Amen.

| Narrator | 1 AND it came to pass that Enoch continued his speech, saying: | Moses 7:1 |

Enoch Behold, our father Adam taught these things, and many have believed and become the sons of God, and many have believed not, and have perished in their sins, and are looking forth with fear, in torment, for the fiery indignation of the wrath of God to be poured out upon them.

References: Moses 6:47-68; Moses 7:1

ENOCH PROPHESIES TO THE PEOPLE
[33]

Narrator	AND from that time forth Enoch began to prophesy, saying unto the people, that:	Moses 7:2-11 Land of Shum

Enoch   As I was journeying, and stood upon the place Mahujah, and cried unto the Lord, there came a voice out of heaven, saying—

The Lord   Turn ye, and get ye upon the mount Simeon*.

Enoch   3 And it came to pass that I turned and went up on the mount; and as I stood upon the mount, I beheld the heavens open, and I was clothed upon with glory; 4 And I saw the Lord; and he stood before my face, and he talked with me, even as a man talketh one with another, face to face; and he said unto me:

The Lord   Look, and I will show unto thee the world for the space of many generations.

Enoch   5 And it came to pass that I beheld in the valley of Shum, and lo, a great people which dwelt in tents, which were the people of Shum. 6 And again the Lord said unto me:

The Lord   Look;

Enoch   and I looked towards the north, and I beheld the people of Canaan, which dwelt in tents. 7 And the Lord said unto me:

The Lord   Prophesy;

Enoch   and I prophesied, saying:

Behold the people of Canaan, which are numerous, shall go forth in battle array against the people of Shum, and shall slay them that they shall utterly be destroyed; and the people of Canaan shall divide themselves in the land, and the land shall be barren and unfruitful, and none other people shall dwell there but the people of Canaan; 8 For behold, the Lord shall curse the land with much heat, and the barrenness thereof shall go forth forever; and there was a blackness came upon all the children of Canaan, that they were despised among all people.

9 And it came to pass that the Lord said unto me:

The Lord   Look;

Enoch   and I looked, and I beheld the land of Sharon, and the land of Enoch, and the land of Omner, and the land of Heni, and the land of Shem, and the land of Haner, and the land of Hanannihah, and all the inhabitants thereof; 10 And the Lord said unto me:

The Lord   Go to this people, and say unto them—

Repent, lest I come out and smite them with a curse, and they die.

Enoch   11 And he gave unto me a commandment that I should baptize in   Moses 7:2-11
the name of the Father, and of the Son, which is full of grace and   Land of Shum
truth, and of the Holy Ghost, which beareth record of the Father
and the Son.

Reference: Moses 7:2-11

* The Hebrew equivalent of Simeon is *Shim'on*, which means "hearing."

ENOCH CALLS ON PEOPLE TO REPENT
[34]

Narrator   AND it came to pass that Enoch continued to call upon all the people, save it were the people of Canaan, to repent; 13 And so great was the faith of Enoch that he led the people of God, and their enemies came to battle against them; and he spake the word of the Lord, and the earth trembled, and the mountains fled, even according to his command; and the rivers of water were turned out of their course; and the roar of the lions was heard out of the wilderness; and all nations feared greatly, so powerful was the word of Enoch, and so great was the power of the language which God had given him.

  14 There also came up a land out of the depth of the sea, and so great was the fear of the enemies of the people of God, that they fled and stood afar off and went upon the land which came up out of the depth of the sea. 15 And the giants of the land, also, stood afar off; and there went forth a curse upon all people that fought against God;

  16 And from that time forth there were wars and bloodshed among them; but the Lord came and dwelt with his people, and they dwelt in righteousness. 17 The fear of the Lord was upon all nations, so great was the glory of the Lord, which was upon his people. And the Lord blessed the land, and they were blessed upon the mountains, and upon the high places, and did flourish.

Moses 7:12-17

Lands beyond Cainan

Reference: Moses 7:12-17

ENOCH'S FOLLOWERS CALLED ZION

[35]

Narrator   AND the Lord called his people ZION, because they were of   Moses 7:18-27
one heart and one mind, and dwelt in righteousness; and   City of Zion
there was no poor among them. 19 And Enoch continued his
preaching in righteousness unto the people of God. And it
came to pass in his days, that he built a city that was called
the City of Holiness, even ZION.

20 And it came to pass that Enoch talked with the Lord; and
he said unto the Lord:

Enoch   Surely Zion shall dwell in safety forever.

Narrator   But the Lord said unto Enoch:

The Lord   Zion have I blessed, but the residue of the people have I cursed.

Narrator   21 And it came to pass that the Lord showed unto Enoch all
the inhabitants of the earth; and he beheld, and lo, Zion, in
process of time, was taken up into heaven. And the Lord
said unto Enoch:

The Lord   Behold mine abode forever.

Narrator   22 And Enoch also beheld the residue of the people which
were the sons of Adam; and they were a mixture of all the
seed of Adam save it was the seed of Cain, for the seed of
Cain were black, and had not place among them. 23 And
after that Zion was taken up into heaven, Enoch beheld, and
lo, all the nations of the earth were before him; 24 And there
came generation upon generation; and Enoch was high and
lifted up, even in the bosom of the Father, and of the Son of
Man; and behold, the power of Satan was upon all the face
of the earth. 25 And he saw angels descending out of heaven;
and he heard a loud voice saying:

Loud Voice   Wo, wo be unto the inhabitants of the earth.

Narrator   26 And he beheld Satan; and he had a great chain in his hand,
and it veiled the whole face of the earth with darkness; and
he looked up and laughed, and his angels rejoiced. 27 And
Enoch beheld angels descending out of heaven, bearing
testimony of the Father and Son; and the Holy Ghost fell on
many, and they were caught up by the powers of heaven into
Zion.

Reference: Moses 7:18-27

ENOCH SHOWN WICKEDNESS OF MAN
[36]

Narrator	AND it came to pass that the God of heaven looked upon the residue of the people, and he wept; and Enoch bore record of it, saying:

Moses 7:28-40
City of Zion

Enoch
How is it that the heavens weep, and shed forth their tears as the rain upon the mountains?

Narrator
29 And Enoch said unto the Lord:

Enoch
How is it that thou canst weep, seeing thou art holy, and from all eternity to all eternity?

30 And were it possible that man could number the particles of the earth, yea, millions of earths like this, it would not be a beginning to the number of thy creations; and thy curtains are stretched out still; and yet thou art there, and thy bosom is there; and also thou art just; thou art merciful and kind forever; 31 And thou hast taken Zion to thine own bosom, from all thy creations, from all eternity to all eternity; and naught but peace, justice, and truth is the habitation of thy throne; and mercy shall go before thy face and have no end; how is it thou canst weep?

Narrator
32 The Lord said unto Enoch:

The Lord
Behold these thy brethren; they are the workmanship of mine own hands, and I gave unto them their knowledge, in the day I created them; and in the Garden of Eden, gave I unto man his agency; 33 And unto thy brethren have I said, and also given commandment,

that they should love one another, and that they should choose me, their Father;

but behold, they are without affection, and they hate their own blood; 34 And the fire of mine indignation is kindled against them; and in my hot displeasure will I send in the floods upon them, for my fierce anger is kindled against them.

God
35 Behold, I am God; Man of Holiness is my name; Man of Counsel is my name; and Endless and Eternal is my name, also.

36 Wherefore, I can stretch forth mine hands and hold all the creations which I have made; and mine eye can pierce them also, and among all the workmanship of mine hands there has not been so great wickedness as among thy brethren. 37 But behold, their sins shall be upon the heads of their fathers; Satan shall be their father, and misery shall be their doom; and the whole heavens shall weep over them, even all the workmanship of mine hands; wherefore should not the heavens weep, seeing these shall suffer?

38 But behold, these which thine eyes are upon shall perish in the floods; and behold, I will shut them up; a prison have I prepared for them. 39 And that which I have chosen hath pled before my face. Wherefore, he suffereth for their sins; inasmuch as they will

God   repent in the day that my Chosen shall return unto me, and until   Moses 7:28-40
that day they shall be in torment; 40 Wherefore, for this shall the   City of Zion
heavens weep, yea, and all the workmanship of mine hands.

Reference: Moses 7:28-40

ENOCH SHOWN MISSION OF NOAH
[37]

Narrator   AND it came to pass that the Lord spake unto Enoch, and   Moses 7:41-46
told Enoch all the doings of the children of men; wherefore   City of Zion
Enoch knew, and looked upon their wickedness, and their
misery, and wept and stretched forth his arms, and his heart
swelled wide as eternity; and his bowels yearned; and all
eternity shook. 42 And Enoch also saw Noah, and his family;
that the posterity of all the sons of Noah should be saved
with a temporal salvation;

43 Wherefore Enoch saw that Noah built an ark; and that the
Lord smiled upon it, and held it in his own hand; but upon
the residue of the wicked the floods came and swallowed
them up.

44 And as Enoch saw this, he had bitterness of soul, and
wept over his brethren, and said unto the heavens:

Enoch   I will refuse to be comforted;

Narrator   but the Lord said unto Enoch:

The Lord   Lift up your heart, and be glad; and look.

Narrator   45 And it came to pass that Enoch looked; and from Noah,
he beheld all the families of the earth; and he cried unto the
Lord, saying:

Enoch   When shall the day of the Lord come? When shall the blood of the
Righteous be shed, that all they that mourn may be sanctified and
have eternal life?

Narrator   46 And the Lord said:

The Lord   It shall be in the meridian of time, in the days of wickedness and
vengeance.

Reference: Moses 7:41-46

ENOCH SHOWN MORTAL MINISTRY OF CHRIST
[38]

Narrator   AND behold, Enoch saw the day of the coming of the Son of   Moses 7:47-58
Man, even in the flesh; and his soul rejoiced, saying: City of Zion

Enoch   The Righteous is lifted up, and the Lamb is slain from the foundation of the world; and through faith I am in the bosom of the Father, and behold, Zion is with me.

Narrator   48 And it came to pass that Enoch looked upon the earth; and he heard a voice from the bowels thereof, saying:

Voice   Wo, wo is me, the mother of men; I am pained, I am weary, because of the wickedness of my children. When shall I rest, and be cleansed from the filthiness which is gone forth out of me? When will my Creator sanctify me, that I may rest, and righteousness for a season abide upon my face?

Narrator   49 And when Enoch heard the earth mourn, he wept, and cried unto the Lord, saying:

Enoch   O Lord, wilt thou not have compassion upon the earth? Wilt thou not bless the children of Noah?

Narrator   50 And it came to pass that Enoch continued his cry unto the Lord, saying:

Enoch   I ask thee, O Lord, in the name of thine Only Begotten, even Jesus Christ, that thou wilt have mercy upon Noah and his seed, that the earth might never more be covered by the floods.

Narrator   51 And the Lord could not withhold; and he covenanted with Enoch, and sware unto him with an oath, that he would stay the floods; that he would call upon the children of Noah; 52 And he sent forth an unalterable decree, that a remnant of his seed should always be found among all nations, while the earth should stand; 53 And the Lord said:

The Lord   Blessed is he through whose seed Messiah shall come;

Narrator   for he saith—

The Lord   I am Messiah, the King of Zion, the Rock of Heaven, which is broad as eternity; whoso cometh in at the gate and climbeth up by me shall never fall; wherefore, blessed are they of whom I have spoken, for they shall come forth with songs of everlasting joy.

Narrator   54 And it came to pass that Enoch cried unto the Lord, saying:

Enoch   When the Son of Man cometh in the flesh, shall the earth rest? I pray thee, show me these things.

Narrator   55 And the Lord said unto Enoch:

The Lord   Look,

Narrator	and he looked and beheld the Son of Man lifted up on the cross, after the manner of men; 56 And he heard a loud voice; and the heavens were veiled; and all the creations of God mourned; and the earth groaned; and the rocks were rent; and the saints arose, and were crowned at the right hand of the Son of Man, with crowns of glory; 57 And as many of the spirits as were in prison came forth, and stood on the right hand of God; and the remainder were reserved in chains of darkness until the judgment of the great day.

Moses 7:47-58
City of Zion

58 And again Enoch wept and cried unto the Lord, saying:

Enoch	When shall the earth rest?

Reference: Moses 7:47-58

ENOCH SHOWN SECOND COMING OF CHRIST
[39]

Narrator   AND Enoch beheld the Son of Man ascend up unto the   Moses 7:59-69
Father; and he called unto the Lord, saying: City of Zion

Enoch   Wilt thou not come again upon the earth? Forasmuch as thou art God, and I know thee, and thou hast sworn unto me, and commanded me that I should ask in the name of thine Only Begotten; thou hast made me, and given unto me a right to thy throne, and not of myself, but through thine own grace; wherefore, I ask thee if thou wilt not come again on the earth.

Narrator   60 And the Lord said unto Enoch:

The Lord   As I live, even so will I come in the last days, in the days of wickedness and vengeance, to fulfil the oath which I have made unto you concerning the children of Noah; 61 And the day shall come that the earth shall rest, but before that day the heavens shall be darkened, and a veil of darkness shall cover the earth; and the heavens shall shake, and also the earth; and great tribulations shall be among the children of men, but my people will I preserve;

God   62 And righteousness will I send down out of heaven; and truth will I send forth out of the earth, to bear testimony of mine Only Begotten; his resurrection from the dead; yea, and also the resurrection of all men;

The Lord   and righteousness and truth will I cause to sweep the earth as with a flood, to gather out mine elect from the four quarters of the earth, unto a place which I shall prepare, an Holy City, that my people may gird up their loins, and be looking forth for the time of my coming; for there shall be my tabernacle, and it shall be called Zion, a New Jerusalem.

Narrator   63 And the Lord said unto Enoch:

The Lord   Then shalt thou and all thy city meet them there, and we will receive them into our bosom, and they shall see us; and we will fall upon their necks, and they shall fall upon our necks, and we will kiss each other; 64 And there shall be mine abode, and it shall be Zion, which shall come forth out of all the creations which I have made; and for the space of a thousand years the earth shall rest.

Narrator   65 And it came to pass that Enoch saw the day of the coming of the Son of Man, in the last days, to dwell on the earth in righteousness for the space of a thousand years; 66 But before that day he saw great tribulations among the wicked; and he also saw the sea, that it was troubled, and men's hearts failing them, looking forth with fear for the judgments of the Almighty God, which should come upon the wicked. 67 And the Lord showed Enoch all things, even unto the end of the world; and he saw the day of the righteous, the hour of their redemption, and received a fulness of joy;

Narrator   68 And all the days of Zion, in the days of Enoch, were three   Moses 7:59-69
hundred and sixty-five years. 69 And Enoch and all his   City of Zion
people walked with God, and he dwelt in the midst of Zion;
and it came to pass that Zion was not, for God received it up
into his own bosom; and from thence went forth the saying,

ZION IS FLED.

1 And all the days of Enoch were four hundred and thirty   Moses 8:1
years.

References: Moses 7:59-69; Moses 8:1

ENOCH BEGETS METHUSELAH
[40]

Narrator   AND it came to pass that Methuselah, the son of Enoch, was   Moses 8:2-7
not taken, that the covenants of the Lord might be fulfilled,   Land of Cainan
which he made to Enoch; for he truly covenanted with
Enoch that Noah should be of the fruit of his loins.

3 And it came to pass that Methuselah prophesied that from
his loins should spring all the kingdoms of the earth
(through Noah), and he took glory unto himself.

4 And there came forth a great famine into the land, and the
Lord cursed the earth with a sore curse, and many of the
inhabitants thereof died.

5 And it came to pass that Methuselah lived one hundred and
eighty-seven years, and begat Lamech; 6 And Methuselah
lived, after he begat Lamech, seven hundred and eighty-two
years, and begat sons and daughters;

7 And all the days of Methuselah were nine hundred and
sixty-nine years, and he died.

_____

References: Moses 8:2-7; Gen. 5:21-27

NOAH

AND this is mine everlasting covenant, that when thy posterity shall embrace the truth, and look upward, then shall Zion look downward, and all the heavens shall shake with gladness, and the earth shall tremble with joy;

JST GENESIS 9:22

LEMECH BEGETS NOAH

[41]

Narrator   AND Lamech lived one hundred and eighty-two years, and   Moses 8:8-14
begat a son, 9 And he called his name Noah, saying: Land of Cainan

Lamech   This son shall comfort us concerning our work and toil of our
hands, because of the ground which the Lord hath cursed.

Narrator   10 And Lamech lived, after he begat Noah, five hundred and
ninety-five years, and begat sons and daughters; 11 And all
the days of Lamech were seven hundred and seventy-seven
years, and he died.

12 And Noah was four hundred and fifty years old, and begat
Japheth; and forty-two years afterward he begat Shem of her
who was the mother of Japheth, and when he was five
hundred years old he begat Ham.

13 And Noah and his sons hearkened unto the Lord, and
gave heed, and they were called the sons of God. 14 And
when these men began to multiply on the face of the earth,
and daughters were born unto them, the sons of men saw
that those daughters were fair, and they took them wives,
even as they chose.

References: Moses 8:8-14; Gen. 5:28-32

NOAH CALLED TO PREACH REPENTANCE
[42]

Narrator	AND the Lord said unto Noah:	Moses 8:15-24
		Land of Cainan
The Lord	The daughters of thy sons have sold themselves; for behold mine anger is kindled against the sons of men, for they will not hearken to my voice.	
Narrator	16 And it came to pass that Noah prophesied, and taught the things of God, even as it was in the beginning. 17 And the Lord said unto Noah:	
The Lord	My Spirit shall not always strive with man, for he shall know that all flesh shall die; yet his days shall be an hundred and twenty years; and if men do not repent, I will send in the floods upon them.	
Narrator	18 And in those days there were giants on the earth, and they sought Noah to take away his life; but the Lord was with Noah, and the power of the Lord was upon him. 19 And the Lord ordained Noah after his own order, and commanded him that he should go forth and declare his Gospel unto the children of men, even as it was given unto Enoch. 20 And it came to pass that Noah called upon the children of men that they should repent; but they hearkened not unto his words; 21 And also, after that they had heard him, they came up before him, saying:	
Children of Men	Behold, we are the sons of God; have we not taken unto ourselves the daughters of men? And are we not eating and drinking, and marrying and giving in marriage? And our wives bear unto us children, and the same are mighty men, which are like unto men of old, men of great renown.	
Narrator	And they hearkened not unto the words of Noah. 22 And God saw that the wickedness of men had become great in the earth; and every man was lifted up in the imagination of the thoughts of his heart, being only evil continually. 23 And it came to pass that Noah continued his preaching unto the people, saying:	
Noah	Hearken, and give heed unto my words; 24 Believe and repent of your sins and be baptized in the name of Jesus Christ, the Son of God, even as our fathers, and ye shall receive the Holy Ghost, that ye may have all things made manifest; and if ye do not this, the floods will come in upon you;	
Narrator	nevertheless they hearkened not.	

References: Moses 8:15-24; Gen. 6:1-10

THE LORD VOWS TO DESTROY ALL FLESH
[43]

Narrator   AND it repented Noah, and his heart was pained that the   Moses 8:25-27
Lord had made man on the earth, and it grieved him at the   Land of Cainan
heart. 26 And the Lord said:

The Lord   I will destroy man whom I have created, from the face of the earth,
both man and beast, and the creeping things, and the fowls of the
air; for it repenteth Noah that I have created them, and that I have
made them; and he hath called upon me; for they have sought his
life.

Narrator   27 And thus Noah found grace in the eyes of the Lord; for
Noah was a just man, and perfect in his generation; and he
walked with God, as did also his three sons, Shem, Ham,
and Japheth.

References: Moses 8:25-27; Gen. 6:11-13

NOAH COMMANDED TO BUILD ARK
[44]

Narrator   THE earth was corrupt before God, and it was filled with   Moses 8:28-30
violence. 29 And God looked upon the earth, and, behold, it   Land of Cainan
was corrupt, for all flesh had corrupted its way upon the
earth. 30 And God said unto Noah:

God   The end of all flesh is come before me, for the earth is filled with
violence, and behold I will destroy all flesh from off the earth.

14 Make thee an ark of gopher wood; rooms [compartments] shalt   Gen. 6:14-22
thou make in the ark, and shalt pitch it within and without with
pitch. 15 And this is the fashion which thou shalt make it of:

The length of the ark shall be three hundred cubits, the breadth
of it fifty cubits, and the height of it thirty cubits. 16 A window*
shalt thou make to the ark, and in a cubit shalt thou finish it
above; and the door of the ark shalt thou set in the side thereof;
with lower, second, and third stories shalt thou make it.

17 And, behold, I, even I, do bring a flood of waters upon the earth,
to destroy all flesh, wherein is the breath of life, from under
heaven; and every thing that is in the earth shall die. 18 But with
thee will I establish my covenant, *even as I have sworn unto thy
father, Enoch, that of thy posterity shall come all nations. And* thou
shalt come into the ark, thou, and thy sons, and thy wife, and thy
sons' wives with thee. 19 And of every living thing of all flesh, two
of every sort shalt thou bring into the ark, to keep them alive with
thee; they shall be male and female. 20 Of fowls after their kind,
and of cattle after their kind, of every creeping thing of the earth
after his kind, two of every sort shall come unto thee, to keep them
alive. 21 And take thou unto thee of all food that is eaten, and thou
shalt gather it to thee; and it shall be for food for thee, and for
them.

Narrator   22 Thus did Noah; according to all that God commanded
him, so did he.

References: Moses 8:28-30; Gen. 6:14-22

* Hebrew: *tsohar*, some rabbis believed it was a precious stone that
shone in the ark.

NOAH'S FAMILY AND ANIMALS ENTER ARK
[45]

Narrator   AND the LORD* said unto Noah,   Gen. 7:1-16

Land of Cainan

The Lord   Come thou and all thy house into the ark; for thee have I seen
righteous before me in this generation. 2 Of every clean beast thou
shalt take to thee by sevens, the male and his female: and of beasts
that are not clean by two, the male and his female. 3 Of fowls also
of the air by sevens, the male and the female; to keep seed alive
upon the face of all the earth. 4 For yet seven days, and I will cause
it to rain upon the earth forty days and forty nights; and every
living substance that I have made will I destroy from off the face of
the earth.

Narrator   5 And Noah did according unto all that the LORD
commanded him. 6 And Noah was six hundred years old
when the flood of waters was upon the earth.

7 And Noah went in, and his sons, and his wife, and his sons'   Noah's Ark
wives with him, into the ark, because of the waters of the
flood. 8 Of clean beasts, and of beasts that are not clean, and
of fowls, and of every thing that creepeth upon the earth,
9 There went in two and two unto Noah into the ark, the
male and the female, as God had commanded Noah.

10 And it came to pass after seven days, that the waters of
the flood were upon the earth.

11 In the six hundredth year of Noah's life, in the second
month, the seventeenth day of the month, the same day were
all the fountains of the great deep broken up [burst open],
and the windows of heaven were opened. 12 And the rain
was upon the earth forty days and forty nights.

13 In the selfsame day entered Noah, and Shem, and Ham,
and Japheth, the sons of Noah, and Noah's wife, and the
three wives of his sons with them, into the ark; 14 They, and
every beast after his kind, and all the cattle after their kind,
and every creeping thing that creepeth upon the earth after
his kind, and every fowl after his kind, every bird of every
sort. 15 And they went in unto Noah into the ark, two and
two of all flesh, wherein is the breath of life. 16 And they
that went in, went in male and female of all flesh, as God
had commanded him: and the LORD shut him in.

Reference: Gen. 7:1-16

* In the King James version, "Jehovah," the premortal Jesus Christ, is
generally denoted by the word "LORD" (small caps). Jehovah is the
covenant (or proper) name of the God of Israel. See the LDS Bible
Dictionary entry for Jehovah.

FLOOD DESTROYS MANY FORMS OF LIFE
[46]

Narrator AND the flood was forty days upon the earth; and the waters   Gen. 7:17-24
increased, and bare up the ark, and it was lift up above the   Noah's Ark
earth [it rose high above the ground]. 18 And the waters
prevailed, and were increased greatly upon the earth; and the
ark went upon the face of the waters. 19 And the waters
prevailed exceedingly upon the earth; and all the high hills,
that were under the whole heaven, were covered. 20 Fifteen
cubits upward did the waters prevail; and the mountains
were covered.

21 And all flesh died that moved upon the earth, both of
fowl, and of cattle, and of beast, and of every creeping thing
that creepeth upon the earth, and every man [the whole of
mankind]: 22 All in whose nostrils was the breath of life, of
all that was in the dry land, died. 23 And every living
substance was destroyed which was upon the face of the
ground, both man, and cattle, and the creeping things, and
the fowl of the heaven; and they were destroyed from the
earth: and Noah only remained alive, and they that were
with him in the ark.

24 And the waters prevailed upon the earth an hundred and
fifty days.

Reference: Gen. 7:17-24

WATERS RECEDE OFF FACE OF EARTH
[47]

Narrator AND God remembered Noah, and every living thing, and all   Gen. 8:1-14
the cattle that was with him in the ark: and God made a wind   Noah's Ark
to pass over the earth, and the waters assuaged [subsided];
2 The fountains also of the deep and the windows of heaven
were stopped, and the rain from heaven was restrained;
3 And the waters returned from off the earth continually: and
after the end of the hundred and fifty days the waters were
abated [had decreased].

4 And the ark rested in the seventh month, on the
seventeenth day of the month, upon the mountains of Ararat.
5 And the waters decreased continually until the tenth
month: in the tenth month, on the first day of the month,
were the tops of the mountains seen.

6 And it came to pass at the end of forty days, that Noah
opened the window of the ark which he had made: 7 And he
sent forth a raven, which went forth to and fro, until the
waters were dried up from off the earth. 8 Also he sent forth
a dove from him, to see if the waters were abated from off
the face of the ground; 9 But the dove found no rest for the
sole of her foot, and she returned unto him into the ark, for
the waters were on the face of the whole earth: then he put
forth his hand, and took her, and pulled her in unto him into
the ark.

10 And he stayed yet other [waited another] seven days; and
again he sent forth the dove out of the ark; 11 And the dove
came in to him in the evening; and, lo, in her mouth was an
olive leaf plucked off: so Noah knew that the waters were
abated from off the earth.

12 And he stayed yet other seven days; and sent forth the
dove; which returned not again unto him any more.

13 And it came to pass in the six hundredth and first year, in
the first month, the first day of the month, the waters were
dried up from off the earth: and Noah removed the covering
of the ark, and looked, and, behold, the face of the ground
was dry. 14 And in the second month, on the seven and
twentieth day of the month, was the earth dried.

Reference: Gen. 8:1-14

NOAH'S FAMILY AND ANIMALS LEAVE ARK
[48]

Narrator AND God spake unto Noah, saying,

Gen. 8:15-22

Noah's Ark

God 16 Go forth of the ark, thou, and thy wife, and thy sons, and thy sons' wives with thee. 17 Bring forth with thee every living thing that is with thee, of all flesh, both of fowl, and of cattle, and of every creeping thing that creepeth upon the earth; that they may breed abundantly in the earth, and be fruitful, and multiply upon the earth.

Narrator 18 And Noah went forth, and his sons, and his wife, and his sons' wives with him: 19 Every beast, every creeping thing, and every fowl, and whatsoever creepeth upon the earth, after their kinds [families], went forth out of the ark.

Near Noah's Ark

20 And Noah builded an altar unto the LORD; and took of every clean beast, and of every clean fowl, and offered burnt offerings on the altar; *and gave thanks unto the Lord, and rejoiced in his heart.* 21 *And the Lord spake unto Noah, and he blessed him.* And *Noah* smelled a sweet savour; and *he* said in his heart,

Noah I *will call on the name of the Lord, that he* will not again curse the ground any more for man's sake [because of man]; for the imagination of man's heart is evil from his youth; *and that he* will *not* again smite any more every thing living, as *he hath* done. 22 While the earth remaineth, seedtime and harvest, and cold and heat, and summer and winter, and day and night shall not cease.

Reference: Gen. 8:15-22

NOAH'S FAMILY COMMANDED TO MULTIPLY
[49]

Narrator   AND God blessed Noah and his sons, and said unto them,   Gen. 9:1-7

God   Be fruitful, and multiply, and replenish [fill] the earth. 2 And the   Near Noah's Ark
            fear of you and the dread of you shall be upon every beast of the
            earth, and upon every fowl of the air, upon all that moveth upon
            the earth, and upon all the fishes of the sea; into your hand are they
            delivered. 3 Every moving thing that liveth shall be meat [food] for
            you; even as the green herb have I given you all things.

            4 But, *the blood of all* flesh *which I have given you for meat, shall
            be shed upon the ground, which taketh life thereof, and the blood
            ye shall* not eat. 5 And surely, *blood shall not be shed, only for
            meat, to save your lives; and the blood* of every beast will I require
            at your hands. 6 *And whoso* sheddeth man's blood, by man shall
            his blood be shed*; for man shall not shed the blood of man. For a
            commandment I give,*

                *that every man's brother shall preserve the life of man, for in
                mine own image have I made* man.

            7 *And a commandment I give unto you,*

                Be ye fruitful, and multiply; bring forth abundantly *on* the earth,
                and multiply therein.

                            ————————

            Reference: Gen. 9:1-7

GOD COVENANTS WITH NOAH'S SEED
[50]

Narrator AND God spake unto Noah, and to his sons with him,   Gen. 9:8-17
saying,   Near Noah's Ark

God 9 And I, behold, I *will* establish my covenant with you, *which I made unto your father Enoch, concerning* your seed after you. 10 And with every living creature that is with you, of the fowl, of the cattle, and of every beast of the earth with you; from all that go out of the ark, to every beast of the earth. 11 And I will establish my covenant with you, *which I made unto Enoch, concerning the remnants of your posterity. Neither* shall all flesh be cut off any more by the waters of a flood; neither shall there any more be a flood to destroy the earth.

Narrator 12 And God said,

God This is the token of the covenant which I make between me and you and every living creature that is with you, for perpetual generations: 13 I do set my bow in the cloud, and it shall be for a token of a covenant between me and the earth.

14 And it shall come to pass, when I bring a cloud over the earth, that the bow shall be seen in the cloud: 15 And I will remember my covenant, which *I have made* between me and you, *for* every living creature of all flesh; and the waters shall no more become a flood to destroy all flesh. 16 And the bow shall be in the cloud; and I will look upon it, that I may remember the everlasting covenant, *which I made unto thy father Enoch; that, when men should keep all my commandments, Zion should again come on the earth, the city of Enoch which I have caught up unto myself.*

And this is mine everlasting covenant, that when thy posterity shall embrace the truth, and look upward, then shall Zion look downward, and all the heavens shall shake with gladness, and the earth shall tremble with joy; And the general assembly of the church of the firstborn shall come down out of heaven, and possess the earth, and shall have place until the end come. And this is mine everlasting covenant, which I made with thy father Enoch. And the bow shall be in the cloud, and I will establish my covenant unto thee, which I have made between *me* and *thee, for* every living creature of all flesh that *shall be* upon the earth.

Narrator 17 And God said unto Noah,

God This is the token of the covenant, which I have established between me and *thee; for* all flesh that *shall be* upon the earth.

———————

Reference: Gen. 9:8-17

NOAH'S DESCENDANTS MULTIPLY

[51]

Narrator AND the sons of Noah, that went forth of the ark, were   Gen. 9:18-29
Shem, and Ham, and Japheth: and Ham is the father of   Near Noah's Ark
Canaan. 19 These are the three sons of Noah: and of them
was the whole earth overspread.

20 And Noah began to be an husbandman, and he planted a
vineyard: 21 And he drank of the wine, and was drunken;
and he was uncovered within his tent. 22 And Ham, the
father of Canaan, saw the nakedness of his father, and told
his two brethren without. 23 And Shem and Japheth took a
garment, and laid it upon both their shoulders, and went
backward, and covered the nakedness of their father; and
their faces were backward, and they saw not their father's
nakedness.

24 And Noah awoke from his wine, and knew what his
younger son had done unto him. 25 And he said,

Noah   Cursed be Canaan; a servant of servants shall he be unto his
brethren.

Narrator   26 And he said,

Noah   Blessed be the LORD God of Shem; and Canaan shall be his
servant, *and a veil of darkness shall cover him, that he shall be
known among all men.* 27 God shall enlarge Japheth, and he shall
dwell in the tents of Shem; and Canaan shall be his servant.

Narrator   28 And Noah lived after the flood three hundred and fifty
years. 29 And all the days of Noah were nine hundred and
fifty years: and he died.

––––––––––

Reference: Gen. 9:18-29

DESCENDANTS OF NOAH'S SONS NAMED
[52]

Narrator NOW these are the generations [genealogical lines] of the   Gen. 10:1-32
sons of Noah, Shem, Ham, and Japheth: and unto them were
sons born after the flood.

Sons of Japheth

2 The sons of Japheth; Gomer, and Magog, and Madai, and
Javan, and Tubal, and Meshech, and Tiras.

3 And the sons of Gomer; Ashkenaz, and Riphath, and
Togarmah.

4 And the sons of Javan; Elishah, and Tarshish, Kittim, and
Dodanim.

5 By [From] these were the isles [coasts, continents] of the
Gentiles divided in their lands; every one after his tongue,
after their families, in their nations.

Sons of Ham

6 And the sons of Ham; Cush [Ethiopians, Egyptians,
Libyans, and Canaanites], and Mizraim [Egypt], and Phut,
and Canaan.

7 And the sons of Cush; Seba, and Havilah, and Sabtah, and
Raamah, and Sabtecha: and the sons of Raamah; Sheba, and
Dedan.

8 And Cush begat Nimrod: he began to be a mighty one in
the earth. 9 He was a mighty hunter before the LORD:
wherefore it is said, Even as Nimrod the mighty hunter
before the LORD. 10 And the beginning of his kingdom was
Babel [later Babylon], and Erech, and Accad, and Calneh, in
the land of Shinar. 11 Out of that land went forth Asshur, and
builded Nineveh, and the city Rehoboth, and Calah, 12 And
Resen between Nineveh and Calah: the same is a great city.

13 And Mizraim begat Ludim, and Anamim, and Lehabim,
and Naphtuhim, 14 And Pathrusim, and Casluhim, (out of
whom came Philistim,) and Caphtorim.

15 And Canaan begat Sidon his firstborn, and Heth, 16 And
the Jebusite, and the Amorite, and the Girgasite, 17 And the
Hivite, and the Arkite, and the Sinite, 18 And the Arvadite,
and the Zemarite, and the Hamathite: and afterward were the
families of the Canaanites spread abroad.

Narrator   19 And the border of the Canaanites was from Sidon, as thou   Gen. 10:1-32
comest to Gerar, unto Gaza; as thou goest, unto Sodom, and
Gomorrah, and Admah, and Zeboim, even unto Lasha.

20 These are the sons of Ham, after their families, after their
tongues, in their countries, and in their nations.

Sons of Shem

21 Unto Shem also, the father of all the children of Eber, the
brother of Japheth the elder, even to him were children born.

22 The children of Shem; Elam, and Asshur, and Arphaxad,
and Lud, and Aram.

23 And the children of Aram; Uz, and Hul, and Gether, and
Mash.

24 And Arphaxad begat Salah; and Salah begat Eber.

25 And unto Eber were born two sons: the name of one was
Peleg [Division]; for in his days was the earth divided; and
his brother's name was Joktan.

26 And Joktan begat Almodad, and Sheleph, and
Hazarmaveth, and Jerah,

27 And Hadoram, and Uzal, and Diklah,

28 And Obal, and Abimael, and Sheba,

29 And Ophir, and Havilah, and Jobab: all these were the
sons of Joktan.

30 And their dwelling was from Mesha, as thou goest unto
Sephar a mount of the east.

31 These are the sons of Shem, after their families, after their
tongues, in their lands, after their nations.

32 These are the families of the sons of Noah, after their
generations, in their nations: and by [from] these were the
nations divided in the earth after the flood.

Reference: Gen. 10:1-32

THE LORD CONFOUNDS THE LANGUAGE
[53]

Narrator AND the whole earth was of one language, and of one speech.

Gen. 11:1-9
Land of Shinar

2 And it came to pass, as they [Noah's descendants] journeyed from the east, that they found a plain in the land of Shinar; and they dwelt there. 3 And they said one to another,

People Go to, let us make brick, and burn them throughly.

Narrator And they had brick for stone, and slime [bitumen] had they for mortar. 4 And they said,

People Go to, let us build us a city and a tower, whose top may reach unto heaven; and let us make us a name, lest we be scattered abroad upon the face of the whole earth.

City of Babel

Narrator 5 And the LORD came down to see the city and the tower, which the children of men builded. 6 And the LORD said,

The Lord Behold, the people is one, and they have all one language; and this they begin to do: and now nothing will be restrained from them, which they have imagined to do. 7 Go to, let us go down, and there confound their language, that they may not understand one another's speech.

Narrator 8 So the LORD scattered them abroad from thence upon the face of all the earth: and they left off to build the city, *and they hearkened not unto the Lord.* 9 Therefore is the name of it called Babel; because the LORD did there confound [mix] the language of all the earth: and from thence did the LORD scatter them abroad upon the face of all the earth.

Reference: Gen. 11:1-9

ABRAHAM

AND I will bless them that bless thee, and curse them that curse thee; and in thee (that is, in thy Priesthood) and in thy seed (that is, thy Priesthood), for I give unto thee a promise that this right shall continue in thee, and in thy seed after thee (that is to say, the literal seed, or the seed of the body) shall all the families of the earth be blessed, even with the blessings of the Gospel, which are the blessings of salvation, even of life eternal.

ABRAHAM 2:11

ABRAHAM'S LINEAGE FROM SHEM NAMED
[54]

Narrator   THESE are the generations of Shem: Shem was an hundred   Gen. 11:10-27
years old, and begat Arphaxad two years after the flood:
11 And Shem lived after he begat Arphaxad five hundred
years, and begat sons and daughters.

12 And Arphaxad lived five and thirty years, and begat
Salah: 13 And Arphaxad lived after he begat Salah four
hundred and three years, and begat sons and daughters.

14 And Salah lived thirty years, and begat Eber: 15 And Salah
lived after he begat Eber four hundred and three years, and
begat sons and daughters.

16 And Eber lived four and thirty years, and begat Peleg:
17 And Eber lived after he begat Peleg four hundred and
thirty years, and begat sons and daughters.

18 And Peleg lived thirty years, and begat Reu: 19 And Peleg
lived after he begat Reu two hundred and nine years, and
begat sons and daughters.

20 And Reu lived two and thirty years, and begat Serug:
21 And Reu lived after he begat Serug two hundred and
seven years, and begat sons and daughters.

22 And Serug lived thirty years, and begat Nahor: 23 And
Serug lived after he begat Nahor two hundred years, and
begat sons and daughters.

24 And Nahor lived nine and twenty years, and begat Terah:
25 And Nahor lived after he begat Terah an hundred and
nineteen years, and begat sons and daughters.

26 And Terah lived seventy years, and begat Abram, Nahor,
and Haran.

27 Now these are the generations of Terah: Terah begat
Abram, Nahor, and Haran; and Haran begat Lot.

Reference: Gen. 11:10-27

ABRAHAM SEEKS BLESSINGS OF THE FATHERS
[55]

Abraham IN the land of the Chaldeans, at the residence of my fathers, Abr. 1:1-7
I, Abraham, saw that it was needful for me to obtain another Land of Chaldea
place of residence;

2 And, finding there was greater happiness and peace and rest for me, I sought for the blessings of the fathers, and the right whereunto I should be ordained to administer the same; having been myself a follower of righteousness, desiring also to be one who possessed great knowledge, and to be a greater follower of righteousness, and to possess a greater knowledge, and to be a father of many nations, a prince of peace, and desiring to receive instructions, and to keep the commandments of God, I became a rightful heir, a High Priest, holding the right belonging to the fathers.

3 It was conferred upon me from the fathers; it came down from the fathers, from the beginning of time, yea, even from the beginning, or before the foundation of the earth, down to the present time, even the right of the firstborn, or the first man, who is Adam, or first father, through the fathers unto me. 4 I sought for mine appointment unto the Priesthood according to the appointment of God unto the fathers concerning the seed.

5 My fathers, having turned from their righteousness, and from the holy commandments which the Lord their God had given unto them, unto the worshiping of the gods of the heathen, utterly refused to hearken to my voice; 6 For their hearts were set to do evil, and were wholly turned to the god of Elkenah, and the god of Libnah, and the god of Mahmackrah, and the god of Korash, and the god of Pharaoh, king of Egypt; 7 Therefore they turned their hearts to the sacrifice of the heathen in offering up their children unto these dumb idols, and hearkened not unto my voice, but endeavored to take away my life by the hand of the priest of Elkenah. The priest of Elkenah was also the priest of Pharaoh.

Reference: Abr. 1:1-7

PHARAOH'S PRIESTS TRY TO SLAY ABRAHAM
[56]

Abraham   NOW, at this time it was the custom of the priest of Pharaoh,   Abr. 1:8-14
the king of Egypt, to offer up upon the altar which was built   Land of Chaldea
in the land of Chaldea, for the offering unto these strange
gods, men, women, and children.

9 And it came to pass that the priest made an offering unto
the god of Pharaoh, and also unto the god of Shagreel, even
after the manner of the Egyptians. Now the god of Shagreel
was the sun. 10 Even the thank-offering of a child did the
priest of Pharaoh offer upon the altar which stood by the hill
called Potiphar's Hill, at the head of the plain of Olishem.

11 Now, this priest had offered upon this altar three virgins at
one time, who were the daughters of Onitah, one of the royal
descent directly from the loins of Ham. These virgins were
offered up because of their virtue; they would not bow down
to worship gods of wood or of stone, therefore they were
killed upon this altar, and it was done after the manner of the
Egyptians.

12 And it came to pass that the priests laid violence upon me,
that they might slay me also, as they did those virgins upon
this altar; and that you may have a knowledge of this altar, I
will refer you to the representation at the commencement of
this record*. 13 It was made after the form of a bedstead,
such as was had among the Chaldeans, and it stood before
the gods of Elkenah, Libnah, Mahmackrah, Korash, and also
a god like unto that of Pharaoh, king of Egypt.

14 That you may have an understanding of these gods, I have
given you the fashion of them in the figures at the
beginning, which manner of figures is called by the
Chaldeans Rahleenos, which signifies hieroglyphics.

Reference: Abr. 1:8-14

* See Facsimile 1 from the Book of Abraham in the Pearl of Great
Price.

THE LORD SAVES ABRAHAM FROM PRIESTS
[57]

Abraham   AND as they [priests of Pharaoh] lifted up their hands upon   Abr. 1:15-19
me, that they might offer me up and take away my life,   Land of Chaldea
behold, I lifted up my voice unto the Lord my God, and the
Lord hearkened and heard, and he filled me with the vision
of the Almighty, and the angel of his presence stood by me,
and immediately unloosed my bands; 16 And his voice was
unto me:

The Lord   Abraham, Abraham, behold, my name is Jehovah, and I have heard
thee, and have come down to deliver thee, and to take thee away
from thy father's house, and from all thy kinsfolk, into a strange
land which thou knowest not of; 17 And this because they have
turned their hearts away from me, to worship the god of Elkenah,
and the god of Libnah, and the god of Mahmackrah, and the god of
Korash, and the god of Pharaoh, king of Egypt; therefore I have
come down to visit them, and to destroy him who hath lifted up his
hand against thee, Abraham, my son, to take away thy life.
18 Behold, I will lead thee by my hand, and I will take thee, to put
upon thee my name, even the Priesthood of thy father, and my
power shall be over thee. 19 As it was with Noah so shall it be with
thee; but through thy ministry my name shall be known in the earth
forever, for I am thy God.

Reference: Abr. 1:15-19

RECORDS PRESERVED BY ABRAHAM
[58]

Abraham

BEHOLD, Potiphar's Hill was in the land of Ur, of Chaldea. And the Lord broke down the altar of Elkenah, and of the gods of the land, and utterly destroyed them, and smote the priest that he died; and there was great mourning in Chaldea, and also in the court of Pharaoh; which Pharaoh signifies king by royal blood.

Abr. 1:20-31
Land of Ur, of Chaldea

21 Now this king of Egypt was a descendant from the loins of Ham, and was a partaker of the blood of the Canaanites by birth. 22 From this descent sprang all the Egyptians, and thus the blood of the Canaanites was preserved in the land.

23 The land of Egypt being first discovered by a woman, who was the daughter of Ham, and the daughter of Egyptus, which in the Chaldean signifies Egypt, which signifies that which is forbidden; 24 When this woman discovered the land it was under water, who afterward settled her sons in it; and thus, from Ham, sprang that race which preserved the curse in the land.

25 Now the first government of Egypt was established by Pharaoh, the eldest son of Egyptus, the daughter of Ham, and it was after the manner of the government of Ham, which was patriarchal. 26 Pharaoh, being a righteous man, established his kingdom and judged his people wisely and justly all his days, seeking earnestly to imitate that order established by the fathers in the first generations, in the days of the first patriarchal reign, even in the reign of Adam, and also of Noah, his father, who blessed him with the blessings of the earth, and with the blessings of wisdom, but cursed him as pertaining to the Priesthood.

27 Now, Pharaoh being of that lineage by which he could not have the right of Priesthood, notwithstanding the Pharaohs would fain claim it from Noah, through Ham, therefore my father was led away by their idolatry; 28 But I shall endeavor, hereafter, to delineate the chronology running back from myself to the beginning of the creation, for the records have come into my hands, which I hold unto this present time.

29 Now, after the priest of Elkenah was smitten that he died, there came a fulfilment of those things which were said unto me concerning the land of Chaldea, that there should be a famine in the land. 30 Accordingly a famine prevailed throughout all the land of Chaldea, and my father was sorely tormented because of the famine, and he repented of the evil

Abraham which he had determined against me, to take away my life. Abr. 1:20-31

31 But the records of the fathers, even the patriarchs, Land of Ur, of concerning the right of Priesthood, the Lord my God Chaldea preserved in mine own hands; therefore a knowledge of the beginning of the creation, and also of the planets, and of the stars, as they were made known unto the fathers, have I kept even unto this day, and I shall endeavor to write some of these things upon this record, for the benefit of my posterity that shall come after me.

Reference: Abr. 1:20-31

ABRAHAM LEAVES UR TO SETTLE IN CANAAN
[59]

Abraham   NOW the Lord God caused the famine to wax sore in the land of Ur, insomuch that Haran, my brother, died; but Terah, my father, yet lived in the land of Ur, of the Chaldees.   Abr. 2:1-5 — Land of Ur, of Chaldea

2 And it came to pass that I, Abraham, took Sarai to wife, and Nahor, my brother, took Milcah to wife, who was the daughter of Haran.

3 Now the Lord had said unto me:

The Lord   Abraham, get thee out of thy country, and from thy kindred, and from thy father's house, unto a land that I will show thee.

Abraham   4 Therefore I left the land of Ur, of the Chaldees, to go into the land of Canaan; and I took Lot, my brother's son, and his wife, and Sarai my wife; and also my father followed after me, unto the land which we denominated Haran.

5 And the famine abated; and my father tarried in Haran and dwelt there, as there were many flocks in Haran; and my father turned again unto his idolatry, therefore he continued in Haran.   Haran

Narrator   30 But Sarai was barren; she had no child. 32 And the days of Terah were two hundred and five years: and Terah died in Haran.   Gen. 11:30, 32

References: Abr. 2:1-5; Gen. 11:28-32; Gen. 12:1

THE LORD BLESSES ABRAHAM'S POSTERITY
[60]

Abraham BUT I, Abraham, and Lot, my brother's son, prayed unto the Abr. 2:6-13
Lord, and the Lord appeared unto me, and said unto me: Haran

The Lord Arise, and take Lot with thee; for I have purposed to take thee away out of Haran, and to make of thee a minister to bear my name in a strange land which I will give unto thy seed after thee for an everlasting possession, when they hearken to my voice. 7 For I am the Lord thy God; I dwell in heaven; the earth is my footstool; I stretch my hand over the sea, and it obeys my voice; I cause the wind and the fire to be my chariot; I say to the mountains—

Depart hence

—and behold, they are taken away by a whirlwind, in an instant, suddenly.

8 My name is Jehovah, and I know the end from the beginning; therefore my hand shall be over thee. 9 And I will make of thee a great nation, and I will bless thee above measure, and make thy name great among all nations, and thou shalt be a blessing unto thy seed after thee, that in their hands they shall bear this ministry and Priesthood unto all nations; 10 And I will bless them through thy name; for as many as receive this Gospel shall be called after thy name, and shall be accounted thy seed, and shall rise up and bless thee, as their father; 11 And I will bless them that bless thee, and curse them that curse thee; and in thee (that is, in thy Priesthood) and in thy seed (that is, thy Priesthood), for I give unto thee a promise that this right shall continue in thee, and in thy seed after thee (that is to say, the literal seed, or the seed of the body) shall all the families of the earth be blessed, even with the blessings of the Gospel, which are the blessings of salvation, even of life eternal.

Abraham 12 Now, after the Lord had withdrawn from speaking to me, and withdrawn his face from me, I said in my heart:

Thy servant has sought thee earnestly; now I have found thee; 13 Thou didst send thine angel to deliver me from the gods of Elkenah, and I will do well to hearken unto thy voice, therefore let thy servant rise up and depart in peace.

References: Abr. 2:6-13; Gen. 12:2-3

THE LORD APPEARS TO ABRAHAM AT BETHEL
[61]

Abraham SO I, Abraham, departed as the Lord had said unto me, and   Abr. 2:14-20
Lot with me; and I, Abraham, was sixty and two years old   Land of Jershon
when I departed out of Haran. 15 And I took Sarai, whom I
took to wife when I was in Ur, in Chaldea, and Lot, my
brother's son, and all our substance that we had gathered,
and the souls that we had won in Haran, and came forth in
the way to the land of Canaan, and dwelt in tents as we came
on our way; 16 Therefore, eternity was our covering and our
rock and our salvation, as we journeyed from Haran by the
way of Jershon*, to come to the land of Canaan.

17 Now I, Abraham, built an altar in the land of Jershon, and
made an offering unto the Lord, and prayed that the famine
might be turned away from my father's house, that they
might not perish.

18 And then we passed from Jershon through the land unto   Shechem
the place of Sechem; it was situated in the plains of Moreh,
and we had already come into the borders of the land of the
Canaanites, and I offered sacrifice there in the plains of
Moreh, and called on the Lord devoutly, because we had
already come into the land of this idolatrous nation. 19 And
the Lord appeared unto me in answer to my prayers, and
said unto me:

The Lord Unto thy seed will I give this land.

Abraham 20 And I, Abraham, arose from the place of the altar which I   East of Bethel
had built unto the Lord, and removed from thence unto a
mountain on the east of Bethel, and pitched my tent there,
Bethel on the west, and Hai on the east; and there I built
another altar unto the Lord, and called again upon the name
of the Lord.

References: Abr. 2:14-20; Gen. 12:4-8

* There is a possibility that Abram traveled southward on the ancient
route by way of Damascus to the site of ancient Jerash (Jershon),
thence down the Jabbok, across the Jordan, and up the Wadi Farah to
Sechem (also spelled Shechem, Sichem, and Sychem).

ABRAHAM JOURNEYS DOWN TO EGYPT
[62]

Abraham   AND I, Abraham, journeyed, going on still towards the   Abr. 2:21-25
south; and there was a continuation of a famine in the land;   Near Egypt
and I, Abraham, concluded to go down into Egypt, to
sojourn there, for the famine became very grievous. 22 And
it came to pass when I was come near to enter into Egypt,
the Lord said unto me:

The Lord   Behold, Sarai, thy wife, is a very fair woman to look upon;
23 Therefore it shall come to pass, when the Egyptians shall see
her, they will say—

     She is his wife;

and they will kill you, but they will save her alive; therefore see
that ye do on this wise: 24 Let her say unto the Egyptians,

     she is thy sister,

and thy soul shall live.

Abraham   25 And it came to pass that I, Abraham, told Sarai, my wife,
all that the Lord had said unto me—

     Therefore say unto them, I pray thee, thou art my sister, that it may
be well with me for thy sake, and my soul shall live because of
thee.

References: Abr. 2:21-25; Gen. 12:9-13

ABRAHAM ENCOUNTERS PHARAOH IN EGYPT
[63]

Narrator   AND it came to pass, that, when Abram was come into   Gen. 12:14-20
Egypt, the Egyptians beheld the woman that she was very   Egypt
fair. 15 The princes also of Pharaoh saw her, and commended
her before Pharaoh: and the woman was taken into
Pharaoh's house.

16 And he entreated Abram well for her sake: and he had
sheep, and oxen, and he asses, and menservants, and
maidservants, and she asses, and camels. 17 And the LORD
plagued Pharaoh and his house with great plagues because
of Sarai Abram's wife. 18 And Pharaoh called Abram, and
said,

Pharaoh   What is this that thou hast done unto me? why didst thou not tell
me that she was thy wife? 19 Why saidst thou, She is my sister? so
I might have taken her to me to wife: now therefore behold thy
wife, take her, and go thy way.

Narrator   20 And Pharaoh commanded his men concerning him: and
they sent him away, and his wife, and all that he had.

———————

Reference: Gen. 12:14-20

ABRAHAM RETURNS TO LAND OF BETHEL
[64]

Narrator   AND Abram went up out of Egypt, he, and his wife, and all   Gen. 13:1-4
that he had, and Lot with him, into the south.   Egypt

2 And Abram was very rich in cattle, in silver, and in gold.

3 And he went on his journeys from the south even to Beth-   Bethel
el, unto the place where his tent had been at the beginning,
between Beth-el and Hai [Ai]; 4 Unto the place of the altar,
which he had made there at the first: and there Abram called
on the name of the LORD.

Reference: Gen. 13:1-4

ABRAHAM AND LOT GO SEPARATE WAYS
[65]

Narrator   AND Lot also, which went with Abram, had flocks, and   Gen. 13:5-13
herds, and tents.   Bethel

6 And the land was not able to bear them, that they might
dwell together: for their substance was great, so that they
could not dwell together. 7 And there was a strife between
the herdmen of Abram's cattle and the herdmen of Lot's
cattle: and the Canaanite and the Perizzite dwelled then in
the land. 8 And Abram said unto Lot,

Abraham   Let there be no strife, I pray thee, between me and thee, and
between my herdmen and thy herdmen; for we be brethren. 9 Is not
the whole land before thee? separate thyself, I pray thee, from me:
if thou wilt take the left hand, then I will go to the right; or if thou
depart to the right hand, then I will go to the left.

Narrator   10 And Lot lifted up his eyes, and beheld all the plain of   Plain of Jordan
Jordan, that it was well watered every where, before the
LORD destroyed Sodom and Gomorrah, even as the garden
of the LORD, like the land of Egypt, as thou comest unto
Zoar. 11 Then Lot chose him all the plain of Jordan; and Lot
journeyed east: and they separated themselves the one from
the other.

12 Abram dwelled in the land of Canaan, and Lot dwelled in
the cities of the plain, and pitched his tent toward Sodom.
13 But the men of Sodom were wicked and sinners before
the LORD exceedingly.

———————

Reference: Gen. 13:5-13

ABRAHAM DWELLS IN LAND OF HEBRON
[66]

Narrator AND the LORD said unto Abram, after that Lot was separated from him,

Gen. 13:14-18
Land of Canaan

The Lord Lift up now thine eyes, and look from the place where thou art northward, and southward, and eastward, and westward *and remember the covenant which I make with thee; for it shall be an everlasting covenant; and thou shalt remember the days of Enoch thy father;* 15 For all the land which thou seest, to thee will I give it, and to thy seed for ever. 16 And I will make thy seed as the dust of the earth: so that if a man can number the dust of the earth, then shall thy seed also be numbered. 17 Arise, walk through the land in the length of it and in the breadth of it; for I will give it unto thee.

Narrator 18 Then Abram removed his tent, and came and dwelt [by the terebinths] in the plain of Mamre, which is in Hebron, and built there an altar unto the LORD.

Hebron

Reference: Gen. 13:14-18

ABRAHAM RESCUES LOT FROM CAPTIVITY

[67]

Narrator AND it came to pass in the days of Amraphel king of Shinar, Gen. 14:1-17
Arioch king of Ellasar, Chedorlaomer king of Elam, and Near Salt Sea
Tidal king of nations; 2 That these made war with Bera king
of Sodom, and with Birsha king of Gomorrah, Shinab king
of Admah, and Shemeber king of Zeboiim, and the king of
Bela, which is Zoar. 3 All these were joined together in the
vale of Siddim, which is the salt sea.

4 Twelve years they served Chedorlaomer, and in the
thirteenth year they rebelled.

5 And in the fourteenth year came Chedorlaomer, and the
kings that were with him, and smote the Rephaims in
Ashteroth Karnaim, and the Zuzims in Ham, and the Emims
in Shaveh Kiriathaim, 6 And the Horites in their mount Seir,
unto El-paran, which is by the wilderness. 7 And they
returned, and came to En-mishpat, which is Kadesh, and
smote all the country of the Amalekites, and also the
Amorites, that dwelt in Hazezon-tamar.

8 And there went out the king of Sodom, and the king of
Gomorrah, and the king of Admah, and the king of Zeboiim,
and the king of Bela (the same is Zoar;) and they joined
battle with them in the vale of Siddim; 9 With Chedorlaomer
the king of Elam, and with Tidal king of nations, and
Amraphel king of Shinar, and Arioch king of Ellasar; four
kings with five. 10 And the vale of Siddim was full of
slimepits [bitumen pits]; and the kings of Sodom and
Gomorrah fled, and fell there; and they that remained fled to
the mountain.

11 And they took all the goods of Sodom and Gomorrah, and
all their victuals, and went their way. 12 And they took Lot,
Abram's brother's son, who dwelt in Sodom, and his goods,
and departed.

13 And there came one that had escaped, and told Abram the Hebron
Hebrew; for he dwelt [by the terebinths] in the plain of
Mamre the Amorite, brother of Eshcol, and brother of Aner:
and these were confederate with Abram.

14 And when Abram heard that his brother was taken
captive, he armed his trained servants [led forth], born in his
own house, three hundred and eighteen, and pursued them
unto Dan.

Narrator   15 And he divided himself against them, he and his servants,   Gen. 14:1-17
by night, and smote them, and pursued them unto Hobah,   Hobah
which is on the left hand [north] of Damascus.

16 And he brought back all the goods, and also brought again   Hebron
his brother Lot, and his goods, and the women also, and the
people.

17 And the king of Sodom went out to meet him after his   Valley of Shaveh
return from the slaughter of Chedorlaomer, and of the kings
that were with him, at the valley of Shaveh, which is the
king's dale.

Reference: Gen. 14:1-17

ABRAHAM PAYS TITHES TO MELCHIZEDEK
[68]

Narrator   AND Melchizedek [King of righteousness] king of Salem brought forth bread and wine: and he *brake bread and blest it; and he blest the wine, he being* the priest of the most high God. 19 And he blessed him, and said,   Gen. 14:18-24   Salem

Melchizedek   Blessed be Abram of the most high God, possessor [creator] of heaven and earth: 20 And blessed be the most high God, which hath delivered thine enemies into thy hand.

Narrator   And he gave him tithes of all.

21 And the king of Sodom said unto Abram,

King of Sodom   Give me the persons, and take the goods to thyself.

Narrator   22 And Abram said to the king of Sodom,

Abraham   I have lift up mine hand unto the LORD, the most high God, the possessor of heaven and earth, 23 That I will not take from a thread even to a shoelatchet, and that I will not take any thing that is thine, lest thou shouldest say, I have made Abram rich: 24 Save only that which the young men have eaten, and the portion of the men which went with me, Aner, Eshcol, and Mamre; let them take their portion.

Narrator   *And Melchizedek lifted up his voice and blessed Abram.*

Now Melchizedek was a man of faith, who wrought righteousness; and when a child he feared God, and stopped the mouths of lions, and quenched the violence of fire.

And thus, having been approved of God, he was ordained an high priest after the order of the covenant which God made with Enoch, It being after the order of the Son of God; which order came, not by man, nor the will of man; neither by father nor mother; neither by beginning of days nor end of years; but of God;

And it was delivered unto men by the calling of his own voice, according to his own will, unto as many as believed on his name. For God having sworn unto Enoch and unto his seed with an oath by himself; that every one being ordained after this order and calling should have power, by faith, to break mountains, to divide the seas, to dry up waters, to turn them out of their course; To put at defiance the armies of nations, to divide the earth, to break every band, to stand in the presence of God; to do all things according to his will, according to his command, subdue principalities and powers; and this by the will of the Son of

Narrator *God which was from before the foundation of the world. And men having this faith, coming up unto this order of God, were translated and taken up into heaven.*

Gen. 14:18-24
Salem

And now, Melchizedek was a priest of this order; therefore he obtained peace in Salem, and was called the Prince of peace. And his people wrought righteousness, and obtained heaven, and sought for the city of Enoch which God had before taken, separating it from the earth, having reserved it unto the latter days, or the end of the world; And hath said, and sworn with an oath,

God *that the heavens and the earth should come together; and the sons of God should be tried so as by fire.*

Narrator *And this Melchizedek, having thus established righteousness, was called the king of heaven by his people, or, in other words, the King of peace.*

And he lifted up his voice, and he blessed Abram, being the high priest, and the keeper of the storehouse of God; Him whom God had appointed to receive tithes for the poor. Wherefore, Abram paid unto him tithes of all that he had, of all the riches which he possessed, which God had given him more than that which he had need.

And it came to pass, that God blessed Abram, and gave unto him riches, and honor, and lands for an everlasting possession; according to the covenant which he had made, and according to the blessing wherewith Melchizedek had blessed him.

Reference: Gen. 14:18-24

ABRAHAM PROMISED NUMEROUS POSTERITY
[69]

Narrator	AFTER these things the word of the LORD came unto Abram in a vision, saying,	Gen. 15:1-11 Hebron

The Lord   Fear not, Abram: I am thy shield, and thy exceeding great reward.

Narrator   2 And Abram said,

Abraham   Lord GOD, what wilt thou give me, seeing I go childless, and the steward of my house is this Eliezer of Damascus?

Narrator   3 And Abram said,

Abraham   Behold, to me thou hast given no seed: and, lo, one born in my house [a son of my house] is mine heir.

Narrator   4 And, behold, the word of the LORD came unto him, saying,

The Lord   This shall not be thine heir; but he that shall come forth out of thine own bowels shall be thine heir.

Narrator   5 And he brought him forth abroad, and said,

The Lord   Look now toward heaven, and tell [count] the stars, if thou be able to number them:

Narrator   and he said unto him,

The Lord   So shall thy seed be.

Narrator   *And Abram said,*

Abraham   *Lord God, how wilt thou give me this land for an everlasting inheritance?*

Narrator   *And the Lord said,*

The Lord   *Though thou wast dead, yet am I not able to give it thee? And if thou shalt die, yet thou shalt possess it, for the day cometh, that the Son of Man shall live; but how can he live if he be not dead? he must first be quickened.*

Narrator   6 And *it came to pass, that Abram looked forth and saw the days of the Son of Man, and was glad, and his soul found rest, and* he believed in the LORD; and *the Lord* counted it to him for righteousness. 7 And he said unto him,

The Lord   I am the LORD that brought thee out of Ur of the Chaldees, to give thee this land to inherit it.

Narrator   8 And he said,

Abraham   Lord GOD, whereby shall I know that I shall inherit it?

Narrator   9 And he said unto him,

| The Lord | Take me an heifer of three years old, and a she goat of three years old, and a ram of three years old, and a turtledove, and a young pigeon. | Gen. 15:1-11 Hebron |

| Narrator | 10 And he took unto him all these, and divided them in the midst, and laid each piece one against another: but the birds divided he not. 11 And when the fowls came down upon the carcases, Abram drove them away. | |

Reference: Gen. 15:1-11

ABRAHAM'S SEED PROMISED A VAST LAND
[70]

Narrator   AND when the sun was going down, a deep sleep fell upon   Gen. 15:12-21
Abram; and, lo, an horror of great darkness fell upon him.   Hebron
13 And he said unto Abram,

The Lord   Know of a surety that thy seed shall be a stranger in a land that is
not theirs, and shall serve them; and they shall afflict them four
hundred years; 14 And also that nation, whom they shall serve, will
I judge: and afterward shall they come out with great substance.
15 And thou shalt go to thy fathers in peace; thou shalt be buried in
a good old age. 16 But in the fourth generation* they shall come
hither again: for the iniquity of the Amorites is not yet full.

Narrator   17 And it came to pass, that, when the sun went down, and it
was dark, behold a smoking furnace, and a burning lamp
that passed between those pieces. 18 In the same day the
LORD made a covenant with Abram, saying,

The Lord   Unto thy seed have I given this land, from the river of Egypt* unto
the great river, the river Euphrates: 19 The Kenites, and the
Kenizzites, and the Kadmonites, 20 And the Hittites, and the
Perizzites, and the Rephaims, 21 And the Amorites, and the
Canaanites, and the Girgashites, and the Jebusites.

Reference: Gen. 15:12-21

* In Ex. 6:16–20 four generations of Levi's descendants are named;
they include (1) Levi, (2) Kohath, (3) Amram, (4) Moses.

** The Wadi El Arish in northern Sinai.

SARAI GIVES HAGAR TO ABRAHAM AS A WIFE
[71]

Narrator NOW Sarai Abram's wife bare him no children: and she had an handmaid, an Egyptian, whose name was Hagar. 2 And Sarai said unto Abram,

Gen. 16:1-9
Hebron

Sarah Behold now, the LORD hath restrained me from bearing: I pray thee, go in unto my maid; it may be that I may obtain children by her.

Narrator And Abram hearkened to the voice of Sarai. 3 And Sarai Abram's wife took Hagar her maid the Egyptian, after Abram had dwelt ten years in the land of Canaan, and gave her to her husband Abram to be his wife. 4 And he went in unto Hagar, and she conceived: and when she saw that she had conceived, her mistress was despised in her eyes. 5 And Sarai said unto Abram,

Sarah My wrong be upon thee: I have given my maid into thy bosom; and when she saw that she had conceived, I was despised in her eyes: the LORD judge between me and thee.

Narrator 6 But Abram said unto Sarai,

Abraham Behold, thy maid is in thy hand; do to her as it pleaseth thee [that which is good in thine eyes].

Narrator And when Sarai dealt hardly with her, she fled from her face. 7 And the angel of the LORD found her by a fountain of water in the wilderness, by the fountain in the way to Shur. 8 And he said,

Between Kadesh and Bered

Angel Hagar, Sarai's maid, whence camest thou? and whither wilt thou go?

Narrator And she said,

Hagar I flee from the face of my mistress Sarai.

Narrator 9 And the angel of the LORD said unto her,

Angel Return to thy mistress, and submit thyself under her hands.

Reference: Gen. 16:1-9

HAGAR BARES ISHMAEL, ABRAHAM'S SON
[72]

Narrator AND the angel of the LORD said unto her [Hagar],   Gen. 16:10-16

Angel I will multiply thy seed exceedingly, that it shall not be numbered   Between Kadesh
for multitude.   and Bered

Narrator 11 And the angel of the LORD said unto her,

Angel Behold, thou art with child, and shalt bear a son, and shalt call his
name Ishmael [God hears]; because the LORD hath heard thy
affliction. 12 And he will be a wild man* [wild ass]; his hand will
be against every man, and every man's hand against him; and he
shall dwell in the presence of all his brethren.

Narrator 13 And she called the name of the LORD that spake unto her,

Hagar Thou God seest me:

Narrator for she said,

Hagar Have I also here looked after him that seeth me?

Narrator 14 Wherefore the well was called Beer-lahai-roi [The well of
him who liveth and seeth me]; behold, it is between Kadesh
and Bered.

15 And Hagar bare Abram a son: and Abram called his son's
name, which Hagar bare, Ishmael. 16 And Abram was
fourscore and six years old, when Hagar bare Ishmael to
Abram.

Reference: Gen. 16:10-16

* Metaphorical here for freedom-loving; probably a nomad.

ABRAM'S NAME CHANGED TO ABRAHAM
[73]

Narrator   AND when Abram was ninety years old and nine, the LORD   Gen. 17:1-8
appeared to Abram, and said unto him,   Hebron

The Lord   I am the Almighty God; walk before me, and be thou perfect.
2 And I will make my covenant between me and thee, and will
multiply thee exceedingly.

Narrator   3 And *it came to pass, that* Abram fell on his face, *and
called upon the name of the Lord. And* God talked with him,
saying,

God   *My people have gone astray from my precepts, and have not kept
mine ordinances, which I gave unto their fathers; And they have
not observed mine anointing, and the burial, or baptism wherewith
I commanded them; But have turned from the commandment, and
taken unto themselves the washing of children, and the blood of
sprinkling; And have said that the blood of the righteous Abel was
shed for sins; and have not known wherein they are accountable
before me.*

4 *But as* for *thee*, behold, *I will make* my covenant with thee, and
thou shalt be a father of many nations. *And this covenant I make,
that thy children may be known among all nations.* 5 Neither shall
thy name any more be called Abram, but thy name shall be
Abraham; for a father of many nations have I made thee. 6 And I
will make thee exceeding fruitful, and I will make nations of thee,
and kings shall come of thee, *and of thy seed.*

7 And I will establish *a covenant of circumcision with thee, and it
shall be* my covenant between me and thee and thy seed after thee
in their generations*; that thou mayest know forever that children
are not accountable before me until they are eight years old. And
thou shalt observe to keep all my covenants wherein I covenanted
with thy fathers; and thou shalt keep the commandments which I
have given thee with mine own mouth, and I will* be a God unto
thee and thy seed after thee. 8 And I will give unto thee, and to thy
seed after thee, the land wherein thou art a stranger, all the land of
Canaan, for an everlasting possession; and I will be their God.

Reference: Gen. 17:1-8

CIRCUMCISION, TOKEN OF GOD'S COVENANT
[74]

Narrator   AND God said unto Abraham,   Gen. 17:9-14

                                                                          Hebron
God   Thou shalt keep my covenant therefore, thou, and thy seed after
            thee in their generations. 10 This is my covenant, which ye shall
            keep, between me and you and thy seed after thee; Every man child
            among you shall be circumcised. 11 And ye shall circumcise the
            flesh of your foreskin; and it shall be a token of the covenant
            betwixt me and you.

            12 And he that is eight days old shall be circumcised among you,
            every man child in your generations, he that is born in the house, or
            bought with money of any stranger, which is not of thy seed. 13 He
            that is born in thy house, and he that is bought with thy money,
            must needs be circumcised: and my covenant shall be in your flesh
            for an everlasting covenant*. 14 And the uncircumcised man child
            whose flesh of his foreskin is not circumcised, that soul shall be cut
            off from his people; he hath broken my covenant.

            _____

            Reference: Gen. 17:9-14

            * The covenant is everlasting, but circumcision as a sign of such a
            covenant was later discontinued.

SARAI PROMISED A SON

[75]

Narrator	AND God said unto Abraham,	Gen. 17:15-22
God	As for Sarai thy wife, thou shalt not call her name Sarai, but Sarah [Princess] shall her name be. 16 And I will bless her, and give thee a son also of her: yea, I will bless her, and she shall be a mother of nations; kings of people shall be of her.	Hebron

Narrator 17 Then Abraham fell upon his face, and *rejoiced*, and said in his heart,

Abraham *There shall* a child be born unto him that is an hundred years old, and Sarah that is ninety years old *shall bear.*

Narrator 18 And Abraham said unto God,

Abraham O that Ishmael might live *uprightly* before thee!

Narrator 19 And God said,

God Sarah thy wife shall bear thee a son indeed; and thou shalt call his name Isaac: and I will establish my covenant with him for an everlasting covenant, and with his seed after him. 20 And as for Ishmael, I have heard thee: Behold, I have blessed him, and will make him fruitful, and will multiply him exceedingly; twelve princes shall he beget, and I will make him a great nation. 21 But my covenant will I establish with Isaac, which Sarah shall bear unto thee at this set time in the next year.

Narrator 22 And he left off talking with him, and God went up from Abraham.

Reference: Gen. 17:15-22

MEN OF ABRAHAM'S HOUSE CIRCUMCISED
[76]

Narrator AND Abraham took Ishmael his son, and all that were born in his house, and all that were bought with his money, every male among the men of Abraham's house; and circumcised the flesh of their foreskin in the selfsame day, as God had said unto him.

Gen. 17:23-27
Hebron

24 And Abraham was ninety years old and nine, when he was circumcised in the flesh of his foreskin. 25 And Ishmael his son was thirteen years old, when he was circumcised in the flesh of his foreskin.

26 In the selfsame day was Abraham circumcised, and Ishmael his son. 27 And all the men of his house, born in the house, and bought with money of the stranger, were circumcised with him.

Reference: Gen. 17:23-27

THE LORD AND ANGELS VISIT ABRAHAM
[77]

Narrator	AND the LORD appeared unto him in the plains of Mamre: and he sat in the tent door in the heat of the day; 2 And he lift up his eyes and looked, and, lo, three *angels which were holy men, and were sent forth after the order of God,* stood by him: and when he saw them, he ran to meet them from the tent door, and bowed himself toward the ground, 3 And said,

Gen. 18:1-22
Hebron

Abraham

My *brethren*, if now I have found favour in thy sight, pass not away, I pray thee, from thy servant: 4 Let a little water, I pray you, be fetched, and wash your feet, and rest yourselves under the tree: 5 And I will fetch a morsel of bread, and comfort [sustain] ye your hearts; after that ye shall pass on: for therefore are ye come to your servant.

Narrator

And they said,

Angels

So do, as thou hast said.

Narrator

6 And Abraham hastened into the tent unto Sarah, and said,

Abraham

Make ready quickly three measures of fine meal, knead it, and make cakes upon the hearth.

Narrator

7 And Abraham ran unto the herd, and fetcht a calf tender and good, and gave it unto a young man; and he hasted to dress it. 8 And he took butter, and milk, and the calf which he had dressed, and set it before them; and he stood by them under the tree, and they did eat. 9 And they said unto him,

Angels

Where is Sarah thy wife?

Narrator

And he said,

Abraham

Behold, in the tent.

Narrator

10 And he said,

The Lord

I will certainly return unto thee according to the time of life; and, lo, Sarah thy wife shall have a son.

Narrator

And Sarah heard it in the tent door, which was behind him. 11 Now Abraham and Sarah were old and well stricken in age; and it ceased to be with Sarah after the manner of women. 12 Therefore Sarah laughed within herself, saying,

Sarah

After I am waxed old shall I have pleasure, my lord being old also?

Narrator

13 And the LORD said unto Abraham,

The Lord

Wherefore did Sarah laugh, saying,

Shall I of a surety bear a child, which am old?

The Lord	14 Is any thing too hard for the LORD? At the time appointed I will return unto thee, according to the time of life, and Sarah shall have a son.

Gen. 18:1-22

Hebron

Narrator 15 Then Sarah denied, saying,

Sarah I laughed not;

Narrator for she was afraid. And he said,

The Lord Nay; but thou didst laugh.

Narrator 16 And the men rose up from thence, and looked toward Sodom: and Abraham went with them to bring them on the way. 17 And the LORD said,

The Lord Shall I hide from Abraham that thing which I do; 18 Seeing that Abraham shall surely become a great and mighty nation, and all the nations of the earth shall be blessed in him? 19 For I know him, that he will command his children and his household after him, and they shall keep the way of the LORD, to do justice and judgment; that the LORD may bring upon Abraham that which he hath spoken of him.

Narrator 20 And the LORD said,

The Lord Because the cry of Sodom and Gomorrah is great, and because their sin is very grievous; 21 I will go down now, and see whether they have done altogether according to the cry of it, which is come unto me; and if not, I will know.

Narrator 22 And the *angels which were holy men, and were sent forth after the order of God,* turned their faces from thence, and went toward Sodom: but Abraham stood yet before the LORD.

Reference: Gen. 18:1-22

FATE OF SODOM AND GOMORRAH DECLARED
[78]

Narrator	AND Abraham drew near, and said,	Gen. 18:23-33
		Hebron

Abraham — Wilt thou also destroy the righteous with the wicked? 24 Peradventure there be fifty righteous within the city: wilt thou also destroy and not spare the place for the fifty righteous that are therein? 25 That be far from thee to do after this manner, to slay the righteous with the wicked: and that the righteous should be as the wicked, that be far from thee: Shall not the Judge of all the earth do right?

Narrator — 26 And the LORD said,

The Lord — If I find in Sodom fifty righteous within the city, then I will spare all the place for their sakes.

Narrator — 27 And Abraham answered and said,

Abraham — Behold now, I have taken upon me to speak unto the Lord, which am but dust and ashes: 28 Peradventure there shall lack five of the fifty righteous: wilt thou destroy all the city for lack of five?

Narrator — And he said,

The Lord — If I find there forty and five, I will not destroy it.

Narrator — 29 And he spake unto him yet again, and said,

Abraham — Peradventure there shall be forty found there.

Narrator — And he said,

The Lord — I will not do it for forty's sake.

Narrator — 30 And he said unto him,

Abraham — Oh let not the Lord be angry, and I will speak: Peradventure there shall thirty be found there. And he said,

The Lord — I will not do it, if I find thirty there.

Narrator — 31 And he said,

Abraham — Behold now, I have taken upon me to speak unto the Lord: Peradventure there shall be twenty found there.

Narrator — And he said,

The Lord — I will not destroy it for twenty's sake.

Narrator — 32 And he said,

Abraham — Oh let not the Lord be angry, and I will speak yet but this once: Peradventure ten shall be found there.

Narrator — And he said,

The Lord — I will not destroy it for ten's sake.

Narrator   33 And the LORD went his way, as soon as he had left   Gen. 18:23-33
communing with Abraham: and Abraham returned unto his   Hebron
place.

Reference: Gen. 18:23-33

ANGELS WARN LOT TO FLEE SODOM
[79]

Narrator	AND there came *three* angels [messengers] to Sodom at even; and Lot sat in the gate of Sodom: and Lot seeing them rose up to meet them; and he bowed himself with his face toward the ground; 2 And he said,

Gen. 19:1-22
Sodom

Lot

Behold now, my lords, turn in, I pray you, into your servant's house, and tarry all night, and wash your feet, and ye shall rise up early, and go on your ways.

Narrator

And they said,

Angels

Nay; but we will abide in the street all night.

Narrator

3 And he pressed upon them greatly; and they turned in unto him, and entered into his house; and he made them a feast, and did bake unleavened bread, and they did eat.

4 But before they lay down, the men of the city, even the men of Sodom, compassed the house round, both old and young, all the people from every quarter: 5 And they called unto Lot, and said unto him,

Men of Sodom

Where are the men which came in to thee this night? bring them out unto us, that we may know* them.

Narrator

6 And Lot went out at the door unto them, and shut the door after him, 7 And said,

Lot

I pray you, brethren, do not so wickedly. 8 Behold now, I have two daughters which have not known man; let me, I pray you, bring them out unto you, and do ye to them as is good in your eyes: only unto these men do nothing; for therefore came they under the shadow of my roof.

Narrator

9 And they said *unto him,*

Men of Sodom

Stand back.

Narrator

And they were angry with him. And they said *among themselves,*

Men of Sodom

This one *man* came in to sojourn *among us,* and he will needs *now make himself to* be a judge; now will we deal worse with *him* than with them.

Narrator

Wherefore they said unto the man,

Men of Sodom

We will have the men, and thy daughters also; and we will do with them as seemeth us good.

Narrator

Now this was after the wickedness of Sodom. And Lot said,

Lot

Behold now, I have two daughters which have not known man; let me, I pray you, plead with my brethren that I may not bring them

Lot   *out unto you; and ye shall not do unto them as seemeth good in your eyes; For God will not justify his servant in this thing; wherefore, let me plead with my brethren, this once only, that unto these men ye do nothing, that they may have peace in my house; for therefore came they under the shadow of my roof.*   Gen. 19:1-22
Sodom

Narrator   And they *were angry with Lot* and came near to break the door. 10 But the *angels of God, which were holy men,* put forth their hand and pulled Lot into the house to them, and shut the door. 11 And they smote the men that were at the door of the house with blindness, both small and great: so that they wearied themselves to find the door. 12 And *these holy* men said unto Lot,

Angels   Hast thou here any besides? son in law, and thy sons, and thy daughters, and whatsoever thou hast in the city, bring them out of this place: 13 For we will destroy this place, because the cry of them is waxen great before the face of the LORD; and the LORD hath sent us to destroy it.

Narrator   14 And Lot went out, and spake unto his sons in law, which married his daughters, and said,

Lot   Up, get you out of this place; for the LORD will destroy this city.

Narrator   But he seemed as one that mocked unto his sons in law.

15 And when the morning arose, then the angels hastened Lot, saying,

Angels   Arise, take thy wife, and thy two daughters, which are here; lest thou be consumed in the iniquity of the city.

Narrator   16 And while he lingered, the men laid hold upon his hand, and upon the hand of his wife, and upon the hand of his two daughters; the LORD being merciful unto him: and they brought him forth, and set him without the city.

17 And it came to pass, when they had brought them forth abroad, that he said,

Angel   Escape for thy life; look not behind thee, neither stay thou in all the plain; escape to the mountain, lest thou be consumed.

Narrator   18 And Lot said unto them,

Lot   Oh, not so, my Lord: 19 Behold now, thy servant hath found grace in thy sight, and thou hast magnified thy mercy, which thou hast shewed unto me in saving my life; and I cannot escape to the mountain, lest some evil take me, and I die: 20 Behold now, this city is near to flee unto, and it is a little one: Oh, let me escape thither, (is it not a little one?) and my soul shall live.

Narrator   21 And he said unto him,

Angel   See, I have accepted thee concerning this thing also, that I will not overthrow this city, for the which thou hast spoken. 22 Haste thee, escape thither; for I cannot do any thing till thou be come thither.

Narrator   Therefore the name of the city was called Zoar [little thing].   Gen. 19:1-22
                                                                              Sodom

_____

Reference: Gen. 19:1-22

* "Know" is used in both Hebrew and English in this kind of context as a
euphemism in place of a sexual word.

FIRE RAINS UPON SODOM AND GOMORRAH

[80]

Narrator THE sun was risen upon the earth when Lot entered into   Gen. 19:23-29
Zoar. 24 Then the LORD rained upon Sodom and upon   City of Zoar
Gomorrah brimstone and fire* [combustible materials] from
the LORD out of heaven; 25 And he overthrew those cities,
and all the plain, and all the inhabitants of the cities, and that
which grew upon the ground.

26 But his wife looked back from behind him, and she
became a pillar of salt.

27 And Abraham gat up early in the morning to the place   Hebron
where he stood before the LORD: 28 And he looked toward
Sodom and Gomorrah, and toward all the land of the plain,
and beheld, and, lo, the smoke of the country went up as the
smoke of a furnace.

29 And it came to pass, when God destroyed the cities of the
plain, that God remembered Abraham, and sent Lot out of
the midst of the overthrow, when he overthrew the cities in
the which Lot dwelt.

Reference: Gen. 19:23-29

* Especially sulphur and pitch.

LOT'S DAUGHTERS PRESERVE THEIR SEED

[81]

Narrator	AND Lot went up out of Zoar, and dwelt in the mountain, and his two daughters with him; for he feared to dwell in Zoar: and he dwelt in a cave, he and his two daughters. 31 And the firstborn *dealt wickedly, and* said unto the younger,

Gen. 19:30-38
Mountain near Zoar

Daughter — Our father is old, and there is not a man in the earth to come in unto us after the manner of all the earth: 32 Come, let us make our father drink wine, and we will lie with him, that we may preserve seed of our father.

Narrator — 33 And they made their father drink wine that night: and the firstborn went in, and lay with her father; and he perceived not when she lay down, nor when she arose.

34 And it came to pass on the morrow, that the firstborn said unto the younger,

Daughter — Behold, I lay yesternight with my father: let us make him drink wine this night also; and go thou in, and lie with him, that we may preserve seed of our father.

Narrator — 35 And they *did wickedly, and* made their father drink wine that night also: and the younger arose, and lay with him; and he perceived not when she lay down, nor when she arose. 36 Thus were both the daughters of Lot with child by their father. 37 And the firstborn bare a son, and called his name Moab: the same is the father of the Moabites unto this day. 38 And the younger, she also bare a son, and called his name Benammi: the same is the father of the children of Ammon unto this day.

Reference: Gen. 19:30-38

ABRAHAM PRAYS FOR ABIMELECH
[82]

Narrator	AND Abraham journeyed from thence toward the south country, and dwelled between Kadesh and Shur, and sojourned in Gerar. 2 And Abraham said of Sarah his wife,	Gen. 20:1-18 Land of Gerar

Abraham   She is my sister:

Narrator   and Abimelech king of Gerar sent, and took Sarah. 3 But God came to Abimelech in a dream by night, and said to him,

God   Behold, thou art but a dead man, for the woman which thou hast taken; for she is a man's wife.

Narrator   4 But Abimelech had not come near her: and he said,

Abimelech   Lord, wilt thou slay also a righteous [an innocent] nation? 5 Said he not unto me,

Abraham   She is my sister?

Abimelech   and she, even she herself said,

Sarah   He is my brother:

Abimelech   in the integrity of my heart and innocency of my hands have I done this.

Narrator   6 And God said unto him in a dream,

God   Yea, I know that thou didst this in the integrity of thy heart; for I also withheld thee from sinning against me: therefore suffered I thee not to touch her. 7 Now therefore restore the man his wife; for he is a prophet, and he shall pray for thee, and thou shalt live: and if thou restore her not, know thou that thou shalt surely die, thou, and all that are thine.

Narrator   8 Therefore Abimelech rose early in the morning, and called all his servants, and told all these things in their ears: and the men were sore afraid. 9 Then Abimelech called Abraham, and said unto him,

Abimelech   What hast thou done unto us? and what have I offended thee, that thou hast brought on me and on my kingdom a great sin? thou hast done deeds unto me that ought not to be done.

Narrator   10 And Abimelech said unto Abraham,

Abilmelech   What sawest thou, that thou hast done this thing?

Narrator   11 And Abraham said,

Abraham   Because I thought, Surely the fear of God is not in this place; and they will slay me for my wife's sake. 12 And yet indeed she is my sister; she is the daughter of my father, but not the daughter of my mother; and she became my wife.

Abraham	13 And it came to pass, when God caused me to wander from my father's house, that I said unto her, This is thy kindness which thou shalt shew unto me; at every place whither we shall come, say of me, He is my brother.	Gen. 20:1-18 Land of Gerar

Narrator

14 And Abimelech took sheep, and oxen, and menservants, and womenservants, and gave them unto Abraham, and restored him Sarah his wife. 15 And Abimelech said,

Abimelech

Behold, my land is before thee: dwell where it pleaseth thee.

Narrator

16 And unto Sarah he said,

Abimelech

Behold, I have given thy brother a thousand pieces of silver: behold, he is to thee a covering of the eyes, unto all that are with thee, and with all other:

Narrator

thus she was reproved.

17 So Abraham prayed unto God: and God healed Abimelech, and his wife, and his maidservants; and they bare children. 18 For the LORD had fast closed up all the wombs of the house of Abimelech, because of Sarah Abraham's wife.

———

Reference: Gen. 20:1-18

SARAH BARES ISAAC, ABRAHAM'S SON
[83]

Narrator   AND the LORD visited Sarah as he had said, and the LORD did unto Sarah as he had spoken. 2 For Sarah conceived, and bare Abraham a son in his old age, at the set time of which God had spoken to him. 3 And Abraham called the name of his son that was born unto him, whom Sarah bare to him, Isaac. 4 And Abraham circumcised his son Isaac being eight days old, as God had commanded him. 5 And Abraham was an hundred years old, when his son Isaac was born unto him. 6 And Sarah said,

Gen. 21:1-8

Land of Gerar

Sarah   God hath made me to laugh [rejoice], so that all that hear will laugh [rejoice] with me.

Narrator   7 And she said,

Sarah   Who would have said unto Abraham, that Sarah should have given children suck? for I have born him a son in his old age.

Narrator   8 And the child grew, and was weaned: and Abraham made a great feast the same day that Isaac was weaned.

———————

Reference: Gen. 21:1-8

HAGAR'S SON ISHMAEL SAVED FROM DEATH
[84]

Narrator   AND Sarah saw the son of Hagar the Egyptian, which she   Gen. 21:9-21
had born unto Abraham, mocking. 10 Wherefore she said   Land of Gerar
unto Abraham,

Sarah   Cast out this bondwoman and her son: for the son of this
bondwoman shall not be heir with my son, even with Isaac.

Narrator   11 And the thing was very grievous in Abraham's sight
because of his son. 12 And God said unto Abraham,

God   Let it not be grievous in thy sight because of the lad, and because
of thy bondwoman; in all that Sarah hath said unto thee, hearken
unto her voice; for in Isaac shall thy seed be called. 13 And also of
the son of the bondwoman will I make a nation, because he is thy
seed.

Narrator   14 And Abraham rose up early in the morning, and took   Wilderness of
bread, and a bottle of water, and gave it unto Hagar, putting   Beersheba
it on her shoulder, and the child, and sent her away: and she
departed, and wandered in the wilderness of Beer-sheba.
15 And the water was spent in the bottle, and she cast the
child under one of the shrubs. 16 And she went, and sat her
down over against him a good way off, as it were a bowshot:
for she said,

Hagar   Let me not see the death of the child.

Narrator   And she sat over against him, and lift up her voice, and
wept. 17 And God heard the voice of the lad; and the angel
of God called to Hagar out of heaven, and said unto her,

Angel   What aileth thee, Hagar? fear not; for God hath heard the voice of
the lad where he is. 18 Arise, lift up the lad, and hold him in thine
hand; for I will make him a great nation.

Narrator   19 And God opened her eyes, and she saw a well of water;
and she went, and filled the bottle with water, and gave the
lad drink.

20 And God was with the lad; and he grew, and dwelt in the   Wilderness of
wilderness, and became an archer. 21 And he dwelt in the   Paran
wilderness of Paran: and his mother took him a wife out of
the land of Egypt.

Reference: Gen. 21:9-21

ABRAHAM AND ABIMELECH RECONCILE
[85]

Narrator	AND it came to pass at that time, that Abimelech and Phichol the chief captain of his host spake unto Abraham, saying,	Gen. 21:22-34
		Beersheba

Abimelech God is with thee in all that thou doest: 23 Now therefore swear unto me here by God that thou wilt not deal falsely with me, nor with my son, nor with my son's son: but according to the kindness that I have done unto thee, thou shalt do unto me, and to the land wherein thou hast sojourned.

Narrator 24 And Abraham said,

Abraham I will swear.

Narrator 25 And Abraham reproved Abimelech because of a well of water, which Abimelech's servants had violently taken away. 26 And Abimelech said,

Abimelech I wot not who hath done this thing: neither didst thou tell me, neither yet heard I of it, but to day.

Narrator 27 And Abraham took sheep and oxen, and gave them unto Abimelech; and both of them made a covenant. 28 And Abraham set seven ewe lambs of the flock by themselves. 29 And Abimelech said unto Abraham,

Abimelech What mean these seven ewe lambs which thou hast set by themselves?

Narrator 30 And he said,

Abraham For these seven ewe lambs shalt thou take of my hand, that they may be a witness unto me, that I have digged this well.

Narrator 31 Wherefore he called that place Beer-sheba [The well of the oath, or well of seven]; because there they sware both of them. 32 Thus they made a covenant at Beer-sheba. *Then Abimelech, and Phichol, the chief captain of his hosts, rose up, and they planted a grove in Beer-sheba, and called there on the name of the Lord;* and they returned into the land of the Philistines.

34 And Abraham *worshipped the everlasting God, and* sojourned in the *land of the* Philistines many days.

Reference: Gen. 21:22-34

ABRAHAM COMMANDED TO SACRIFICE ISAAC
[86]

Narrator	AND it came to pass after these things, that God did tempt [test, or prove] Abraham, and said unto him,	Gen. 22:1-19 Beersheba
God	Abraham:	
Narrator	and he said,	
Abraham	Behold, here I am.	
Narrator	2 And he said,	
God	Take now thy son, thine only son Isaac, whom thou lovest, and get thee into the land of Moriah [Salem]; and offer him there for a burnt offering upon one of the mountains which I will tell thee of.	
Narrator	3 And Abraham rose up early in the morning, and saddled his ass, and took two of his young men with him, and Isaac his son, and clave the wood for the burnt offering, and rose up, and went unto the place of which God had told him.	
	4 Then on the third day Abraham lifted up his eyes, and saw the place afar off. 5 And Abraham said unto his young men,	Land of Moriah
Abraham	Abide ye here with the ass; and I and the lad will go yonder and worship, and come again to you.	
Narrator	6 And Abraham took the wood of the burnt offering, and laid it upon Isaac his son; and he took the fire in his hand, and a knife; and they went both of them together. 7 And Isaac spake unto Abraham his father, and said,	
Isaac	My father:	
Narrator	and he said,	
Abraham	Here am I, my son [Yes, my son].	
Narrator	And he said,	
Isaac	Behold the fire and the wood: but where is the lamb for a burnt offering?	
Narrator	8 And Abraham said,	
Abraham	My son, God will provide himself a lamb for a burnt offering:	
Narrator	so they went both of them together. 9 And they came to the place which God had told him of; and Abraham built an altar there, and laid the wood in order, and bound Isaac his son, and laid him on the altar upon the wood. 10 And Abraham stretched forth his hand, and took the knife to slay his son. 11 And the angel of the LORD called unto him out of heaven, and said,	

Angel	Abraham, Abraham:

Gen. 22:1-19
Land of Moriah

Narrator   and he said,

Abraham   Here am I.

Narrator   12 And he said,

Angel   Lay not thine hand upon the lad, neither do thou any thing unto him: for now I know that thou fearest God, seeing thou hast not withheld thy son, thine only son from me.

Narrator   13 And Abraham lifted up his eyes, and looked, and behold behind him a ram caught in a thicket by his horns: and Abraham went and took the ram, and offered him up for a burnt offering in the stead of his son. 14 And Abraham called the name of that place Jehovah-jireh [The Lord will see, or provide]: as it is said to this day, In the mount of the LORD it shall be seen [manifest].

15 And the angel of the LORD called unto Abraham out of heaven the second time, 16 And said,

Angel   By myself have I sworn, saith the LORD, for because thou hast done this thing, and hast not withheld thy son, thine only son: 17 That in blessing I will bless thee, and in multiplying I will multiply thy seed as the stars of the heaven, and as the sand which is upon the sea shore; and thy seed shall possess the gate of his enemies; 18 And in thy seed shall all the nations of the earth be blessed; because thou hast obeyed my voice.

Narrator   19 So Abraham returned unto his young men, and they rose up and went together to Beer-sheba; and Abraham dwelt at Beer-sheba.

Beersheba

Reference: Gen. 22:1-19

REBEKAH BORN TO NAHOR'S DAUGHTER
[87]

Narrator   AND it came to pass after these things, that it was told   Gen. 22:20-24
Abraham, saying,   Beersheba

Person   Behold, Milcah, she hath also born children unto thy brother
Nahor;

Narrator   21 Huz his firstborn, and Buz his brother, and Kemuel the
father of Aram, 22 And Chesed, and Hazo, and Pildash, and
Jidlaph, and Bethuel.

23 And Bethuel begat Rebekah: these eight Milcah did bear
to Nahor, Abraham's brother.

24 And his concubine, whose name was Reumah, she bare
also Tebah, and Gaham, and Thahash, and Maachah.

Reference: Gen. 22:20-24

SARAH BURIED IN CAVE OF MACHPELAH
[88]

Narrator	AND Sarah was an hundred and seven and twenty years old: these were the years of the life of Sarah. 2 And Sarah died in Kirjath-arba; the same is Hebron in the land of Canaan: and Abraham came to mourn for Sarah, and to weep for her. 3 And Abraham stood up from before his dead, and spake unto the sons of Heth, saying,	Gen. 23:1-20 Hebron

Abraham

4 I am a stranger [resident alien] and a sojourner with you: give me a possession of a buryingplace with you, that I may bury my dead out of my sight.

Narrator

5 And the children of Heth answered Abraham, saying unto him,

Children of Heth

6 Hear us, my lord: thou art a mighty prince among us [a prince of God]: in the choice of our sepulchres bury thy dead; none of us shall withhold from thee his sepulchre, but that thou mayest bury thy dead.

Narrator

7 And Abraham stood up, and bowed himself to the people of the land, even to the children of Heth. 8 And he communed with them, saying,

Abraham

If it be your mind that I should bury my dead out of my sight; hear me, and entreat for me to Ephron the son of Zohar, 9 That he may give me the cave of Machpelah, which he hath, which is in the end of his field; for as much money as it is worth he shall give it me for a possession of a buryingplace amongst you.

Narrator

10 And Ephron dwelt among the children of Heth: and Ephron the Hittite answered Abraham in the audience of the children of Heth, even of all that went in at the gate of his city, saying,

Ephron

11 Nay, my lord, hear me: the field give I thee, and the cave that is therein, I give it thee; in the presence of the sons of my people give I it thee: bury thy dead.

Narrator

12 And Abraham bowed down himself before the people of the land. 13 And he spake unto Ephron in the audience of the people of the land, saying,

Abraham

But if thou wilt give it, I pray thee, hear me: I will give thee money for the field; take it of me, and I will bury my dead there.

Narrator

14 And Ephron answered Abraham, saying unto him,

Ephron

15 My lord, hearken unto me: the land is worth four hundred shekels of silver; what is that betwixt me and thee? bury therefore thy dead.

Narrator   16 And Abraham hearkened unto Ephron; and Abraham   Gen. 23:1-20
weighed to Ephron the silver, which he had named in the   Hebron
audience of the sons of Heth, four hundred shekels of silver,
current money with the merchant.

17 And the field of Ephron, which was in Machpelah, which
was before Mamre, the field, and the cave which was
therein, and all the trees that were in the field, that were in
all the borders round about, were made sure 18 Unto
Abraham for a possession in the presence of the children of
Heth, before all that went in at the gate of his city. 19 And
after this, Abraham buried Sarah his wife in the cave of the
field of Machpelah before Mamre: the same is Hebron in the
land of Canaan. 20 And the field, and the cave that is therein,
were made sure unto Abraham for a possession of a
buryingplace by the sons of Heth.

Reference: Gen. 23:1-20

ISAAC

AND I will make thy seed [Isaac] to multiply as the stars of heaven, and will give unto thy seed all these countries; and in thy seed shall all the nations of the earth be blessed; Because that Abraham obeyed my voice, and kept my charge, my commandments, my statutes, and my laws.

GENESIS 26:4-5

SERVANT SEEKS WIFE FOR ISAAC
[89]

Narrator | AND Abraham was old, and well stricken [advanced] in age: and the LORD had blessed Abraham in all things. 2 And Abraham said unto his eldest servant of his house, that ruled over all that he had, | Gen. 24:1-9
Beersheba

Abraham | Put, I pray thee, thy hand under my *hand*: 3 And I will make thee swear by the LORD, the God of heaven, and the God of the earth, that thou shalt not take a wife unto my son of the daughters of the Canaanites, among whom I dwell: 4 But thou shalt go unto my country, and to my kindred, and take a wife unto my son Isaac.

Narrator | 5 And the servant said unto him,

Servant | Peradventure the woman will not be willing to follow me unto this land: must I needs bring thy son again unto the land from whence thou camest?

Narrator | 6 And Abraham said unto him,

Abraham | Beware thou that thou bring not my son thither again. 7 The LORD God of heaven, which took me from my father's house, and from the land of my kindred, and which spake unto me, and that sware unto me, saying,

God | Unto thy seed will I give this land; he shall send his angel before thee, and thou shalt take a wife unto my son from thence.

Abraham | 8 And if the woman will not be willing to follow thee, then thou shalt be clear from this my oath: only bring not my son thither again.

Narrator | 9 And the servant put his hand under the *hand* of Abraham his master, and sware to him concerning that matter.

Reference: Gen. 24:1-9

SERVANT GUIDED TO REBEKAH
[90]

Narrator AND the servant took ten camels of the camels of his master [Isaac], and departed; for all the goods of his master were in his hand: and he arose, and went to Mesopotamia [Aram-Naharaim; Aram of the two rivers], unto the city of Nahor. 11 And he made his camels to kneel down without the city by a well of water at the time of the evening, even the time that women go out to draw water. 12 And he said,

Gen. 24:10-28
City of Nahor
(Haran)

Servant O LORD God of my master Abraham, I pray thee, send me good speed this day, and shew kindness unto my master Abraham. 13 Behold, I stand here by the well of water; and the daughters of the men of the city come out to draw water: 14 And let it come to pass, that the damsel to whom I shall say,

Let down thy pitcher, I pray thee, that I may drink;

and she shall say,

Drink, and I will give thy camels drink also:

let the same be she that thou hast appointed for thy servant Isaac; and thereby shall I know that thou hast shewed kindness unto my master.

Narrator 15 And it came to pass, before he had done speaking, that, behold, Rebekah came out, who was born to Bethuel, son of Milcah, the wife of Nahor, Abraham's brother, with her pitcher upon her shoulder. 16 And the damsel was very fair to look upon, a virgin, neither had any man known *the like unto* her: and she went down to the well, and filled her pitcher, and came up. 17 And the servant ran to meet her, and said,

Servant Let me, I pray thee, drink a little water of thy pitcher.

Narrator 18 And she said,

Rebekah Drink, my lord:

Narrator and she hasted, and let down her pitcher upon her hand, and gave him drink. 19 And when she had done giving him drink, she said,

Rebekah I will draw water for thy camels also, until they have done drinking.

Narrator 20 And she hasted, and emptied her pitcher into the trough, and ran again unto the well to draw water, and drew for all his camels. 21 And the man wondering at her held his peace, to wit whether the LORD had made his journey prosperous or not.

Narrator   22 And it came to pass, as the camels had done drinking, that the man took a golden earring [ring] of half a shekel weight, and two bracelets for her hands of ten shekels weight of gold; 23 And said,

Gen. 24:10-28
City of Nahor
(Haran)

Servant   Whose daughter art thou? tell me, I pray thee: is there room in thy father's house for us to lodge in?

Narrator   24 And she said unto him,

Rebekah   I am the daughter of Bethuel the son of Milcah, which she bare unto Nahor.

Narrator   25 She said moreover unto him,

Rebekah   We have both straw and provender enough, and room to lodge in.

Narrator   26 And the man bowed down his head, and worshipped the LORD. 27 And he said,

Servant   Blessed be the LORD God of my master Abraham, who hath not left destitute my master of his mercy and his truth: I being in the way, the LORD led me to the house of my master's brethren.

Narrator   28 And the damsel ran, and told them of her mother's house these things.

Reference: Gen. 24:10-28

SERVANT RELATES HIS ERRAND TO FAMILY
[91]

Narrator	AND Rebekah had a brother, and his name was Laban: and Laban ran out unto the man, unto the well.	Gen. 24:29-52 City of Nahor (Haran)
	30 And it came to pass, when he saw the earring and bracelets upon his sister's hands, and when he heard the words of Rebekah his sister, saying,	
Rebekah	Thus spake the man unto me;	
Narrator	that he came unto the man; and, behold, he stood by the camels at the well. 31 And he said,	
Laban	Come in, thou blessed of the LORD; wherefore standest thou without? for I have prepared the house, and room for the camels.	
Narrator	32 And the man came into the house: and he ungirded his camels, and gave straw and provender for the camels, and water to wash his feet, and the men's feet that were with him. 33 And there was set meat before him to eat: but he said,	
Servant	I will not eat, until I have told mine errand.	
Narrator	And he said,	
Laban	Speak on.	
Narrator	34 And he said,	
Servant	I am Abraham's servant. 35 And the LORD hath blessed my master greatly; and he is become great: and he hath given him flocks, and herds, and silver, and gold, and menservants, and maidservants, and camels, and asses. 36 And Sarah my master's wife bare a son to my master when she was old: and unto him hath he given all that he hath. 37 And my master made me swear, saying,	
Abraham	Thou shalt not take a wife to my son of the daughters of the Canaanites, in whose land I dwell: 38 But thou shalt go unto my father's house, and to my kindred, and take a wife unto my son.	
Servant	39 And I said unto my master, Peradventure the woman will not follow me. 40 And he said unto me,	
Abraham	The LORD, before whom I walk, will send his angel with thee, and prosper thy way; and thou shalt take a wife for my son of my kindred, and of my father's house: 41 Then shalt thou be clear from this my oath, when thou comest to my kindred; and if they give not thee one, thou shalt be clear from my oath.	
Servant	42 And I came this day unto the well, and said,	
	O LORD God of my master Abraham, if now thou do prosper my way which I go: 43 Behold, I stand by the well of water; and it shall come to pass, that when the virgin cometh forth to draw water, and I say to her,	

Servant	Give me, I pray thee, a little water of thy pitcher to drink;	Gen. 24:29-52
	44 And she say to me,	City of Nahor (Haran)

Rebekah   Both drink thou, and I will also draw for thy camels:

Servant   let the same be the woman whom the LORD hath appointed out for my master's son.

45 And before I had done speaking in mine heart, behold, Rebekah came forth with her pitcher on her shoulder; and she went down unto the well, and drew water: and I said unto her,

Let me drink, I pray thee.

46 And she made haste, and let down her pitcher from her shoulder, and said,

Rebekah   Drink, and I will give thy camels drink also:

Servant   so I drank, and she made the camels drink also. 47 And I asked her, and said,

Whose daughter art thou?

And she said,

Rebekah   The daughter of Bethuel, Nahor's son, whom Milcah bare unto him:

Servant   and I put the earring upon her face [ring on her nose], and the bracelets upon her hands. 48 And I bowed down my head, and worshipped the LORD, and blessed the LORD God of my master Abraham, which had led me in the right way to take my master's brother's daughter unto his son. 49 And now if ye will deal kindly and truly with my master, tell me: and if not, tell me; that I may turn to the right hand, or to the left.

Narrator   50 Then Laban and Bethuel answered and said,

Laban / Bethuel   The thing proceedeth from the LORD: we cannot speak unto thee bad or good. 51 Behold, Rebekah is before thee, take her, and go, and let her be thy master's son's wife, as the LORD hath spoken.

Narrator   52 And it came to pass, that, when Abraham's servant heard their words, he worshipped the LORD, bowing himself to the earth.

Reference: Gen. 24:29-52

REBEKAH AGREES TO RETURN WITH SERVANT
[92]

Narrator AND the servant [of Isaac] brought forth jewels of silver, and   Gen. 24:53-61
jewels of gold [things of silver and gold], and raiment, and   City of Nahor
gave them to Rebekah: he gave also to her brother and to her   (Haran)
mother precious things. 54 And they did eat and drink, he
and the men that were with him, and tarried all night; and
they rose up in the morning, and he said,

Servant Send me away unto my master.

Narrator 55 And her brother and her mother said,

Laban / Bethuel Let the damsel abide with us a few days, at the least ten; after that
she shall go.

Narrator 56 And he said unto them,

Servant Hinder me not, seeing the LORD hath prospered my way; send me
away that I may go to my master.

Narrator 57 And they said,

Laban / Bethuel We will call the damsel, and inquire at her mouth.

Narrator 58 And they called Rebekah, and said unto her,

Laban / Bethuel Wilt thou go with this man?

Narrator And she said,

Rebekah I will go.

Narrator 59 And they sent away Rebekah their sister, and her nurse,
and Abraham's servant, and his men. 60 And they blessed
Rebekah, and said unto her,

Laban / Bethuel Thou art our sister, be thou the mother of thousands of millions,
and let thy seed possess the gate of those which hate them.

Narrator 61 And Rebekah arose, and her damsels, and they rode upon
the camels, and followed the man: and the servant took
Rebekah, and went his way.

Reference: Gen. 24:53-61

REBEKAH BECOMES ISAAC'S WIFE
[93]

Narrator   AND Isaac came from the way of the well Lahai-roi; for he   Gen. 24:62-67
dwelt in the south country. 63 And Isaac went out to meditate   South Country
in the field at the eventide: and he lifted up his eyes, and   (Beersheba)
saw, and, behold, the camels were coming. 64 And Rebekah
lifted up her eyes, and when she saw Isaac, she lighted
[dismounted] off the camel. 65 For she had said unto the
servant,

Rebekah   What man is this that walketh in the field to meet us?

Narrator   And the servant had said,

Servant   It is my master:

Narrator   therefore she took a veil, and covered herself. 66 And the
servant told Isaac all things that he had done. 67 And Isaac
brought her into his mother Sarah's tent, and took Rebekah,
and she became his wife; and he loved her: and Isaac was
comforted after his mother's death.

Reference: Gen. 24:62-67

ABRAHAM BURIED IN CAVE OF MACHPELAH
[94]

Narrator THEN again Abraham took a wife, and her name was
Keturah. 2 And she bare him Zimran, and Jokshan, and
Medan, and Midian, and Ishbak, and Shuah. 3 And Jokshan
begat Sheba, and Dedan.

And the sons of Dedan were Asshurim, and Letushim, and
Leummim.

4 And the sons of Midian; Ephah, and Epher, and Hanoch,
and Abida, and Eldaah.

All these were the children of Keturah.

5 And Abraham gave all that he had unto Isaac. 6 But unto
the sons of the concubines, which Abraham had, Abraham
gave gifts, and sent them away from Isaac his son, while he
yet lived, eastward, unto the east country. 7 And these are the
days of the years of Abraham's life which he lived, an
hundred threescore and fifteen years. 8 Then Abraham gave
up the ghost, and died in a good old age, an old man, and
full of years; and was gathered to his people.

9 And his sons Isaac and Ishmael buried him in the cave of
Machpelah, in the field of Ephron the son of Zohar the
Hittite, which is before Mamre; 10 The field which Abraham
purchased of the sons of Heth: there was Abraham buried,
and Sarah his wife.

11 And it came to pass after the death of Abraham, that God
blessed his son Isaac; and Isaac dwelt by the well Lahai-roi.

Margin notes:
Gen. 25:1-11
Beersheba

Hebron

South Country
(Beersheba)

Reference: Gen. 25:1-11

ISHMAEL'S DESCENDANTS NAMED
[95]

Narrator   NOW these are the generations of Ishmael, Abraham's son,   Gen. 25:12-18
whom Hagar the Egyptian, Sarah's handmaid, bare unto
Abraham:

13 And these are the names of the sons of Ishmael, by their
names, according to their generations: the firstborn of
Ishmael, Nebajoth; and Kedar, and Adbeel, and Mibsam,
14 And Mishma, and Dumah, and Massa, 15 Hadar, and
Tema, Jetur, Naphish, and Kedemah:

16 These are the sons of Ishmael, and these are their names,
by their towns, and by their castles; twelve princes
according to their nations. 17 And these are the years of the
life of Ishmael, an hundred and thirty and seven years: and
he gave up the ghost and died; and was gathered unto his
people. 18 And they dwelt from Havilah unto Shur, that is
before Egypt, as thou goest toward Assyria: and he died in
the presence of all his brethren.

Reference: Gen. 25:12-18

REBEKAH BARES TWINS, ESAU AND JACOB
[96]

Narrator AND these are the generations of Isaac, Abraham's son: Gen. 25:19-26
Abraham begat Isaac: 20 And Isaac was forty years old when   South Country
he took Rebekah to wife, the daughter of Bethuel the Syrian   (Beersheba)
of Padan-aram, the sister to Laban the Syrian.

21 And Isaac entreated the LORD for his wife, because she
was barren: and the LORD was intreated of him, and
Rebekah his wife conceived. 22 And the children struggled
together within her; and she said,

Rebekah If it be so, why am I thus?

Narrator And she went to inquire of the LORD. 23 And the LORD said
unto her,

The Lord Two nations are in thy womb, and two manner of people shall be
separated from thy bowels; and the one people shall be stronger
than the other people; and the elder shall serve the younger.

Narrator 24 And when her days to be delivered were fulfilled, behold,
there were twins in her womb. 25 And the first came out red,
all over like an hairy garment; and they called his name
Esau. 26 And after that came his brother out, and his hand
took hold on Esau's heel; and his name was called Jacob:
and Isaac was threescore years old when she bare them.

Reference: Gen. 25:19-26

ESAU SELLS HIS BIRTHRIGHT TO JACOB
[97]

Narrator   AND the boys grew: and Esau was a cunning hunter, a man   Gen. 25:27-34
of the field; and Jacob was a plain [whole, complete, perfect,   South Country
simple] man, dwelling in tents. 28 And Isaac loved Esau,   (Beersheba)
because he did eat of his venison: but Rebekah loved Jacob.

29 And Jacob sod pottage: and Esau came from the field, and
he was faint: 30 And Esau said to Jacob,

Esau   Feed me, I pray thee, with that same red pottage; for I am faint:

Narrator   therefore was his name called Edom [Red]. 31 And Jacob
said,

Jacob   Sell me this day thy birthright.

Narrator   32 And Esau said,

Esau   Behold, I am at the point to die: and what profit shall this birthright
do to me?

Narrator   33 And Jacob said,

Jacob   Swear to me this day;

Narrator   and he sware unto him: and he sold his birthright unto
Jacob. 34 Then Jacob gave Esau bread and pottage of
lentiles; and he did eat and drink, and rose up, and went his
way: thus Esau despised his birthright.

Reference: Gen. 25:27-34

THE LORD PROSPERS ISAAC
[98]

Narrator AND there was a famine in the land, beside the first famine that was in the days of Abraham. And Isaac went unto Abimelech king of the Philistines unto Gerar. 2 And the LORD appeared unto him, and said,

Gen. 26:1-25

Land of Gerar

The Lord Go not down into Egypt; dwell in the land which I shall tell thee of: 3 Sojourn in this land, and I will be with thee, and will bless thee; for unto thee, and unto thy seed, I will give all these countries, and I will perform the oath which I sware unto Abraham thy father; 4 And I will make thy seed to multiply as the stars of heaven, and will give unto thy seed all these countries; and in thy seed shall all the nations of the earth be blessed; 5 Because that Abraham obeyed my voice, and kept my charge, my commandments, my statutes, and my laws.

Narrator 6 And Isaac dwelt in Gerar: 7 And the men of the place asked him of his wife; and he said,

Isaac She is my sister:

Narrator for he feared to say,

Isaac She is my wife;

Narrator lest, said he,

Isaac the men of the place should kill me for Rebekah; because she was fair to look upon.

Narrator 8 And it came to pass, when he had been there a long time, that Abimelech king of the Philistines looked out at a window, and saw, and, behold, Isaac was sporting with Rebekah his wife. 9 And Abimelech called Isaac, and said,

Abimelech Behold, of a surety she is thy wife: and how saidst thou,

Isaac She is my sister?

Narrator And Isaac said unto him,

Isaac Because I said, Lest I die for her.

Narrator 10 And Abimelech said,

Abimelech What is this thou hast done unto us? one of the people might lightly have lien [lain] with thy wife, and thou shouldest have brought guiltiness upon us.

Narrator 11 And Abimelech charged all his people, saying,

Isaac He that toucheth this man or his wife shall surely be put to death.

Narrator 12 Then Isaac sowed in that land, and received in the same year an hundredfold: and the LORD blessed him. 13 And the man waxed great, and went forward, and grew until he

Narrator	became very great [continually increased in wealth until he was very wealthy]: 14 For he had possession of flocks, and possession of herds, and great store of servants: and the Philistines envied him. 15 For all the wells which his father's servants had digged in the days of Abraham his father, the Philistines had stopped them, and filled them with earth. 16 And Abimelech said unto Isaac,	Gen. 26:1-25 Land of Gerar
Abimelech	Go from us; for thou art much mightier than we.	
Narrator	17 And Isaac departed thence, and pitched his tent in the valley of Gerar, and dwelt there. 18 And Isaac digged again the wells of water, which they had digged in the days of Abraham his father; for the Philistines had stopped them after the death of Abraham: and he called their names after the names by which his father had called them. 19 And Isaac's servants digged in the valley, and found there a well of springing water. 20 And the herdmen of Gerar did strive with Isaac's herdmen, saying,	Valley of Gerar
Herdmen	The water is ours:	
Narrator	and he called the name of the well Esek [Strife]; because they strove with him. 21 And they digged another well, and strove for that also: and he called the name of it Sitnah [Opposition]. 22 And he removed from thence, and digged another well; and for that they strove not: and he called the name of it Rehoboth [Broad open places]; and he said,	
Isaac	For now the LORD hath made room for us, and we shall be fruitful in the land.	
Narrator	23 And he went up from thence to Beer-sheba. 24 And the LORD appeared unto him the same night, and said,	Beersheba
The Lord	I am the God of Abraham thy father: fear not, for I am with thee, and will bless thee, and multiply thy seed for my servant Abraham's sake.	
Narrator	25 And he builded an altar there, and called upon the name of the LORD, and pitched his tent there: and there Isaac's servants digged a well.	

Reference: Gen. 26:1-25

ISAAC AND ABIMELECH MAKE COVENANT
[99]

Narrator	THEN Abimelech went to him from Gerar, and Ahuzzath one of his friends, and Phichol the chief captain of his army. 27 And Isaac said unto them,

Gen. 26:26-33
Beersheba

Isaac

Wherefore come ye to me, seeing ye hate me, and have sent me away from you?

Narrator

28 And they said,

Abimelech's People

We saw certainly that the LORD was with thee: and we said, Let there be now an oath betwixt us, even betwixt us and thee, and let us make a covenant with thee; 29 That thou wilt do us no hurt, as we have not touched thee, and as we have done unto thee nothing but good, and have sent thee away in peace: thou art now the blessed of the LORD.

Narrator

30 And he made them a feast, and they did eat and drink. 31 And they rose up betimes in the morning [arose early], and sware one to another: and Isaac sent them away, and they departed from him in peace.

32 And it came to pass the same day, that Isaac's servants came, and told him concerning the well which they had digged, and said unto him,

Servants

We have found water.

Narrator

33 And he called it Shebah: therefore the name of the city is Beer-sheba [Well of an oath] unto this day.

———

Reference: Gen. 26:26-33

ESAU TAKES JUDITH, A HITTITE, TO WIFE
[100]

Narrator AND Esau was forty years old when he took to wife Judith   Gen. 26:34-35
the daughter of Beeri the Hittite, and Bashemath the
daughter of Elon the Hittite: 35 Which were a grief of mind*
[bitterness of spirit] unto Isaac and to Rebekah.

Reference: Gen. 26:34-35

* Meaning great sorrow or grief.

JACOB

I AM the LORD God of Abraham thy father, and the God of
Isaac: the land whereon thou liest, to thee will I give it, and
to thy seed; And thy seed shall be as the dust of the earth,
and thou shalt spread abroad to the west, and to the east, and
to the north, and to the south: and in thee and in thy seed
shall all the families of the earth be blessed.

GENESIS 28:13-14

REBEKAH LEADS ISAAC IN JACOB'S BLESSING
[101]

Narrator	AND it came to pass, that when Isaac was old, and his eyes were dim, so that he could not see, he called Esau his eldest son, and said unto him,

Gen. 27:1-29
Beersheba

Isaac   My son:

Narrator   and he said unto him,

Esau   Behold, here am I.

Narrator   2 And he said,

Isaac   Behold now, I am old, I know not the day of my death: 3 Now therefore take, I pray thee, thy weapons, thy quiver and thy bow, and go out to the field, and take [hunt] me some venison; 4 And make me savoury meat, such as I love, and bring it to me, that I may eat; that my soul may bless thee before I die.

Narrator   5 And Rebekah heard when Isaac spake to Esau his son. And Esau went to the field to hunt for venison, and to bring it. 6 And Rebekah spake unto Jacob her son, saying,

Rebekah   Behold, I heard thy father speak unto Esau thy brother, saying,

Isaac   7 Bring me venison, and make me savoury meat, that I may eat, and bless thee before the LORD before my death.

Rebekah   8 Now therefore, my son, obey my voice according to that which I command thee. 9 Go now to the flock, and fetch me from thence two good kids of the goats; and I will make them savoury meat for thy father, such as he loveth: 10 And thou shalt bring it to thy father, that he may eat, and that he may bless thee before his death.

Narrator   11 And Jacob said to Rebekah his mother,

Jacob   Behold, Esau my brother is a hairy man, and I am a smooth man: 12 My father peradventure will feel me, and I shall seem to him as a deceiver; and I shall bring a curse upon me, and not a blessing.

Narrator   13 And his mother said unto him,

Rebekah   Upon me be thy curse, my son: only obey my voice, and go fetch me them.

Narrator   14 And he went, and fetched, and brought them to his mother: and his mother made savoury meat, such as his father loved.

15 And Rebekah took goodly raiment of her eldest son Esau, which were with her in the house, and put them upon Jacob her younger son:

16 And she put the skins of the kids of the goats upon his hands, and upon the smooth of his neck: 17 And she gave the

Narrator	savoury meat and the bread, which she had prepared, into the hand of her son Jacob. 18 And he came unto his father, and said,	Gen. 27:1-29 Beersheba
Jacob	My father:	
Narrator	and he said,	
Isaac	Here am I; who art thou, my son?	
Narrator	19 And Jacob said unto his father,	
Jacob	I am Esau thy firstborn; I have done according as thou badest me: arise, I pray thee, sit and eat of my venison, that thy soul may bless me.	
Narrator	20 And Isaac said unto his son,	
Isaac	How is it that thou hast found it so quickly, my son?	
Narrator	And he said,	
Jacob	Because the LORD thy God brought it to me.	
Narrator	21 And Isaac said unto Jacob,	
Isaac	Come near, I pray thee, that I may feel thee, my son, whether thou be my very son Esau or not.	
Narrator	22 And Jacob went near unto Isaac his father; and he felt him, and said,	
Isaac	The voice is Jacob's voice, but the hands are the hands of Esau.	
Narrator	23 And he discerned him not, because his hands were hairy, as his brother Esau's hands: so he blessed him. 24 And he said,	
Isaac	Art thou my very son Esau?	
Narrator	And he said,	
Jacob	I am.	
Narrator	25 And he said,	
Isaac	Bring it near to me, and I will eat of my son's venison, that my soul may bless thee.	
Narrator	And he brought it near to him, and he did eat: and he brought him wine, and he drank. 26 And his father Isaac said unto him,	
Isaac	Come near now, and kiss me, my son.	
Narrator	27 And he came near, and kissed him: and he smelled the smell of his raiment, and blessed him, and said,	
Isaac	See, the smell of my son is as the smell of a field which the LORD hath blessed: 28 Therefore God give thee of the dew of heaven, and the fatness of the earth, and plenty of corn and wine: 29 Let people	

Isaac   serve thee, and nations bow down to thee: be lord over thy   Gen. 27:1-29
brethren, and let thy mother's sons bow down to thee: cursed be   Beersheba
every one that curseth thee, and blessed be he that blesseth thee.

Reference: Gen. 27:1-29

AS FIRSTBORN, ESAU DESIRES A BLESSING
[102]

Narrator   AND it came to pass, as soon as Isaac had made an end of blessing Jacob, and Jacob was yet scarce gone out from the presence of Isaac his father, that Esau his brother came in from his hunting. 31 And he also had made savoury meat, and brought it unto his father, and said unto his father,   Gen. 27:30-40   Beersheba

Esau   Let my father arise, and eat of his son's venison, that thy soul may bless me.

Narrator   32 And Isaac his father said unto him,

Isaac   Who art thou?

Narrator   And he said,

Esau   I am thy son, thy firstborn Esau.

Narrator   33 And Isaac trembled very exceedingly, and said,

Isaac   Who? where is he that hath taken venison [hunted game], and brought it me, and I have eaten of all before thou camest, and have blessed him? yea, and he shall be blessed.

Narrator   34 And when Esau heard the words of his father, he cried with a great and exceeding bitter cry, and said unto his father,

Esau   Bless me, even me also, O my father.

Narrator   35 And he said,

Isaac   Thy brother came with subtilty, and hath taken away thy blessing.

Narrator   36 And he said,

Esau   Is not he rightly named Jacob [A supplanter]? for he hath supplanted me these two times: he took away my birthright; and, behold, now he hath taken away my blessing.

Narrator   And he said,

Esau   Hast thou not reserved a blessing for me?

Narrator   37 And Isaac answered and said unto Esau,

38 And Esau said unto his father,

Esau   Hast thou but one blessing, my father? bless me, even me also, O my father.

Narrator   And Esau lifted up his voice, and wept. 39 And Isaac his father answered and said unto him,

Isaac   Behold, thy dwelling shall be the fatness of the earth, and of the dew of heaven from above; 40 And by thy sword shalt thou live,

Isaac   and shalt serve thy brother; and it shall come to pass when thou   Gen. 27:30-40
shalt have the dominion, that thou shalt break his yoke from off thy   Beersheba
neck.

Reference: Gen. 27:30-40

ESAU PURPOSES TO SLAY JACOB
[103]

Narrator   AND Esau hated Jacob because of the blessing wherewith   Gen. 27:41-45
his father blessed him: and Esau said in his heart,   Beersheba

Esau   The days of mourning for my father are at hand; then will I slay my brother Jacob.

Narrator   42 And these words of Esau her elder son were told to Rebekah: and she sent and called Jacob her younger son, and said unto him,

Rebekah   Behold, thy brother Esau, as touching thee, doth comfort himself, purposing to kill thee. 43 Now therefore, my son, obey my voice; and arise, flee thou to Laban my brother to Haran; 44 And tarry with him a few days, until thy brother's fury turn away; 45 Until thy brother's anger turn away from thee, and he forget that which thou hast done to him: then I will send, and fetch thee from thence: why should I be deprived also of you both in one day?

Reference: Gen. 27:41-45

JACOB SEEKS WIFE OF LABAN'S DAUGHTERS
[104]

Narrator	AND Rebekah said to Isaac,	Gen. 27:46
Rebekah	I am weary of my life because of the daughters of Heth: if Jacob take a wife of the daughters of Heth, such as these which are of the daughters of the land, what good shall my life do me?	Beersheba
Narrator	1 AND Isaac called Jacob, and blessed him, and charged him, and said unto him,	Gen. 28:1-5
Isaac	Thou shalt not take a wife of the daughters of Canaan. 2 Arise, go to Padan-aram, to the house of Bethuel thy mother's father; and take thee a wife from thence of the daughters of Laban thy mother's brother. 3 And God Almighty bless thee, and make thee fruitful, and multiply thee, that thou mayest be a multitude of people; 4 And give thee the blessing of Abraham, to thee, and to thy seed with thee; that thou mayest inherit the land wherein thou art a stranger, which God gave unto Abraham.	
Narrator	5 And Isaac sent away Jacob: and he went to Padan-aram unto Laban, son of Bethuel the Syrian [Aramean], the brother of Rebekah, Jacob's and Esau's mother.	Padan-aram (Haran)

References: Gen. 27:46; Gen. 28:1-5

ESAU MARRIES A DAUGHTER OF ISHMAEL
[105]

Narrator   WHEN Esau saw that Isaac had blessed Jacob, and sent him   Gen. 28:6-9
away to Padan-aram, to take him a wife from thence; and   Beersheba
that as he blessed him he gave him a charge, saying,

Isaac   Thou shalt not take a wife of the daughters of Canaan;

Narrator   7 And that Jacob obeyed his father and his mother, and was
gone to Padan-aram;

8 And Esau seeing that the daughters of Canaan pleased not   Land of Canaan
Isaac his father; 9 Then went Esau unto Ishmael, and took
unto the wives which he had Mahalath the daughter of
Ishmael Abraham's son, the sister of Nebajoth, to be his
wife.

Reference: Gen. 28:6-9

THE LORD BLESSES JACOB
[106]

Narrator   AND Jacob went out from Beer-sheba, and went toward   Gen. 28:10-15
Haran. 11 And he lighted upon a certain place, and tarried   Bethel
there all night, because the sun was set; and he took of the
stones of that place, and put them for his pillows, and lay
down in that place to sleep. 12 And he dreamed, and behold a
ladder set up on the earth, and the top of it reached to
heaven: and behold the angels of God ascending and
descending on it. 13 And, behold, the LORD stood above it
[beside him], and said,

The Lord   I am the LORD God of Abraham thy father, and the God of Isaac:
the land whereon thou liest, to thee will I give it, and to thy seed;
14 And thy seed shall be as the dust of the earth, and thou shalt
spread abroad to the west, and to the east, and to the north, and to
the south: and in thee and in thy seed shall all the families of the
earth be blessed. 15 And, behold, I am with thee, and will keep thee
in all places whither thou goest, and will bring thee again into this
land; for I will not leave thee, until I have done that which I have
spoken to thee of.

Reference: Gen. 28:10-15

JACOB VOWS TO GIVE TENTH OF HIS GOODS
[107]

Narrator AND Jacob awaked out of his sleep, and he said,

Gen. 28:16-22

Bethel

Jacob   Surely the LORD is in this place; and I knew it not.

Narrator 17 And he was afraid, and said,

Jacob   How dreadful is this place! this is none other but the house of God, and this is the gate of heaven.

Narrator 18 And Jacob rose up early in the morning, and took the stone that he had put for his pillows, and set it up for a pillar, and poured oil upon the top of it. 19 And he called the name of that place Beth-el [House of God]: but the name of that city was called Luz at the first. 20 And Jacob vowed a vow, saying,

Jacob   If God will be with me, and will keep me in this way that I go, and will give me bread to eat, and raiment to put on, 21 So that I come again to my father's house in peace; then shall the LORD be my God: 22 And this stone, which I have set for a pillar, shall be God's house: and of all that thou shalt give me I will surely give the tenth unto thee.

Reference: Gen. 28:16-22

JACOB MEETS RACHEL IN HARAN
[108]

Narrator	THEN Jacob went on his journey, and came into the land of the people of the east. 2 And he looked, and behold a well in the field, and, lo, there were three flocks of sheep lying by it; for out of that well they watered the flocks: and a great stone was upon the well's mouth. 3 And thither were all the flocks gathered: and they rolled the stone from the well's mouth, and watered the sheep, and put the stone again upon the well's mouth in his place. 4 And Jacob said unto them,	Gen. 29:1-14 Haran

Jacob   My brethren, whence be ye?

Narrator   And they said,

Shepherds   Of Haran are we.

Narrator   5 And he said unto them,

Jacob   Know ye Laban the son of Nahor?

Narrator   And they said,

Shepherds   We know him.

Narrator   6 And he said unto them,

Jacob   Is he well?

Narrator   And they said,

Shepherds   He is well: and, behold, Rachel his daughter cometh with the sheep.

Narrator   7 And he said,

Jacob   Lo, it is yet high day, neither is it time that the cattle should be gathered together: water ye the sheep, and go and feed them.

Narrator   8 And they said,

Shepherds   We cannot, until all the flocks [shepherds] be gathered together, and till they roll the stone from the well's mouth; then we water the sheep.

Narrator   9 And while he yet spake with them, Rachel came with her father's sheep: for she kept them.

10 And it came to pass, when Jacob saw Rachel the daughter of Laban his mother's brother, and the sheep of Laban his mother's brother, that Jacob went near, and rolled the stone from the well's mouth, and watered the flock of Laban his mother's brother. 11 And Jacob kissed Rachel, and lifted up his voice, and wept. 12 And Jacob told Rachel that he was her father's brother, and that he was Rebekah's son: and she ran and told her father.

Narrator	13 And it came to pass, when Laban heard the tidings of Jacob his sister's son, that he ran to meet him, and embraced him, and kissed him, and brought him to his house. And he told Laban all these things. 14 And Laban said to him,

Gen. 29:1-14

Haran

Laban   Surely thou art my bone and my flesh.

Narrator   And he abode with him the space of a month.

Reference: Gen. 29:1-14

JACOB SERVES LABAN SEVEN YEARS
[109]

Narrator	AND Laban said unto Jacob,	Gen. 29:15-20
Laban	Because thou art my brother, shouldest thou therefore serve me for nought? tell me, what shall thy wages be?	Haran

Narrator 16 And Laban had two daughters: the name of the elder was Leah, and the name of the younger was Rachel. 17 Leah was tender eyed; but Rachel was beautiful and well favoured. 18 And Jacob loved Rachel; and said,

Jacob I will serve thee seven years for Rachel thy younger daughter.

Narrator 19 And Laban said,

Laban It is better that I give her to thee, than that I should give her to another man: abide with me.

Narrator 20 And Jacob served seven years for Rachel; and they seemed unto him but a few days, for the love he had to her.

Reference: Gen. 29:15-20

JACOB REQUIRED TO FIRST MARRY LEAH
[110]

Narrator AND Jacob said unto Laban,   Gen. 29:21-24

Haran

Jacob Give me my wife, for my days are fulfilled, that I may go in unto her.

Narrator 22 And Laban gathered together all the men of the place, and made a feast.

23 And it came to pass in the evening, that he took Leah his daughter, and brought her to him; and he went in unto her. 24 And Laban gave unto his daughter Leah Zilpah his maid for an handmaid.

Reference: Gen. 29:21-24

JACOB SERVES MORE YEARS FOR RACHEL
[111]

Narrator   AND it came to pass, that in the morning, behold, it was   Gen. 29:25-30
            Leah: and he said to Laban,   Haran

Jacob   What is this thou hast done unto me? did not I serve with thee for
            Rachel? wherefore then hast thou beguiled me?

Narrator   26 And Laban said,

Laban   It must not be so done in our country, to give the younger before
            the firstborn. 27 Fulfil her week, and we will give thee this also for
            the service which thou shalt serve with me yet seven other years.

Narrator   28 And Jacob did so, and fulfilled her week: and he gave him
            Rachel his daughter to wife also. 29 And Laban gave to
            Rachel his daughter Bilhah his handmaid to be her maid.
            30 And he went in also unto Rachel, and he loved also
            Rachel more than Leah, and served with him yet seven other
            years.

Reference: Gen. 29:25-30

LEAH BARES FOUR SONS
[112]

Narrator AND when the LORD saw that Leah was hated, he opened   Gen. 29:31-35
her womb: but Rachel was barren. 32 And Leah conceived,   Haran
and bare a son, and she called his name Reuben [Look, a
son]: for she said,

Leah Surely the LORD hath looked upon my affliction; now therefore my
husband will love me.

Narrator 33 And she conceived again, and bare a son; and said,

Leah Because the LORD hath heard that I was hated, he hath therefore
given me this son also:

Narrator and she called his name Simeon [Hearing]. 34 And she
conceived again, and bare a son; and said,

Leah Now this time will my husband be joined unto me, because I have
born him three sons:

Narrator therefore was his name called Levi [Joined, or Pledged].
35 And she conceived again, and bare a son: and she said,

Leah Now will I praise the LORD:

Narrator therefore she called his name Judah [Praise]; and left
bearing.

Reference: Gen. 29:31-35

JACOB MARRIES BILHAH AND ZILPAH
[113]

Narrator	AND when Rachel saw that she bare Jacob no children, Rachel envied her sister; and said unto Jacob,	Gen. 30:1-13 Haran
Rachel	Give me children, or else I die.	
Narrator	2 And Jacob's anger was kindled against Rachel: and he said,	
Jacob	Am I in God's stead, who hath withheld from thee the fruit of the womb?	
Narrator	3 And she said,	
Rachel	Behold my maid Bilhah, go in unto her; and she shall bear upon my knees, that I may also have children by her [be built up by her].	
Narrator	4 And she gave him Bilhah her handmaid to wife: and Jacob went in unto her. 5 And Bilhah conceived, and bare Jacob a son. 6 And Rachel said,	
Rachel	God hath judged me, and hath also heard my voice, and hath given me a son:	
Narrator	therefore called she his name Dan [He has judged, or vindicated]. 7 And Bilhah Rachel's maid conceived again, and bare Jacob a second son. 8 And Rachel said,	
Rachel	With great wrestlings [of God] have I wrestled with my sister, and I have prevailed:	
Narrator	and she called his name Naphtali [My wrestling]. 9 When Leah saw that she had left bearing, she took Zilpah her maid, and gave her Jacob to wife. 10 And Zilpah Leah's maid bare Jacob a son. 11 And Leah said,	
Leah	A troop cometh:	
Narrator	and she called his name Gad* [Good fortune]. 12 And Zilpah Leah's maid bare Jacob a second son. 13 And Leah said,	
Leah	Happy am I, for the daughters will call me blessed:	
Narrator	and she called his name Asher [Happy, Blessed].	

Reference: Gen. 30:1-13

* Wordplay on the Hebrew words gedud, "troop," and gad, "fortune."

LEAH BARES MORE SONS AND A DAUGHTER
[114]

Narrator	AND Reuben went in the days of wheat harvest, and found mandrakes in the field, and brought them unto his mother Leah. Then Rachel said to Leah,	Gen. 30:14-21 Haran

Rachel   Give me, I pray thee, of thy son's mandrakes.

Narrator   15 And she said unto her,

Leah   Is it a small matter that thou hast taken my husband? and wouldest thou take away my son's mandrakes also?

Narrator   And Rachel said,

Rachel   Therefore he shall lie with thee to night for thy son's mandrakes.

Narrator   16 And Jacob came out of the field in the evening, and Leah went out to meet him, and said,

Leah   Thou must come in unto me; for surely I have hired thee with my son's mandrakes.

Narrator   And he lay with her that night. 17 And God hearkened unto Leah, and she conceived, and bare Jacob the fifth son. 18 And Leah said,

Leah   God hath given me my hire [recompense], because I have given my maiden to my husband:

Narrator   and she called his name Isaachar [There is recompense]. 19 And Leah conceived again, and bare Jacob the sixth son. 20 And Leah said,

Leah   God hath endued me with a good dowry; now will my husband dwell with me [honor me, exalt me], because I have born him six sons:

Narrator   and she called his name Zebulun*. 21 And afterwards she bare a daughter, and called her name Dinah.

Reference: Gen. 30:14-21

* The Hebrew *zevul* means "exalted abode."

RACHEL BARES A SON NAMED JOSEPH
[115]

Narrator	AND God remembered Rachel, and God hearkened to her, and opened her womb. 23 And she conceived, and bare a son; and said,

Gen. 30:22-24
Haran

Rachel	God hath taken away my reproach:
Narrator	24 And she called his name Joseph*; and said,
Rachel	The LORD shall add to me another son.

Reference: Gen. 30:22-24

* "Joseph" relates both to the Hebrew root *yasaph*, "to add," and to *asaph*, meaning both "to take away" and "to gather." The context plays upon all of these meanings.

JACOB AND LABAN DIVIDE THEIR FLOCKS

[116]

Narrator AND it came to pass, when Rachel had born Joseph, that Jacob said unto Laban,

Gen. 30:25-43

Haran

Jacob Send me away, that I may go unto mine own place, and to my country. 26 Give me my wives and my children, for whom I have served thee, and let me go: for thou knowest my service which I have done thee.

Narrator 27 And Laban said unto him,

Laban I pray thee, if I have found favour in thine eyes, tarry: for I have learned by experience that the LORD hath blessed me for thy sake.

Narrator 28 And he said,

Laban Appoint me thy wages, and I will give it.

Narrator 29 And he said unto him,

Jacob Thou knowest how I have served thee, and how thy cattle was with me. 30 For it was little which thou hadst before I came, and it is now increased unto a multitude; and the LORD hath blessed thee since my coming: and now when shall I provide for mine own house also?

Narrator 31 And he said,

Laban What shall I give thee?

Narrator And Jacob said,

Jacob Thou shalt not give me any thing: if thou wilt do this thing for me, I will again feed and keep thy flock: 32 I will pass through all thy flock to day, removing from thence all the speckled and spotted cattle* [sheep], and all the brown cattle among the sheep, and the spotted and speckled among the goats: and of such shall be my hire. 33 So shall my righteousness answer for me in time to come, when it shall come for my hire before thy face: every one that is not speckled and spotted among the goats, and brown among the sheep, that shall be counted stolen with me.

Narrator 34 And Laban said,

Laban Behold, I would it might be according to thy word.

Narrator 35 And he removed that day the he goats that were ringstraked and spotted, and all the she goats that were speckled and spotted, and every one that had some white in it, and all the brown among the sheep, and gave them into the hand of his sons. 36 And he set three days' journey betwixt himself and Jacob: and Jacob fed the rest of Laban's flocks.

Narrator

37 And Jacob took him rods of green poplar, and of the hazel [almond] and chestnut tree; and pilled [peeled] white strakes in them, and made the white appear which was in the rods. 38 And he set the rods which he had pilled before the flocks in the gutters in the watering troughs when the flocks came to drink, that they should conceive when they came to drink. 39 And the flocks conceived before the rods, and brought forth cattle ringstraked, speckled, and spotted. 40 And Jacob did separate the lambs, and set the faces of the flocks toward the ringstraked, and all the brown in the flock of Laban; and he put his own flocks by themselves, and put them not unto Laban's cattle.

41 And it came to pass, whensoever the stronger cattle did conceive, that Jacob laid the rods before the eyes of the cattle in the gutters, that they might conceive among the rods. 42 But when the cattle were feeble, he put them not in: so the feebler were Laban's, and the stronger Jacob's.

43 And the man increased exceedingly, and had much cattle, and maidservants, and menservants, and camels, and asses.

Gen. 30:25-43

Haran

Reference: Gen. 30:25-43

* "Cattle" is older English for "flock" or "herd" as part of one's property, or "stock."

JACOB RETURNS TO CANAAN
[117]

Narrator	AND he heard the words of Laban's sons, saying,

Gen. 31:1-16

Haran

Laban's Sons Jacob hath taken away all that was our father's; and of that which was our father's hath he gotten all this glory [wealth].

Narrator 2 And Jacob beheld the countenance of Laban, and, behold, it was not toward him as before. 3 And the LORD said unto Jacob,

The Lord Return unto the land of thy fathers, and to thy kindred; and I will be with thee.

Narrator 4 And Jacob sent and called Rachel and Leah to the field unto his flock, 5 And said unto them,

Jacob I see your father's countenance, that it is not toward me as before; but the God of my father hath been with me. 6 And ye know that with all my power I have served your father. 7 And your father hath deceived me, and changed my wages ten times; but God suffered him not to hurt me. 8 If he said thus,

Laban The speckled shall be thy wages; then all the cattle bare speckled:

Jacob and if he said thus, he ringstraked shall be thy hire; then bare all the cattle ringstraked.

9 Thus God hath taken away the cattle of your father, and given them to me.

10 And it came to pass at the time that the cattle [flock] conceived, that I lifted up mine eyes, and saw in a dream, and, behold, the rams which leaped upon the cattle were ringstraked, speckled, and grisled. 11 And the angel of God spake unto me in a dream, saying,

Angel Jacob:

Jacob And I said,

Here am I.

12 And he said,

Angel Lift up now thine eyes, and see, all the rams which leap upon the cattle [flock] are ringstraked, speckled, and grisled: for I have seen all that Laban doeth unto thee. 13 I am the God of Beth-el, where thou anointedst the pillar, and where thou vowedst a vow unto me: now arise, get thee out from this land, and return unto the land of thy kindred.

Narrator 14 And Rachel and Leah answered and said unto him,

Rachel and Leah Is there yet any portion or inheritance for us in our father's house? 15 Are we not counted of him strangers? for he hath sold us, and

Rachel and Leah

hath quite devoured also our money. 16 For all the riches which God hath taken from our father, that is ours, and our children's: now then, whatsoever God hath said unto thee, do.

Gen. 31:1-16

Haran

Reference: Gen. 31:1-16

LABAN ACCUSES JACOB OF STEALING IMAGES
[118]

Narrator THEN Jacob rose up, and set his sons and his wives upon camels; 18 And he carried away all his cattle, and all his goods which he had gotten, the cattle of his getting, which he had gotten in Padan-aram, for to go to Isaac his father in the land of Canaan. 19 And Laban went to shear his sheep: and Rachel had stolen the images that were her father's. 20 And Jacob stole away unawares to Laban the Syrian [Aramean], in that he told him not that he fled.

Gen. 31:17-42
Haran

21 So he fled with all that he had; and he rose up, and passed over the river, and set his face toward the mount Gilead.

Near Mount Gilead

22 And it was told Laban on the third day that Jacob was fled. 23 And he took his brethren with him, and pursued after him seven days' journey; and they overtook him in the mount Gilead. 24 And God came to Laban the Syrian in a dream by night, and said unto him,

God Take heed that thou speak not to Jacob either good or bad.

Narrator 25 Then Laban overtook Jacob. Now Jacob had pitched his tent in the mount: and Laban with his brethren pitched in the mount of Gilead. 26 And Laban said to Jacob,

Mount Gilead

Laban What hast thou done, that thou hast stolen away unawares to me, and carried away my daughters, as captives taken with the sword? 27 Wherefore didst thou flee away secretly, and steal away from me; and didst not tell me, that I might have sent thee away with mirth, and with songs, with tabret, and with harp? 28 And hast not suffered me to kiss my sons and my daughters? thou hast now done foolishly in so doing. 29 It is in the power of my hand to do you hurt: but the God of your father spake unto me yesternight, saying,

God Take thou heed that thou speak not to Jacob either good or bad.

Laban 30 And now, though thou wouldest needs be gone, because thou sore longedst after thy father's house, yet wherefore hast thou stolen my gods?

Narrator 31 And Jacob answered and said to Laban,

Jacob Because I was afraid: for I said,

Peradventure thou wouldest take by force thy daughters from me.

32 With whomsoever thou findest thy gods, let him not live: before our brethren discern thou what is thine with me, and take it to thee.

Narrator For Jacob knew not that Rachel had stolen them. 33 And Laban went into Jacob's tent, and into Leah's tent, and into the two maidservants' tents; but he found them not. Then

Narrator   went he out of Leah's tent, and entered into Rachel's tent. 34 Now Rachel had taken the images, and put them in the camel's furniture, and sat upon them. And Laban searched all the tent, but found them not. 35 And she said to her father,   Gen. 31:17-42   Mount Gilead

Rachel   Let it not displease my lord that I cannot rise up before thee; for the custom of women is upon me.

Narrator   And he searched, but found not the images. 36 And Jacob was wroth, and chode with Laban: and Jacob answered and said to Laban,

Jacob   What is my trespass? what is my sin, that thou hast so hotly pursued after me? 37 Whereas thou hast searched all my stuff, what hast thou found of all thy household stuff? set it here before my brethren and thy brethren, that they may judge betwixt us both.

38 This twenty years have I been with thee; thy ewes and thy she goats have not cast their young, and the rams of thy flock have I not eaten. 39 That which was torn of beasts I brought not unto thee; I bare the loss of it; of my hand didst thou require it, whether stolen by day, or stolen by night. 40 Thus I was; in the day the drought consumed me, and the frost by night; and my sleep departed from mine eyes.

41 Thus have I been twenty years in thy house; I served thee fourteen years for thy two daughters, and six years for thy cattle: and thou hast changed my wages ten times. 42 Except the God of my father, the God of Abraham, and the fear of Isaac, had been with me, surely thou hadst sent me away now empty. God hath seen mine affliction and the labour of my hands, and rebuked thee yesternight.

Reference: Gen. 31:17-42

JACOB AND LABAN MAKE COVENANT
[119]

Narrator   AND Laban answered and said unto Jacob,

Laban   These daughters are my daughters, and these children are my children, and these cattle are my cattle, and all that thou seest is mine: and what can I do this day unto these my daughters, or unto their children which they have born? 44 Now therefore come thou, let us make a covenant, I and thou; and let it be for a witness between me and thee.

Narrator   45 And Jacob took a stone, and set it up for a pillar. 46 And Jacob said unto his brethren,

Jacob   Gather stones;

Narrator   and they took stones, and made an heap: and they did eat there upon the heap. 47 And Laban called it Jegar-sahadutha [The heap of witness (Aramaic)]: but Jacob called it Galeed [The heap of witness (Hebrew)]. 48 And Laban said,

Laban   This heap is a witness between me and thee this day.

Narrator   Therefore was the name of it called Galeed; 49 And Mizpah [the lookout point]; for he said,

Mizpah   The LORD watch between me and thee, when we are absent one from another. 50 If thou shalt afflict my daughters, or if thou shalt take other wives beside my daughters, no man is with us; see, God is witness betwixt me and thee.

Narrator   51 And Laban said to Jacob,

Laban   Behold this heap, and behold this pillar, which I have cast betwixt me and thee; 52 This heap be witness, and this pillar be witness, that I will not pass over this heap to thee, and that thou shalt not pass over this heap and this pillar unto me, for harm. 53 The God of Abraham, and the God of Nahor, the God of their father, judge betwixt us.

Narrator   And Jacob sware by the fear of his father Isaac. 54 Then Jacob offered sacrifice upon the mount, and called his brethren to eat bread: and they did eat bread, and tarried all night in the mount. 55 And early in the morning Laban rose up, and kissed his sons and his daughters, and blessed them: and Laban departed, and returned unto his place.

Gen. 31:43-55

Mount Gilead

Reference: Gen. 31:43-55

JACOB FEARS MEETING ESAU
[120]

Narrator | AND Jacob went on his way, and the angels of God met him. Gen. 32:1-23
2 And when Jacob saw them, he said, Mahanaim

Jacob | This is God's host [camp]:

Narrator | and he called the name of that place Mahanaim [Two hosts, or camps]. 3 And Jacob sent messengers before him to Esau his brother unto the land of Seir, the country of Edom. 4 And he commanded them, saying,

Jacob | Thus shall ye speak unto my lord Esau;

Thy servant Jacob saith thus,

I have sojourned with Laban, and stayed there until now: 5 And I have oxen, and asses, flocks, and menservants, and womenservants: and I have sent to tell my lord, that I may find grace in thy sight.

Narrator | 6 And the messengers returned to Jacob, saying,

Messengers | We came to thy brother Esau, and also he cometh to meet thee, and four hundred men with him.

Narrator | 7 Then Jacob was greatly afraid and distressed: and he divided the people that was with him, and the flocks, and herds, and the camels, into two bands; 8 And said,

Jacob | If Esau come to the one company, and smite it, then the other company which is left shall escape.

Narrator | 9 And Jacob said,

Jacob | O God of my father Abraham, and God of my father Isaac, the LORD which saidst unto me,

The Lord | Return unto thy country, and to thy kindred, and I will deal well with thee:

Jacob | 10 I am not worthy of the least of all the mercies [I am unworthy of all the mercies], and of all the truth, which thou hast shewed unto thy servant; for with my staff I passed over this Jordan; and now I am become two bands. 11 Deliver me, I pray thee, from the hand of my brother, from the hand of Esau: for I fear him, lest he will come and smite me, and the mother with the children. 12 And thou saidst,

The Lord | I will surely do thee good, and make thy seed as the sand of the sea, which cannot be numbered for multitude.

Narrator | 13 And he lodged there that same night; and took of that which came to his hand a present for Esau his brother; 14 Two hundred she goats, and twenty he goats, two hundred ewes, and twenty rams, 15 Thirty milch camels with their

Narrator	colts, forty kine, and ten bulls, twenty she asses, and ten foals. 16 And he delivered them into the hand of his servants, every drove by themselves; and said unto his servants,

Gen. 32:1-23
Mahanaim

Jacob Pass over before me, and put a space betwixt drove and drove.

Narrator 17 And he commanded the foremost, saying,

Jacob When Esau my brother meeteth thee, and asketh thee, saying,

Whose art thou? and whither goest thou? and whose are these before thee?

18 Then thou shalt say,

They be thy servant Jacob's; it is a present sent unto my lord Esau: and, behold, also he is behind us.

Narrator 19 And so commanded he the second, and the third, and all that followed the droves, saying,

Jacob On this manner shall ye speak unto Esau, when ye find him. 20 And say ye moreover,

Behold, thy servant Jacob is behind us.

Narrator For he said,

Jacob I will appease him with the present that goeth before me, and afterward I will see his face; peradventure he will accept of me.

Narrator 21 So went the present over before him: and himself lodged that night in the company.

22 And he rose up that night, and took his two wives, and his two womenservants, and his eleven sons, and passed over the ford Jabbok. 23 And he took them, and sent them over the brook, and sent over that he had.

Ford Jabbok

Reference: Gen. 32:1-23

JACOB'S NAME TO BE CHANGED TO ISRAEL
[121]

Narrator   AND Jacob was left alone; and there wrestled a man with   Gen. 32:24-32
him until the breaking of the day. 25 And when he saw that   Peniel
he prevailed not against him, he touched the hollow of his
thigh; and the hollow of Jacob's thigh was out of joint, as he
wrestled with him. 26 And he said,

Man   Let me go, for the day breaketh.

Narrator   And he said,

Jacob   I will not let thee go, except thou bless me.

Narrator   27 And he said unto him,

Man   What is thy name?

Narrator   And he said,

Jacob   Jacob.

Narrator   28 And he said,

Man   Thy name shall be called no more Jacob, but Israel*: for as a
prince hast thou power with God and with men, and hast prevailed
[persevered with God].

Narrator   29 And Jacob asked him, and said,

Jacob   Tell me, I pray thee, thy name.

Narrator   And he said,

Man   Wherefore is it that thou dost ask after my name?

Narrator   And he blessed him there. 30 And Jacob called the name of
the place Peniel [The face of God]: for I have seen God face
to face, and my life is preserved. 31 And as he passed over
Penuel the sun rose upon him, and he halted upon his thigh.
32 Therefore the children of Israel eat not of the sinew which
shrank, which is upon the hollow of the thigh, unto this day:
because he touched the hollow of Jacob's thigh in the sinew
that shrank.

Reference: Gen. 32:24-32

* He perseveres (with) God; it may also mean, Let God prevail.

JACOB AND ESAU RECONCILE
[122]

Narrator   AND Jacob lifted up his eyes, and looked, and, behold, Esau came, and with him four hundred men. And he divided the children unto Leah, and unto Rachel, and unto the two handmaids. 2 And he put the handmaids and their children foremost, and Leah and her children after, and Rachel and Joseph hindermost. 3 And he passed over before them, and bowed himself to the ground seven times, until he came near to his brother. 4 And Esau ran to meet him, and embraced him, and fell on his neck, and kissed him: and they wept. 5 And he lifted up his eyes, and saw the women and the children; and said,

        Gen. 33:1-15
        Peniel

Esau   Who are those with thee?

Narrator   And he said,

Jacob   The children which God hath graciously given thy servant.

Narrator   6 Then the handmaidens came near, they and their children, and they bowed themselves. 7 And Leah also with her children came near, and bowed themselves: and after came Joseph near and Rachel, and they bowed themselves. 8 And he said,

Esau   What meanest thou by all this drove which I met?

Narrator   And he said,

Jacob   These are to find grace in the sight of my lord.

Narrator   9 And Esau said,

Esau   I have enough, my brother; keep that thou hast unto thyself.

Narrator   10 And Jacob said,

Jacob   Nay, I pray thee, if now I have found grace in thy sight, then receive my present at my hand: for therefore I have seen thy face, as though I had seen the face of God, and thou wast pleased with me. 11 Take, I pray thee, my blessing that is brought to thee; because God hath dealt graciously with me, and because I have enough.

Narrator   And he urged him, and he took it. 12 And he said,

Esau   Let us take our journey, and let us go, and I will go before thee.

Narrator   13 And he said unto him,

Jacob   My lord knoweth that the children are tender, and the flocks and herds with young are with me: and if men should overdrive them one day, all the flock will die. 14 Let my lord, I pray thee, pass over

| Jacob | before his servant: and I will lead on softly, according as the cattle that goeth before me and the children be able to endure, until I come unto my lord unto Seir. | Gen. 33:1-15 Peniel |

Narrator   15 And Esau said,

Esau   Let me now leave with thee some of the folk that are with me.

Narrator   And he said,

Jacob   What needeth it? let me find grace in the sight of my lord.

Reference: Gen. 33:1-15

JACOB SETTLES AT SHECHEM IN CANAAN
[123]

Narrator   So Esau returned that day on his way unto Seir. 17 And   Gen. 33:16-20
Jacob journeyed to Succoth [Booths], and built him an   Succoth
house, and made booths for his cattle: therefore the name of
the place is called Succoth.

18 And Jacob came to Shalem, a city of Shechem, which is   Shechem
in the land of Canaan, when he came from Padan-aram; and
pitched his tent before the city. 19 And he bought a parcel of
a field, where he had spread his tent, at the hand of the
children of Hamor, Shechem's father, for an hundred pieces
of money. 20 And he erected there an altar, and called it El-
elohe-Israel [El (God) is the God of Israel].

Reference: Gen. 33:16-20

SHECHEM, A HIVITE, DEFILES DINAH
[124]

Narrator	AND Dinah the daughter of Leah, which she bare unto Jacob, went out to see the daughters of the land. 2 And when Shechem the son of Hamor the Hivite, prince of the country, saw her, he took her, and lay with her, and defiled her. 3 And his soul clave unto Dinah the daughter of Jacob, and he loved the damsel, and spake kindly unto the damsel. 4 And Shechem spake unto his father Hamor, saying,

Gen. 34:1-24
Shechem

Shechem   Get me this damsel to wife.

Narrator   5 And Jacob heard that he had defiled Dinah his daughter: now his sons were with his cattle in the field: and Jacob held his peace until they were come. 6 And Hamor the father of Shechem went out unto Jacob to commune with him. 7 And the sons of Jacob came out of the field when they heard it: and the men were grieved, and they were very wroth, because he had wrought folly in Israel in lying with Jacob's daughter; which thing ought not to be done. 8 And Hamor communed with them, saying,

Hamor   The soul of my son Shechem longeth for your daughter: I pray you give her him to wife. 9 And make ye marriages with us, and give your daughters unto us, and take our daughters unto you. 10 And ye shall dwell with us: and the land shall be before you; dwell and trade ye therein, and get you possessions therein.

Narrator   11 And Shechem said unto her father and unto her brethren,

Shechem   Let me find grace in your eyes, and what ye shall say unto me I will give. 12 Ask me never so much dowry [ever so high a dowry] and gift, and I will give according as ye shall say unto me: but give me the damsel to wife.

Narrator   13 And the sons of Jacob answered Shechem and Hamor his father deceitfully, and said, because he had defiled Dinah their sister: 14 And they* said unto them,

Sons of Jacob   We cannot do this thing, to give our sister to one that is uncircumcised; for that were a reproach unto us: 15 But in this will we consent unto you: If ye will be as we be, that every male of you be circumcised; 16 Then will we give our daughters unto you, and we will take your daughters to us, and we will dwell with you, and we will become one people. 17 But if ye will not hearken unto us, to be circumcised; then will we take our daughter, and we will be gone.

Narrator   18 And their words pleased Hamor, and Shechem Hamor's son. 19 And the young man deferred not to do the thing, because he had delight in Jacob's daughter: and he was more honourable than all the house of his father.

| Narrator | 20 And Hamor and Shechem his son came unto the gate of their city, and communed with the men of their city, saying, | Gen. 34:1-24 Shechem |

Hamor and Shechem

21 These men are peaceable with us; therefore let them dwell in the land, and trade therein; for the land, behold, it is large enough for them; let us take their daughters to us for wives, and let us give them our daughters. 22 Only herein will the men consent unto us for to dwell with us, to be one people, if every male among us be circumcised, as they are circumcised. 23 Shall not their cattle and their substance and every beast of theirs be ours? only let us consent unto them, and they will dwell with us.

Narrator

24 And unto Hamor and unto Shechem his son hearkened all that went out of the gate of his city; and every male was circumcised, all that went out of the gate of his city.

Reference: Gen. 34:1-24

* Septuagint: Simeon and Levi, brothers of Dinah, sons of Leah.

SIMEON AND LEVI REVENGE DEFILEMENT
[125]

Narrator — AND it came to pass on the third day, when they [men of city] were sore, that two of the sons of Jacob, Simeon and Levi, Dinah's brethren, took each man his sword, and came upon the city boldly, and slew all the males. 26 And they slew Hamor and Shechem his son with the edge of the sword, and took Dinah out of Shechem's house, and went out. 27 The sons of Jacob came upon the slain, and spoiled the city, because they had defiled their sister. 28 They took their sheep, and their oxen, and their asses, and that which was in the city, and that which was in the field, 29 And all their wealth, and all their little ones, and their wives took they captive, and spoiled even all that was in the house. 30 And Jacob said to Simeon and Levi,

Gen. 34:25-31

Shechem

Jacob — Ye have troubled me to make me to stink among the inhabitants of the land, among the Canaanites and the Perizzites: and I being few in number, they shall gather themselves together against me, and slay me; and I shall be destroyed, I and my house.

Narrator — 31 And they said,

Simeon and Levi — Should he deal with our sister as with an harlot?

———————

Reference: Gen. 34:25-31

GOD DIRECTS JACOB TO BETHEL
[126]

Narrator   AND God said unto Jacob,

                                                   Gen. 35:1-8

                                                   Shechem

God   Arise, go up to Beth-el, and dwell there: and make there an altar unto God, that appeared unto thee when thou fleddest from the face of Esau thy brother.

Narrator   2 Then Jacob said unto his household, and to all that were with him,

Jacob   Put away the strange gods that are among you, and be clean, and change your garments: 3 And let us arise, and go up to Beth-el; and I will make there an altar unto God, who answered me in the day of my distress, and was with me in the way which I went.

Narrator   4 And they gave unto Jacob all the strange gods which were in their hand, and all their earrings which were in their ears; and Jacob hid them under the oak which was by Shechem. 5 And they journeyed: and the terror of God was upon the cities that were round about them, and they did not pursue after the sons of Jacob.

6 So Jacob came to Luz, which is in the land of Canaan, that   Bethel
is, Beth-el, he and all the people that were with him. 7 And he built there an altar, and called the place El-beth-el: because there God appeared unto him, when he fled from the face of his brother. 8 But Deborah Rebekah's nurse died, and she was buried beneath Beth-el under an oak: and the name of it was called Allon-bachuth [Oak of weeping].

Reference: Gen. 35:1-8

GOD GIVES JACOB THE NAME OF ISRAEL
[127]

Narrator   AND God appeared unto Jacob again, when he came out of   Gen. 35:9-15
            Padan-aram, and blessed him. 10 And God said unto him,   Bethel

God   Thy name is Jacob: thy name shall not be called any more Jacob,
            but Israel shall be thy name:

Narrator   and he called his name Israel. 11 And God said unto him,

God   I am God Almighty [El Shaddai]: be fruitful and multiply; a nation
            and a company of nations shall be of thee, and kings shall come
            out of thy loins; 12 And the land which I gave Abraham and Isaac,
            to thee I will give it, and to thy seed after thee will I give the land.

Narrator   13 And God went up from him in the place where he talked
            with him. 14 And Jacob set up a pillar in the place where he
            talked with him, even a pillar of stone: and he poured a
            drink offering thereon, and he poured oil thereon. 15 And
            Jacob called the name of the place where God spake with
            him, Beth-el.

Reference: Gen. 35:9-15

RACHEL TRAVAILS AND BARES BENJAMIN
[128]

Narrator   AND they [Jacob and his people] journeyed from Beth-el;   Gen. 35:16-18
and there was but a little way to come to Ephrath: and   Near Bethlehem
Rachel travailed, and she had hard labour.

17 And it came to pass, when she was in hard labour, that the
midwife said unto her,

Midwife   Fear not; thou shalt have this son also.

Narrator   18 And it came to pass, as her soul was in departing, (for she
died) that she called his name Ben-oni [Son of my sorrow, or
distress]: but his father called him Benjamin [Son at the
right (hand)].

Reference: Gen. 35:16-18

RACHEL BURIED NEAR BETHLEHEM
[129]

Narrator   AND Rachel died, and was buried in the way to Ephrath,   Gen. 35:19-20
which is Beth-lehem. 20 And Jacob set a pillar upon her   Near Bethlehem
grave: that is the pillar of Rachel's grave unto this day.

Reference: Gen. 35:19-20

JACOB'S TWELVE SONS NAMED
[130]

Narrator   AND Israel journeyed, and spread his tent beyond the tower   Gen. 35:21-26
of Edar. 22 And it came to pass, when Israel dwelt in that   Near Edar
land, that Reuben went and lay with Bilhah his father's
concubine: and Israel heard it. Now the sons of Jacob were
twelve:

23 The sons of Leah; Reuben, Jacob's firstborn, and Simeon,
and Levi, and Judah, and Isaachar, and Zebulun:

24 The sons of Rachel; Joseph, and Benjamin*:

25 And the sons of Bilhah, Rachel's handmaid; Dan, and
Naphtali:

26 And the sons of Zilpah, Leah's handmaid; Gad, and
Asher:

these are the sons of Jacob, which were born to him in
Padan-aram.

Reference: Gen. 35:21-26

* Benjamin, Rachel's son, was not born in Padan-aram (Haran) but
near Bethlehem (see events 128, 129)

ISAAC DIES AND BURIED IN HEBRON
[131]

Narrator   AND Jacob came unto Isaac his father unto Mamre, unto the   Gen. 35:27-29
city of Arbah, which is Hebron, where Abraham and Isaac   Hebron
sojourned. 28 And the days of Isaac were an hundred and
fourscore years. 29 And Isaac gave up the ghost, and died,
and was gathered unto his people, being old and full of days:
and his sons Esau and Jacob buried him.

Reference: Gen. 35:27-29

DESCENDANTS OF ESAU NAMED
[132]

Narrator   NOW these are the generations of Esau, who is Edom. 2 Esau   Gen. 36:1-43
took his wives of the daughters of Canaan;

Wives of Esau

Adah the daughter of Elon the Hittite, and Aholibamah the
daughter of Anah the daughter of Zibeon the Hivite; 3 And
Bashemath Ishmael's daughter, sister of Nebajoth.

Sons of Esau

4 And Adah bare to Esau Eliphaz; and Bashemath bare
Reuel; 5 And Aholibamah bare Jeush, and Jaalam, and
Korah: these are the sons of Esau, which were born unto
him in the land of Canaan.

6 And Esau took his wives, and his sons, and his daughters,
and all the persons of his house, and his cattle, and all his
beasts, and all his substance, which he had got in the land of
Canaan; and went into the country from the face of his
brother Jacob. 7 For their riches were more than that they
might dwell together; and the land wherein they were
strangers could not bear them because of their cattle. 8 Thus
dwelt Esau in mount Seir: Esau is Edom. 9 And these are the
generations [genealogical lines] of Esau the father of the
Edomites in mount Seir:

10 These are the names of Esau's sons; Eliphaz the son of
Adah the wife of Esau, Reuel the son of Bashemath the wife
of Esau.

> 11 And the sons of Eliphaz were Teman, Omar, Zepho, and Gatam,
> and Kenaz. 12 And Timna was concubine to Eliphaz Esau's son;
> and she bare to Eliphaz Amalek: these were the sons of Adah
> Esau's wife.

> 13 And these are the sons of Reuel; Nahath, and Zerah, Shammah,
> and Mizzah: these were the sons of Bashemath Esau's wife.

14 And these were the sons of Aholibamah, the daughter of
Anah the daughter of Zibeon, Esau's wife: and she bare to
Esau Jeush, and Jaalam, and Korah.

Dukes of Esau

15 These were dukes [tribal chiefs] of the sons of Esau: the
sons of Eliphaz the firstborn son of Esau; duke Teman, duke
Omar, duke Zepho, duke Kenaz, 16 Duke Korah, duke
Gatam, and duke Amalek: these are the dukes that came of
Eliphaz in the land of Edom; these were the sons of Adah.

Narrator   17 And these are the sons of Reuel Esau's son; duke Nahath,   Gen. 36:1-43
duke Zerah, duke Shammah, duke Mizzah: these are the
dukes that came of Reuel in the land of Edom; these are the
sons of Bashemath Esau's wife.

18 And these are the sons of Aholibamah Esau's wife; duke
Jeush, duke Jaalam, duke Korah: these were the dukes that
came of Aholibamah the daughter of Anah, Esau's wife.

19 These are the sons of Esau, who is Edom, and these are
their dukes.

Sons of Seir

20 These are the sons of Seir the Horite, who inhabited the
land; Lotan, and Shobal, and Zibeon, and Anah, 21 And
Dishon, and Ezer, and Dishan: these are the dukes of the
Horites, the children of Seir in the land of Edom.

22 And the children of Lotan were Hori and Hemam; and
Lotan's sister was Timna.

23 And the children of Shobal were these; Alvan, and
Manahath, and Ebal, Shepho, and Onam.

24 And these are the children of Zibeon; both Ajah, and
Anah: this was that Anah that found the mules in the
wilderness, as he fed the asses of Zibeon his father.

25 And the children of Anah were these; Dishon, and
Aholibamah the daughter of Anah.

26 And these are the children of Dishon; Hemdan, and
Eshban, and Ithran, and Cheran.

27 The children of Ezer are these; Bilhan, and Zaavan, and
Akan.

28 The children of Dishan are these; Uz, and Aran.

Dukes of Seir

29 These are the dukes that came of the Horites; duke Lotan,
duke Shobal, duke Zibeon, duke Anah, 30 Duke Dishon,
duke Ezer, duke Dishan: these are the dukes that came of
Hori, among their dukes in the land of Seir.

Kings of the land of Edom

31 And these are the kings that reigned in the land of Edom,
before there reigned any king over the children of Israel.

32 And Bela the son of Beor reigned in Edom: and the name
of his city was Dinhabah. 33 And Bela died, and

Narrator   Jobab the son of Zerah of Bozrah reigned in his stead.   Gen. 36:1-43
34 And Jobab died, and

Husham of the land of Temani reigned in his stead. 35 And Husham died, and

Hadad the son of Bedad, who smote Midian in the field of Moab, reigned in his stead: and the name of his city was Avith. 36 And Hadad died, and

Samlah of Masrekah reigned in his stead. 37 And Samlah died, and

Saul of Rehoboth by the river reigned in his stead. 38 And Saul died, and

Baal-hanan the son of Achbor reigned in his stead. 39 And Baal-hanan the son of Achbor died, and

Hadar reigned in his stead: and the name of his city was Pau; and his wife's name was Mehetabel, the daughter of Matred, the daughter of Mezahab.

40 And these are the names of the dukes that came of Esau, according to their families, after their places, by their names; duke Timnah, duke Alvah, duke Jetheth, 41 Duke Aholibamah, duke Elah, duke Pinon, 42 Duke Kenaz, duke Teman, duke Mibzar, 43 Duke Magdiel, duke Iram: these be the dukes of Edom, according to their habitations in the land of their possession: he is Esau the father of the Edomites.

Reference: Gen. 36:1-43

JOSEPH

WHEREFORE the fruit of thy loins shall write, and the fruit of the loins of Judah shall write; and that which shall be written by the fruit of thy loins, and also that which shall be written by the fruit of the loins of Judah, shall grow together unto the confounding of false doctrines, and laying down of contentions, and establishing peace among the fruit of thy loins, and bringing them to a knowledge of their fathers in the latter days; and also to the knowledge of my covenants, saith the Lord.

JST GENESIS 50:31

JACOB FAVORS JOSEPH
[133]

Narrator AND Jacob dwelt in the land [of his father's sojournings]   Gen. 37:1-4
wherein his father was a stranger, in the land of Canaan.   Hebron
2 These are the generations [genealogical lines] of Jacob.

Joseph, being seventeen years old, was feeding the flock
with his brethren; and the lad was with the sons of Bilhah,
and with the sons of Zilpah, his father's wives: and Joseph
brought unto his father their evil report.

3 Now Israel loved Joseph more than all his children,
because he was the son of his old age: and he made him a
coat of many colours*. 4 And when his brethren saw that
their father loved him more than all his brethren, they hated
him, and could not speak peaceably unto him.

Reference: Gen. 37:1-4

The Septuagint word indicates many colors, but the Hebrew term may
indicate simply a long coat with sleeves.

JOSEPH DREAMS FAMILY WILL OBEY HIM
[134]

Narrator | AND Joseph dreamed a dream, and he told it his brethren: and they hated him yet the more. 6 And he said unto them, Gen. 37:5-11 Hebron

Joseph | Hear, I pray you, this dream which I have dreamed: 7 For, behold, we were binding sheaves in the field, and, lo, my sheaf arose, and also stood upright; and, behold, your sheaves stood round about, and made obeisance to my sheaf.

Narrator | 8 And his brethren said to him,

Brethren | Shalt thou indeed reign over us? or shalt thou indeed have dominion over us?

Narrator | And they hated him yet the more for his dreams, and for his words. 9 And he dreamed yet another dream, and told it his brethren, and said,

Joseph | Behold, I have dreamed a dream more; and, behold, the sun and the moon and the eleven stars made obeisance to me.

Narrator | 10 And he told it to his father, and to his brethren: and his father rebuked him, and said unto him,

Jacob | What is this dream that thou hast dreamed? Shall I and thy mother and thy brethren indeed come to bow down ourselves to thee to the earth?

Narrator | 11 And his brethren envied him; but his father observed the saying.

Reference: Gen. 37:5-11

JOSEPH SOLD TO ISHMEELITE MERCHANTS
[135]

Narrator	AND his [Joseph's] brethren went to feed their father's flock in Shechem. 13 And Israel said unto Joseph,	Gen. 37:12-28 Hebron
Jacob	Do not thy brethren feed the flock in Shechem? come, and I will send thee unto them.	
Narrator	And he said to him,	
Joseph	Here am I.	
Narrator	14 And he said to him,	
Jacob	Go, I pray thee, see whether it be well with thy brethren, and well with the flocks; and bring me word again.	
Narrator	So he sent him out of the vale of Hebron, and he came to Shechem. 15 And a certain man found him, and, behold, he was wandering in the field: and the man asked him, saying,	Shechem
Man	What seekest thou?	
Narrator	16 And he said,	
Joseph	I seek my brethren: tell me, I pray thee, where they feed their flocks.	
Narrator	17 And the man said,	
Man	They are departed hence; for I heard them say,	
Brethren	Let us go to Dothan.	
Narrator	And Joseph went after his brethren, and found them in Dothan. 18 And when they saw him afar off, even before he came near unto them, they conspired against him to slay him. 19 And they said one to another,	Dothan
Brethren	Behold, this dreamer [master of dreams] cometh. 20 Come now therefore, and let us slay him, and cast him into some pit, and we will say,	
	Some evil beast hath devoured him:	
	and we shall see what will become of his dreams.	
Narrator	21 And Reuben heard it, and he delivered him out of their hands; and said,	
Reuben	Let us not kill him.	
Narrator	22 And Reuben said unto them,	
Reuben	Shed no blood, but cast him into this pit that is in the wilderness, and lay no hand upon him; that he might rid him out of their hands, to deliver him to his father again.	

Narrator 23 And it came to pass, when Joseph was come unto his brethren, that they stript Joseph out of his coat, his coat of many colours that was on him; 24 And they took him, and cast him into a pit: and the pit was empty, there was no water in it. 25 And they sat down to eat bread: and they lifted up their eyes and looked, and, behold, a company of Ishmeelites came from Gilead with their camels bearing spicery and balm and myrrh, going to carry it down to Egypt. 26 And Judah said unto his brethren,

Gen. 37:12-28

Dothan

Judah What profit is it if we slay our brother, and conceal his blood? 27 Come, and let us sell him to the Ishmeelites, and let not our hand be upon him; for he is our brother and our flesh.

Narrator And his brethren were content [hearkened]. 28 Then there passed by Midianites merchantmen; and they drew and lifted up Joseph out of the pit, and sold Joseph to the Ishmeelites for twenty pieces of silver: and they brought Joseph into Egypt.

Reference: Gen. 37:12-28

JACOB TOLD JOSEPH WAS KILLED BY BEASTS
[136]

Narrator AND Reuben returned unto the pit; and, behold, Joseph was   Gen. 37:29-36
not in the pit; and he rent his clothes. 30 And he returned   Dothan
unto his brethren, and said,

Reuben The child is not; and I, whither shall I go?

Narrator 31 And they took Joseph's coat, and killed a kid of the goats,
and dipped the coat in the blood;

32 And they sent the coat of many colours, and they brought   Hebron
it to their father; and said,

Brethren This have we found: know now whether it be thy son's coat or no.

Narrator 33 And he knew it, and said,

Jacob It is my son's coat; an evil beast hath devoured him; Joseph is
without doubt rent in pieces.

Narrator 34 And Jacob rent his clothes, and put sackcloth upon his
loins, and mourned for his son many days. 35 And all his
sons and all his daughters rose up to comfort him; but he
refused to be comforted; and he said,

Jacob For I will go down into the grave unto my son mourning.

Narrator Thus his father wept for him.

36 And the Midianites sold him into Egypt unto Potiphar, an   Egypt
officer [eunuch] of Pharaoh's, and captain of the guard*.

Reference: Gen. 37:29-36

* Which often designates a royal official: chief of the butchers, or the
cooks; probably the chief steward.

SHUAH BARES JUDAH THREE SONS
[137]

Narrator   AND it came to pass at that time, that Judah went down from   Gen. 38:1-5
his brethren, and turned in to a certain Adullamite, whose   Hebron
name was Hirah. 2 And Judah saw there a daughter of a
certain Canaanite, whose name was Shuah; and he took her,
and went in unto her. 3 And she conceived, and bare a son;
and he called his name Er. 4 And she conceived again, and
bare a son; and she called his name Onan. 5 And she yet
again conceived, and bare a son; and called his name
Shelah: and he was at Chezib, when she bare him.

Reference: Gen. 38:1-5

TAMAR BARES JUDAH TWIN SONS
[138]

Narrator	AND Judah took a wife for Er his firstborn, whose name was Tamar. 7 And Er, Judah's firstborn, was wicked in the sight of the LORD; and the LORD slew him. 8 And Judah said unto Onan,	Gen. 38:6-30 Hebron
Judah	Go in unto thy brother's wife, and marry her, and raise up seed to thy brother.	
Narrator	9 And Onan knew that the seed should not be his; and it came to pass, when he went in unto his brother's wife, that he spilled it on the ground, lest that he should give seed to his brother. 10 And the thing which he did displeased the LORD: wherefore he slew him also. 11 Then said Judah to Tamar his daughter in law,	
Judah	Remain a widow at thy father's house, till Shelah my son be grown:	
Narrator	for he said,	
Judah	Lest peradventure he die also, as his brethren did.	
Narrator	And Tamar went and dwelt in her father's house. 12 And in process of time the daughter of Shuah Judah's wife died; and Judah was comforted, and went up unto his sheepshearers to Timnath, he and his friend Hirah the Adullamite. 13 And it was told Tamar, saying,	Timnath
Person	Behold thy father in law goeth up to Timnath to shear his sheep.	
Narrator	14 And she put her widow's garments off from her, and covered her with a veil, and wrapped herself, and sat in an open place, which is by the way to Timnath; for she saw that Shelah was grown, and she was not given unto him to wife. 15 When Judah saw her, he thought her to be an harlot; because she had covered her face. 16 And he turned unto her by the way, and said,	
Judah	Go to, I pray thee, let me come in unto thee; (for he knew not that she was his daughter in law.)	
Narrator	And she said,	
Judah	What wilt thou give me, that thou mayest come in unto me?	
Narrator	17 And he said,	
Judah	I will send thee a kid from the flock.	
Narrator	And she said,	
Tamar	Wilt thou give me a pledge, till thou send it?	

Narrator	18 And he said,
Judah	What pledge shall I give thee?
Narrator	And she said,
Tamar	Thy signet, and thy bracelets, and thy staff that is in thine hand.
Narrator	And he gave it her, and came in unto her, and she conceived by him. 19 And she arose, and went away, and laid by her veil from her, and put on the garments of her widowhood.
	20 And Judah sent the kid by the hand of his friend the Adullamite, to receive his pledge from the woman's hand: but he found her not.
	21 Then he asked the men of that place, saying,
Friend of Judah	Where is the harlot, that was openly by the way side?
Narrator	And they said,
Men	There was no harlot in this place.
Narrator	22 And he returned to Judah, and said,
Friend of Judah	I cannot find her; and also the men of the place said, that there was no harlot in this place.
Narrator	23 And Judah said,
Judah	Let her take it to her, lest we be shamed: behold, I sent this kid, and thou hast not found her.
Narrator	24 And it came to pass about three months after, that it was told Judah, saying,
Person	Tamar thy daughter in law hath played the harlot; and also, behold, she is with child by whoredom.
Narrator	And Judah said,
Judah	Bring her forth, and let her be burnt.
Narrator	25 When she was brought forth, she sent to her father in law, saying,
Tamar	By the man, whose these are, am I with child:
Narrator	and she said,
Tamar	Discern, I pray thee, whose are these, the signet, and bracelets, and staff.
Narrator	26 And Judah acknowledged them, and said,
Judah	She hath been more righteous than I; because that I gave her not to Shelah my son.
Narrator	And he knew her again no more. 27 And it came to pass in the time of her travail, that, behold, twins were in her womb.

Gen. 38:6-30

Timnath

Hebron

Timnath

Hebron

Narrator   28 And it came to pass, when she travailed, that the one put   Gen. 38:6-30
out his hand: and the midwife took and bound upon his hand   Hebron
a scarlet thread, saying,

Midwife   This came out first.

Narrator   29 And it came to pass, as he drew back his hand, that, behold, his brother came out: and she said,

Midwife   How hast thou broken forth? this breach be upon thee:

Narrator   therefore his name was called Pharez. 30 And afterward came out his brother, that had the scarlet thread upon his hand: and his name was called Zarah.

Reference: Gen. 38:6-30

JOSEPH BECOMES POTIPHAR'S OVERSEER
[139]

Narrator AND Joseph was brought down to Egypt; and Potiphar, an   Gen. 39:1-6
officer of Pharaoh, captain of the guard, an Egyptian, bought   Egypt
him of the hands of the Ishmeelites, which had brought him
down thither.

2 And the LORD was with Joseph, and he was a prosperous
man; and he was in the house of his master the Egyptian.
3 And his master saw that the LORD was with him, and that
the LORD made all that he did to prosper in his hand. 4 And
Joseph found grace in his sight, and he served him: and he
made him overseer over his house, and all that he had he put
into his hand.

5 And it came to pass from the time that he had made him
overseer in his house, and over all that he had, that the LORD
blessed the Egyptian's house for Joseph's sake; and the
blessing of the LORD was upon all that he had in the house,
and in the field. 6 And he left all that he had in Joseph's
hand; and he knew not ought he had, save the bread which
he did eat. And Joseph was a goodly person, and well
favoured.

Reference: Gen. 39:1-6

Note: Potiphar is "an officer of Pharaoh," not the name of Pharaoh
(Gen. 39:1; see events 139, 140).

JOSEPH RESISTS POTIPHAR'S WIFE

[140]

Narrator	AND it came to pass after these things, that his master's wife cast her eyes upon Joseph; and she said,

Gen. 39:7-19

Egypt

Potiphar's Wife — Lie with me.

Narrator — 8 But he refused, and said unto his master's wife,

Joseph — Behold, my master *knoweth* not what is with me in the house, and he hath committed all that he hath to my hand; 9 There is none greater in this house than I; neither hath he kept back any thing from me but thee, because thou art his wife: how then can I do this great wickedness, and sin against God?

Narrator — 10 And it came to pass, as she spake to Joseph day by day, that he hearkened not unto her, to lie by her, or to be with her.

11 And it came to pass about this time, that Joseph went into the house to do his business; and there was none of the men of the house there within. 12 And she caught him by his garment, saying,

Potiphar's Wife — Lie with me:

Narrator — and he left his garment in her hand, and fled, and got him out.

13 And it came to pass, when she saw that he had left his garment in her hand, and was fled forth, 14 That she called unto the men of her house, and spake unto them, saying,

Potiphar's Wife — See, he hath brought in an Hebrew unto us to mock us; he came in unto me to lie with me, and I cried with a loud voice: 15 And it came to pass, when he heard that I lifted up my voice and cried, that he left his garment with me, and fled, and got him out.

Narrator — 16 And she laid up his garment by her, until his lord came home. 17 And she spake unto him according to these words, saying,

Potiphar's Wife — The Hebrew servant, which thou hast brought unto us, came in unto me to mock me: 18 And it came to pass, as I lifted up my voice and cried, that he left his garment with me, and fled out.

Narrator — 19 And it came to pass, when his master heard the words of his wife, which she spake unto him, saying,

Potiphar's Wife — After this manner did thy servant to me;

Narrator — that his wrath was kindled.

Reference: Gen. 39:7-19

JOSEPH PLACED IN PRISON
[141]

Narrator AND Joseph's master took him, and put him into the prison, Gen. 39:20-23
a place where the king's prisoners were bound: and he was Egypt
there in the prison.

21 But the LORD was with Joseph, and shewed him mercy,
and gave him favour in the sight of the keeper of the prison.
22 And the keeper of the prison committed to Joseph's hand
all the prisoners that were in the prison; and whatsoever they
did there, he was the *overseer* of it. 23 The keeper of the
prison looked not to any thing that was under his hand;
because the LORD was with him, and that which he did, the
LORD made it to prosper.

Reference: Gen. 39:20-23

JOSEPH INTERPRETS TWO DREAMS
[142]

Narrator	AND it came to pass after these things, that the butler of the king of Egypt and his baker had offended their lord the king of Egypt. 2 And Pharaoh was wroth against two of his officers, against the chief of the butlers, and against the chief of the bakers. 3 And he put them in ward in the house of the captain of the guard, into the prison, the place where Joseph was bound. 4 And the captain of the guard charged Joseph with them, and he served them: and they continued a season in ward.

Gen. 40:1-19

Egypt

5 And they dreamed a dream both of them, each man his dream in one night, each man according to the interpretation of his dream, the butler and the baker of the king of Egypt, which were bound in the prison. 6 And Joseph came in unto them in the morning, and looked upon them, and, behold, they were sad. 7 And he asked Pharaoh's officers that were with him in the ward of his lord's house, saying,

Joseph	Wherefore look ye so sadly to day?
Narrator	8 And they said unto him,
Butler and Baker	We have dreamed a dream, and there is no interpreter of it.
Narrator	And Joseph said unto them,
Joseph	Do not interpretations belong to God? tell me them, I pray you.
Narrator	9 And the chief butler told his dream to Joseph, and said to him,
Butler	In my dream, behold, a vine was before me; 10 And in the vine were three branches: and it was as though it budded, and her blossoms shot forth; and the clusters thereof brought forth ripe grapes: 11 And Pharaoh's cup was in my hand: and I took the grapes, and pressed them into Pharaoh's cup, and I gave the cup into Pharaoh's hand.
Narrator	12 And Joseph said unto him,
Joseph	This is the interpretation of it: The three branches are three days: 13 Yet within three days shall Pharaoh lift up thine head, and restore thee unto thy place: and thou shalt deliver Pharaoh's cup into his hand, after the former manner when thou wast his butler. 14 But think on me when it shall be well with thee, and shew kindness, I pray thee, unto me, and make mention of me unto Pharaoh, and bring me out of this house: 15 For indeed I was stolen away out of the land of the Hebrews: and here also have I done nothing that they should put me into the dungeon.
Narrator	16 When the chief baker saw that the interpretation was good, he said unto Joseph,

Baker	I also was in my dream, and, behold, I had three white baskets on my head: 17 And in the uppermost basket there was of all manner of bakemeats for Pharaoh; and the birds did eat them out of the basket upon my head.	Gen. 40:1-19 Egypt

Narrator   18 And Joseph answered and said,

Joseph   This is the interpretation thereof: The three baskets are three days: 19 Yet within three days shall Pharaoh lift up thy head from off thee, and shall hang thee on a tree; and the birds shall eat thy flesh from off thee.

Reference: Gen. 40:1-19

PHARAOH'S CHIEF BAKER HANGED
[143]

Narrator   AND it came to pass the third day, which was Pharaoh's   Gen. 40:20-23
birthday, that he made a feast unto all his servants: and he   Egypt
lifted up the head of the chief butler and of the chief baker
among his servants. 21 And he restored the chief butler unto
his butlership again; and he gave the cup into Pharaoh's
hand: 22 But he hanged the chief baker: as Joseph had
interpreted to them. 23 Yet did not the chief butler remember
Joseph, but forgat him.

Reference: Gen. 40:20-23

PHARAOH DREAMS OF KINE AND CORN
[144]

Narrator   AND it came to pass at the end of two full years, that   Gen. 41:1-13
Pharaoh dreamed: and, behold, he stood by the river. 2 And,   Egypt
behold, there came up out of the river seven well favoured
kine [cows] and fatfleshed; and they fed in a meadow. 3 And,
behold, seven other kine came up after them out of the river,
ill favoured and leanfleshed; and stood by the other kine
upon the brink of the river. 4 And the ill favoured and
leanfleshed kine did eat up the seven well favoured and fat
kine. So Pharaoh awoke.

5 And he slept and dreamed the second time: and, behold,
seven ears of corn came up upon one stalk, rank and good.
6 And, behold, seven thin ears and blasted with the east wind
sprung up after them. 7 And the seven thin ears devoured the
seven rank and full ears. And Pharaoh awoke, and, behold, it
was a dream.

8 And it came to pass in the morning that his spirit was
troubled; and he sent and called for all the magicians of
Egypt, and all the wise men thereof: and Pharaoh told them
his dream; but there was none that could interpret them unto
Pharaoh.

9 Then spake the chief butler unto Pharaoh, saying,

Butler   I do remember my faults this day: 10 Pharaoh was wroth with his
servants, and put me in ward in the captain of the guard's house,
both me and the chief baker: 11 And we dreamed a dream in one
night, I and he; we dreamed each man according to the
interpretation of his dream. 12 And there was there with us a young
man, an Hebrew, servant to the captain of the guard; and we told
him, and he interpreted to us our dreams; to each man according to
his dream he did interpret. 13 And it came to pass, as he interpreted
to us, so it was; me he restored unto mine office, and him he
hanged.

Reference: Gen. 41:1-13

PHARAOH CALLS JOSEPH TO INTERPRET DREAM
[145]

Butler THEN Pharaoh sent and called Joseph, and they brought him   Gen. 41:14-24
hastily out of the dungeon: and he shaved himself, and   Egypt
changed his raiment, and came in unto Pharaoh. 15 And
Pharaoh said unto Joseph,

Pharaoh I have dreamed a dream, and there is none that can interpret it: and
I have heard say of thee, that thou canst understand a dream to
interpret it.

Narrator 16 And Joseph answered Pharaoh, saying,

Joseph It is not in me: God shall give Pharaoh an answer of peace.

Narrator 17 And Pharaoh said unto Joseph,

Pharaoh In my dream, behold, I stood upon the bank of the river: 18 And,
behold, there came up out of the river seven kine, fatfleshed and
well favoured; and they fed in a meadow: 19 And, behold, seven
other kine came up after them, poor and very ill favoured and
leanfleshed, such as I never saw in all the land of Egypt for
badness: 20 And the lean and the ill favoured kine did eat up the
first seven fat kine: 21 And when they had eaten them up, it could
not be known that they had eaten them; but they were still ill
favoured, as at the beginning. So I awoke.

22 And I saw in my dream, and, behold, seven ears came up in one
stalk, full and good: 23 And, behold, seven ears, withered, thin, and
blasted with the east wind, sprung up after them: 24 And the thin
ears devoured the seven good ears: and I told this unto the
magicians; but there was none that could declare it to me.

—————

Reference: Gen. 41:14-24

JOSEPH INTERPRETS PHARAOH'S DREAM
[146]

Narrator   AND Joseph said unto Pharaoh,

Gen. 41:25-36

Egypt

Joseph   The dream of Pharaoh is one: God hath shewed Pharaoh what he is about to do. 26 The seven good kine are seven years; and the seven good ears are seven years: the dream is one. 27 And the seven thin and ill favoured kine that came up after them are seven years; and the seven empty ears blasted with the east wind shall be seven years of famine. 28 This is the thing which I have spoken unto Pharaoh: What God is about to do he sheweth unto Pharaoh. 29 Behold, there come seven years of great plenty throughout all the land of Egypt: 30 And there shall arise after them seven years of famine; and all the plenty shall be forgotten in the land of Egypt; and the famine shall consume the land; 31 And the plenty shall not be known in the land by reason of that famine following; for it shall be very grievous.

32 And for that the dream was doubled unto Pharaoh twice; it is because the thing is established by God, and God will shortly bring it to pass. 33 Now therefore let Pharaoh look out a man discreet and wise, and set him over the land of Egypt. 34 Let Pharaoh do this, and let him appoint officers over the land, and take up the fifth part of the land of Egypt in the seven plenteous years. 35 And let them gather all the food of those good years that come, and lay up corn under the hand of Pharaoh, and let them keep food in the cities. 36 And that food shall be for store to the land against the seven years of famine, which shall be in the land of Egypt; that the land perish not through the famine.

Reference: Gen. 41:25-36

JOSEPH PLACED OVER LAND OF EGYPT
[147]

Narrator | AND the thing was good in the eyes of Pharaoh, and in the eyes of all his servants. 38 And Pharaoh said unto his servants,

Gen. 41:37-44

Egypt

Pharaoh | Can we find such a one as this is, a man in whom the Spirit of God is?

Narrator | 39 And Pharaoh said unto Joseph,

Pharaoh | Forasmuch as God hath shewed thee all this, there is none so discreet and wise as thou art: 40 Thou shalt be over my house, and according unto thy word shall all my people be ruled: only in the throne will I be greater than thou.

Narrator | 41 And Pharaoh said unto Joseph,

Pharaoh | See, I have set thee over all the land of Egypt.

Narrator | 42 And Pharaoh took off his ring from his hand, and put it upon Joseph's hand, and arrayed him in vestures of fine linen, and put a gold chain about his neck; 43 And he made him to ride in the second chariot which he had; and they cried before him,

People | Bow the knee:

Narrator | and he made him ruler over all the land of Egypt. 44 And Pharaoh said unto Joseph,

Pharaoh | I am Pharaoh, and without thee shall no man lift up his hand or foot in all the land of Egypt.

Reference: Gen. 41:37-44

JOSEPH MARRIES ASENATH AND STORES FOOD
[148]

Narrator AND Pharaoh called Joseph's name Zaphnath-paaneah; and   Gen. 41:45-49
he gave him to wife Asenath the daughter of Poti-pherah   Egypt
priest of On. And Joseph went out over all the land of Egypt.
46 And Joseph was thirty years old when he stood before
Pharaoh king of Egypt. And Joseph went out from the
presence of Pharaoh, and went throughout all the land of
Egypt.

47 And in the seven plenteous years the earth brought forth
by handfuls. 48 And he gathered up all the food of the seven
years, which were in the land of Egypt, and laid up the food
in the cities: the food of the field, which was round about
every city, laid he up in the same. 49 And Joseph gathered
corn as the sand of the sea, very much, until he left
numbering; for it was without number.

Reference: Gen. 41:45-49

ASENATH BARES MANASSEH AND EPHRAIM
[149]

Narrator	AND unto Joseph were born two sons before the years of famine came, which Asenath the daughter of Poti-pherah priest of On bare unto him. 51 And Joseph called the name of the firstborn Manasseh: For God, said

Gen. 41:50-52
Egypt

Joseph   he, hath made me forget all my toil, and all my father's house.

Narrator   52 And the name of the second called he Ephraim:

Joseph   For God hath caused me to be fruitful in the land of my affliction.

Reference: Gen. 41:50-52

DURING FAMINE, JOSEPH PROVIDES FOOD
[150]

Narrator   AND the seven years of plenteousness, that was in the land   Gen. 41:53-57
of Egypt, were ended. 54 And the seven years of dearth   Egypt
began to come, according as Joseph had said: and the dearth
was in all lands; but in all the land of Egypt there was bread.
55 And when all the land of Egypt was famished, the people
cried to Pharaoh for bread: and Pharaoh said unto all the
Egyptians,

Pharaoh   Go unto Joseph; what he saith to you, do.

Narrator   56 And the famine was over all the face of the earth: And
Joseph opened all the storehouses, and sold unto the
Egyptians; and the famine waxed sore in the land of Egypt.
57 And all countries came into Egypt to Joseph for to buy
corn; because that the famine was so sore in all lands.

Reference: Gen. 41:53-57

JACOB SENDS SONS TO BUY GRAIN IN EGYPT
[151]

Narrator	NOW when Jacob saw that there was corn in Egypt, Jacob said unto his sons,	Gen. 42:1-13 Hebron
Jacob	Why do ye look one upon another?	
Narrator	2 And he said,	
Jacob	Behold, I have heard that there is corn in Egypt: get you down thither, and buy for us from thence; that we may live, and not die.	
Narrator	3 And Joseph's ten brethren went down to buy corn in Egypt. 4 But Benjamin, Joseph's brother, Jacob sent not with his brethren; for he said,	
Jacob	Lest peradventure mischief befall him.	
Narrator	5 And the sons of Israel came to buy corn among those that came: for the famine was in the land of Canaan. 6 And Joseph was the governor over the land, and he it was that sold to all the people of the land: and Joseph's brethren came, and bowed down themselves before him with their faces to the earth. 7 And Joseph saw his brethren, and he knew them, but made himself strange unto them, and spake roughly unto them; and he said unto them,	Egypt
Joseph	Whence come ye?	
Narrator	And they said,	
Brethren	From the land of Canaan to buy food.	
Narrator	8 And Joseph knew his brethren, but they knew not him. 9 And Joseph remembered the dreams which he dreamed of them, and said unto them,	
Joseph	Ye are spies; to see the nakedness of the land ye are come.	
Narrator	10 And they said unto him,	
Brethren	Nay, my lord, but to buy food are thy servants come. 11 We are all one man's sons; we are true men, thy servants are no spies.	
Narrator	12 And he said unto them,	
Joseph	Nay, but to see the nakedness of the land ye are come.	
Narrator	13 And they said,	
Brethren	Thy servants are twelve brethren, the sons of one man in the land of Canaan; and, behold, the youngest is this day with our father, and one is not.	

Reference: Gen. 42:1-13

BROTHERS TO PROVE THEY ARE NOT SPIES
[152]

Narrator	AND Joseph said unto them,	Gen. 42:14-20
Joseph	That is it that I spake unto you, saying,	Egypt

Ye are spies:

15 Hereby ye shall be proved: By the life of Pharaoh ye shall not go forth hence, except your youngest brother come hither. 16 Send one of you, and let him fetch your brother, and ye shall be kept in prison, that your words may be proved, whether there be any truth in you: or else by the life of Pharaoh surely ye are spies.

Narrator   17 And he put them all together into ward three days. 18 And Joseph said unto them the third day,

Joseph   This do, and live; for I fear God: 19 If ye be true men, let one of your brethren be bound in the house of your prison: go ye, carry corn for the famine of your houses: 20 But bring your youngest brother unto me; so shall your words be verified, and ye shall not die.

Narrator   And they did so.

Reference: Gen. 42:14-20

JOSEPH SENDS GRAIN TO JACOB
[153]

Narrator   AND they [Joseph's brethren] said one to another,   Gen. 42:21-28

Egypt

Brethren   We are verily guilty concerning our brother, in that we saw the anguish of his soul, when he besought us, and we would not hear; therefore is this distress come upon us.

Narrator   22 And Reuben answered them, saying,

Reuben   Spake I not unto you, saying,

> Do not sin against the child;

and ye would not hear? therefore, behold, also his blood is required.

Narrator   23 And they knew not that Joseph understood them; for he spake unto them by an interpreter. 24 And he turned himself about from them, and wept; and returned to them again, and communed with them, and took from them Simeon, and bound him before their eyes.

25 Then Joseph commanded to fill their sacks with corn, and to restore every man's money into his sack, and to give them provision for the way: and thus did he unto them. 26 And they laded their asses with the corn, and departed thence.

27 And as one of them opened his sack to give his ass   Between Egypt
provender in the inn, he espied his money; for, behold, it   and Hebron
was in his sack's mouth. 28 And he said unto his brethren,

Brother   My money is restored; and, lo, it is even in my sack:

Narrator   and their heart failed them, and they were afraid, saying one to another,

Brethren   What is this that God hath done unto us?

———————

Reference: Gen. 42:21-28

BROTHERS TO RETURN WITH BENJAMIN
[154]

Narrator	AND they came unto Jacob their father unto the land of Canaan, and told him all that befell unto them; saying,	Gen. 42:29-38 Hebron

Brethren 30 The man, who is the lord of the land, spake roughly to us, and took us for spies of the country. 31 And we said unto him,

> We are true men; we are no spies: 32 We be twelve brethren, sons of our father; one is not, and the youngest is this day with our father in the land of Canaan.

33 And the man, the lord of the country, said unto us,

Joseph Hereby shall I know that ye are true men; leave one of your brethren here with me, and take food for the famine of your households, and be gone: 34 And bring your youngest brother unto me: then shall I know that ye are no spies, but that ye are true men: so will I deliver you your brother, and ye shall traffick in the land.

Narrator 35 And it came to pass as they emptied their sacks, that, behold, every man's bundle of money was in his sack: and when both they and their father saw the bundles of money, they were afraid. 36 And Jacob their father said unto them,

Jacob Me have ye bereaved of my children: Joseph is not, and Simeon is not, and ye will take Benjamin away: all these things are against me.

Narrator 37 And Reuben spake unto his father, saying,

Reuben Slay my two sons, if I bring him not to thee: deliver him into my hand, and I will bring him to thee again.

Narrator 38 And he said,

Jacob My son shall not go down with you; for his brother is dead, and he is left alone: if mischief befall him by the way in the which ye go, then shall ye bring down my gray hairs with sorrow to the grave.

Reference: Gen. 42:29-38

JACOB ALLOWS BENJAMIN GO TO EGYPT
[155]

Narrator	AND the famine was sore in the land. 2 And it came to pass, when they had eaten up the corn which they had brought out of Egypt, their father said unto them,	Gen. 43:1-14 Hebron

Jacob Go again, buy us a little food.

Narrator 3 And Judah spake unto him, saying,

Judah The man did solemnly protest unto us, saying,

Joseph   Ye shall not see my face, except your brother be with you.

Judah 4 If thou wilt send our brother with us, we will go down and buy thee food: 5 But if thou wilt not send him, we will not go down: for the man said unto us,

Joseph   Ye shall not see my face, except your brother be with you.

Narrator 6 And Israel* [Jacob] said,

Jacob Wherefore dealt ye so ill with me, as to tell the man whether ye had yet a brother?

Narrator 7 And they said,

Brethren The man asked us straitly of our state, and of our kindred, saying,

Joseph   Is your father yet alive? have ye another brother?

Brethren and we told him according to the tenor of these words: could we certainly know that he would say,

Joseph   Bring your brother down?

Narrator 8 And Judah said unto Israel his father,

Judah Send the lad with me, and we will arise and go; that we may live, and not die, both we, and thou, and also our little ones. 9 I will be surety for him; of my hand shalt thou require him: if I bring him not unto thee, and set him before thee, then let me bear the blame for ever: 10 For except we had lingered, surely now we had returned this second time.

Narrator 11 And their father Israel said unto them,

Jacob If it must be so now, do this; take of the best fruits in the land in your vessels, and carry down the man a present, a little balm, and a little honey, spices, and myrrh, nuts, and almonds: 12 And take double money in your hand; and the money that was brought again in the mouth of your sacks, carry it again in your hand; peradventure it was an oversight:

    13 Take also your brother, and arise, go again unto the man:

Jacob   14 And God Almighty give you mercy before the man, that he may   Gen. 43:1-14
         send away your other brother, and Benjamin. If I be bereaved of   Hebron
         my children, I am bereaved.

Reference: Gen. 43:1-14

* This is the first mention of the name Israel for Jacob. For consistency, we continue to use the name Jacob in the event names and margin annotations (see Prologue).

BROTHERS DINE WITH JOSEPH
[156]

Narrator	AND the men [Joseph's brethren] took that present, and they took double money in their hand, and Benjamin; and rose up, and went down to Egypt, and stood before Joseph. 16 And when Joseph saw Benjamin with them, he said to the ruler of his house,	Gen. 43:15-34 Egypt

Joseph

Bring these men home, and slay, and make ready; for these men shall dine with me at noon.

Narrator

17 And the man did as Joseph bade; and the man brought the men into Joseph's house. 18 And the men were afraid, because they were brought into Joseph's house; and they said,

Brethren

Because of the money that was returned in our sacks at the first time are we brought in; that he may seek occasion against us, and fall upon us, and take us for bondmen, and our asses.

Narrator

19 And they came near to the steward of Joseph's house, and they communed with him at the door of the house, 20 And said,

Brethren

O sir, we came indeed down at the first time to buy food: 21 And it came to pass, when we came to the inn, that we opened our sacks, and, behold, every man's money was in the mouth of his sack, our money in full weight: and we have brought it again in our hand. 22 And other money have we brought down in our hands to buy food: we cannot tell who put our money in our sacks.

Narrator

23 And he said,

Steward

Peace be to you, fear not: your God, and the God of your father, hath given you treasure in your sacks: I had your money.

Narrator

And he brought Simeon out unto them. 24 And the man brought the men into Joseph's house, and gave them water, and they washed their feet; and he gave their asses provender. 25 And they made ready the present against Joseph came at noon: for they heard that they should eat bread there. 26 And when Joseph came home, they brought him the present which was in their hand into the house, and bowed themselves to him to the earth. 27 And he asked them of their welfare, and said,

Joseph

Is your father well, the old man of whom ye spake? Is he yet alive?

Narrator

28 And they answered,

Brethren

Thy servant our father is in good health, he is yet alive.

Narrator	And they bowed down their heads, and made obeisance. 29 And he lifted up his eyes, and saw his brother Benjamin, his mother's son, and said,	Gen. 43:15-34 Egypt
Joseph	Is this your younger brother, of whom ye spake unto me?	
Narrator	And he said,	
Joseph	God be gracious unto thee, my son.	
Narrator	30 And Joseph made haste; for his bowels did yearn upon his brother: and he sought where to weep; and he entered into his chamber, and wept there. 31 And he washed his face, and went out, and refrained himself, and said,	
Joseph	Set on bread.	
Narrator	32 And they set on for him by himself, and for them by themselves, and for the Egyptians, which did eat with him, by themselves: because the Egyptians might not eat bread with the Hebrews; for that is an abomination unto the Egyptians.	
	33 And they sat before him, the firstborn according to his birthright, and the youngest according to his youth: and the men marvelled one at another. 34 And he took and sent messes unto them from before him: but Benjamin's mess was five times so much as any of theirs. And they drank, and were merry with him.	

Reference: Gen. 43:15-34

JOSEPH HINDERS RETURN TO HEBRON
[157]

Narrator | AND he [Joseph] commanded the steward of his house, saying,

Gen. 44:1-13

Egypt

Joseph | Fill the men's sacks with food, as much as they can carry, and put every man's money in his sack's mouth. 2 And put my cup, the silver cup, in the sack's mouth of the youngest, and his corn money.

Narrator | And he did according to the word that Joseph had spoken. 3 As soon as the morning was light, the men were sent away, they and their asses. 4 And when they were gone out of the city, and not yet far off, Joseph said unto his steward,

Joseph | Up, follow after the men; and when thou dost overtake them, say unto them,

Wherefore have ye rewarded evil for good? 5 Is not this it in which my lord drinketh, and whereby indeed he divineth? ye have done evil in so doing.

Narrator | 6 And he overtook them, and he spake unto them these same words. 7 And they said unto him,

Between Egypt and Hebron

Brethren | Wherefore saith my lord these words? God forbid that thy servants should do according to this thing: 8 Behold, the money, which we found in our sacks' mouths, we brought again unto thee out of the land of Canaan: how then should we steal out of thy lord's house silver or gold? 9 With whomsoever of thy servants it be found, both let him die, and we also will be my lord's bondmen.

Narrator | 10 And he said,

Steward | Now also let it be according unto your words: he with whom it is found shall be my servant; and ye shall be blameless.

Narrator | 11 Then they speedily took down every man his sack to the ground, and opened every man his sack. 12 And he searched, and began at the eldest, and left at the youngest: and the cup was found in Benjamin's sack. 13 Then they rent their clothes, and laded every man his ass, and returned to the city.

Reference: Gen. 44:1-13

JUDAH OFFERED AS BENJAMIN'S BONDSMAN
[158]

Narrator	AND Judah and his brethren came to Joseph's house; for he was yet there: and they fell before him on the ground. 15 And Joseph said unto them,	Gen. 44:14-34 Egypt

Joseph   What deed is this that ye have done? wot ye not that such a man as I can certainly divine?

Narrator   16 And Judah said,

Judah   What shall we say unto my lord? what shall we speak? or how shall we clear ourselves? God hath found out the iniquity of thy servants: behold, we are my lord's servants, both we, and he also with whom the cup is found.

Narrator   17 And he said,

Joseph   God forbid that I should do so: but the man in whose hand the cup is found, he shall be my servant; and as for you, get you up in peace unto your father.

Narrator   18 Then Judah came near unto him, and said,

Judah   Oh my lord, let thy servant, I pray thee, speak a word in my lord's ears, and let not thine anger burn against thy servant: for thou art even as Pharaoh. 19 My lord asked his servants, saying,

Joseph   Have ye a father, or a brother?

Judah   20 And we said unto my lord,

Brethren   We have a father, an old man, and a child of his old age, a little one; and his brother is dead, and he alone is left of his mother, and his father loveth him.

Judah   21 And thou saidst unto thy servants,

Joseph   Bring him down unto me, that I may set mine eyes upon him.

Judah   22 And we said unto my lord,

Brethren   The lad cannot leave his father: for if he should leave his father, his father would die.

Judah   23 And thou saidst unto thy servants,

Joseph   Except your youngest brother come down with you, ye shall see my face no more.

Judah   24 And it came to pass when we came up unto thy servant my father, we told him the words of my lord. 25 And our father said,

Jacob   Go again, and buy us a little food.

Judah   26 And we said,

Brethren	We cannot go down: if our youngest brother be with us, then will we go down: for we may not see the man's face, except our youngest brother be with us.	Gen. 44:14-34 Egypt

Judah   27 And thy servant my father said unto us,

Jacob   Ye know that my wife bare me two sons: 28 And the one went out from me, and I said, Surely he is torn in pieces; and I saw him not since: 29 And if ye take this also from me, and mischief befall him, ye shall bring down my gray hairs with sorrow to the grave.

Judah   30 Now therefore when I come to thy servant my father, and the lad be not with us; seeing that his life is bound up in the lad's life; 31 It shall come to pass, when he seeth that the lad is not with us, that he will die: and thy servants shall bring down the gray hairs of thy servant our father with sorrow to the grave. 32 For thy servant became surety for the lad unto my father, saying,

If I bring him not unto thee, then I shall bear the blame to my father for ever.

33 Now therefore, I pray thee, let thy servant abide instead of the lad a bondman to my lord; and let the lad go up with his brethren. 34 For how shall I go up to my father, and the lad be not with me? lest peradventure I see the evil that shall come on my father.

———————

Reference: Gen. 44:14-34

JOSEPH REVEALS HIMSELF TO HIS BROTHERS
[159]

Judah THEN Joseph could not refrain himself before all them that stood by him; and he cried,

Gen. 45:1-15
Egypt

Joseph Cause every man to go out from me.

Narrator And there stood no man with him, while Joseph made himself known unto his brethren. 2 And he wept aloud: and the Egyptians and the house of Pharaoh heard. 3 And Joseph said unto his brethren,

Joseph I am Joseph; doth my father yet live?

Narrator And his brethren could not answer him; for they were troubled at his presence. 4 And Joseph said unto his brethren,

Joseph Come near to me, I pray you.

Narrator And they came near. And he said,

Joseph I am Joseph your brother, whom ye sold into Egypt. 5 Now therefore be not grieved, nor angry with yourselves, that ye sold me hither: for God did send me before you to preserve life. 6 For these two years hath the famine been in the land: and yet there are five years, in the which there shall neither be earing nor harvest.

7 And God sent me before you to preserve you a posterity in the earth, and to save your lives by a great deliverance. 8 So now it was not you that sent me hither, but God: and he hath made me a father to Pharaoh, and lord of all his house, and a ruler throughout all the land of Egypt. 9 Haste ye, and go up to my father, and say unto him, Thus saith thy son Joseph,

God hath made me lord of all Egypt: come down unto me, tarry not: 10 And thou shalt dwell in the land of Goshen, and thou shalt be near unto me, thou, and thy children, and thy children's children, and thy flocks, and thy herds, and all that thou hast:

11 And there will I nourish thee; for yet there are five years of famine; lest thou, and thy household, and all that thou hast, come to poverty. 12 And, behold, your eyes see, and the eyes of my brother Benjamin, that it is my mouth that speaketh unto you. 13 And ye shall tell my father of all my glory in Egypt, and of all that ye have seen; and ye shall haste and bring down my father hither.

Narrator 14 And he fell upon his brother Benjamin's neck, and wept; and Benjamin wept upon his neck. 15 Moreover he kissed all his brethren, and wept upon them: and after that his brethren talked with him.

Reference: Gen. 45:1-15

PHARAOH INVITES JACOB'S FAMILY TO EGYPT
[160]

Narrator   AND the fame thereof was heard in Pharaoh's house, saying,   Gen. 45:16-28
Joseph's brethren are come: and it pleased Pharaoh well, and   Egypt
his servants. 17 And Pharaoh said unto Joseph,

Pharaoh   Say unto thy brethren,

This do ye; lade your beasts, and go, get you unto the land of
Canaan; 18 And take your father and your households, and
come unto me: and I will give you the good of the land of
Egypt, and ye shall eat the fat of the land. 19 Now thou art
commanded, this do ye; take you wagons out of the land of
Egypt for your little ones, and for your wives, and bring your
father, and come. 20 Also regard not your stuff; for the good of
all the land of Egypt is yours.

Narrator   21 And the children of Israel did so: and Joseph gave them
wagons, according to the commandment of Pharaoh, and
gave them provision for the way. 22 To all of them he gave
each man changes of raiment; but to Benjamin he gave three
hundred pieces of silver, and five changes of raiment. 23 And
to his father he sent after this manner; ten asses laden with
the good things of Egypt, and ten she asses laden with corn
and bread and meat for his father by the way. 24 So he sent
his brethren away, and they departed: and he said unto them,

Joseph   See that ye fall not out by the way.

Narrator   25 And they went up out of Egypt, and came into the land of   Hebron
Canaan unto Jacob their father, 26 And told him, saying,

Brethren   Joseph is yet alive, and he is governor over all the land of Egypt.

Narrator   And Jacob's heart fainted, for he believed them not. 27 And
they told him all the words of Joseph, which he had said
unto them: and when he saw the wagons which Joseph had
sent to carry him, the spirit of Jacob their father revived:
28 And Israel said,

Jacob   It is enough; Joseph my son is yet alive: I will go and see him
before I die.

_____

Reference: Gen. 45:16-28

GOD SENDS JACOB'S FAMILY TO EGYPT
[161]

Narrator   AND Israel took his journey with all that he had, and came to   Gen. 46:1-7
Beer-sheba, and offered sacrifices unto the God of his father   Beersheba
Isaac. 2 And God spake unto Israel in the visions of the
night, and said,

God   Jacob, Jacob.

Narrator   And he said,

Jacob   Here am I.

Narrator   3 And he said,

God   I am God, the God of thy father: fear not to go down into Egypt;
for I will there make of thee a great nation: 4 I will go down with
thee into Egypt; and I will also surely bring thee up again: and
Joseph shall put his hand upon thine eyes.

Narrator   5 And Jacob rose up from Beer-sheba: and the sons of Israel
carried Jacob their father, and their little ones, and their
wives, in the wagons which Pharaoh had sent to carry him.

6 And they took their cattle, and their goods, which they had   Egypt
gotten in the land of Canaan, and came into Egypt, Jacob,
and all his seed with him: 7 His sons, and his sons' sons with
him, his daughters, and his sons' daughters, and all his seed
brought he with him into Egypt.

Reference: Gen. 46:1-7

JACOB'S DESCENDANTS IN EGYPT NAMED
[162]

Narrator AND these are the names of the children of Israel, which   Gen. 46:8-27
came into Egypt, Jacob and his sons:

Leah's Sons

Reuben, Jacob's firstborn. 9 And the sons of Reuben;
Hanoch, and Phallu, and Hezron, and Carmi.

10 And the sons of Simeon; Jemuel, and Jamin, and Ohad,
and Jachin, and Zohar, and Shaul the son of a Canaanitish
woman.

11 And the sons of Levi; Gershon, Kohath, and Merari.

12 And the sons of Judah; Er, and Onan, and Shelah, and
Pharez, and Zerah: but Er and Onan died in the land of
Canaan. And the sons of Pharez were Hezron and Hamul.

13 And the sons of Isaachar; Tola, and Phuvah, and Job, and
Shimron.

14 And the sons of Zebulun; Sered, and Elon, and Jahleel.

15 These be the sons of Leah, which she bare unto Jacob in
Padan-aram, with his daughter Dinah: all the souls of his
sons and his daughters were thirty and three.

Zilpah's Sons

16 And the sons of Gad; Ziphion, and Haggi, Shuni, and
Ezbon, Eri, and Arodi, and Areli.

17 And the sons of Asher; Jimnah, and Ishuah, and Isui, and
Beriah, and Serah their sister: and the sons of Beriah; Heber,
and Malchiel.

18 These are the sons of Zilpah, whom Laban gave to Leah
his daughter, and these she bare unto Jacob, even sixteen
souls.

Rachel's Sons

19 The sons of Rachel Jacob's wife; Joseph, and Benjamin.

20 And unto Joseph in the land of Egypt were born
Manasseh and Ephraim, which Asenath the daughter of Poti-
pherah priest of On bare unto him.

21 And the sons of Benjamin were Belah, and Becher, and
Ashbel, Gera, and Naaman, Ehi, and Rosh, Muppim, and
Huppim, and Ard.

Narrator   22 These are the sons of Rachel, which were born to Jacob: Gen. 46:8-27
all the souls were fourteen.

Bilhah's Sons

23 And the sons of Dan; Hushim.

24 And the sons of Naphtali; Jahzeel, and Guni, and Jezer, and Shillem.

25 These are the sons of Bilhah, which Laban gave unto Rachel his daughter, and she bare these unto Jacob: all the souls were seven.

---

26 All the souls that came with Jacob into Egypt, which   Egypt
came out of his loins, besides Jacob's sons' wives, all the souls were threescore and six; 27 And the sons of Joseph, which were born him in Egypt, were two souls: all the souls of the house of Jacob, which came into Egypt, were threescore and ten.

Reference: Gen. 46:8-27

JOSEPH MEETS HIS FATHER AND WEEPS
[163]

Narrator	AND he [Jacob] sent Judah before him unto Joseph, to direct his face unto Goshen; and they came into the land of Goshen. 29 And Joseph made ready his chariot, and went up to meet Israel his father, to Goshen, and presented himself unto him; and he fell on his neck, and wept on his neck a good while. 30 And Israel said unto Joseph,

Gen. 46:28-34

Land of Goshen

Jacob

Now let me die, since I have seen thy face, because thou art yet alive.

Narrator

31 And Joseph said unto his brethren, and unto his father's house,

Joseph

I will go up, and shew Pharaoh, and say unto him,

My brethren, and my father's house, which were in the land of Canaan, are come unto me; 32 And the men are shepherds, for their trade hath been to feed cattle; and they have brought their flocks, and their herds, and all that they have.

33 And it shall come to pass, when Pharaoh shall call you, and shall say,

What is your occupation?

34 That ye shall say,

Thy servants' trade hath been about cattle from our youth even until now, both we, and also our fathers:

that ye may dwell in the land of Goshen; for every shepherd is an abomination unto the Egyptians.

Reference: Gen. 46:28-34

JACOB'S FAMILY SETTLES IN GOSHEN
[164]

Narrator   THEN Joseph came and told Pharaoh, and said,

Gen. 47:1-6

Egypt

Joseph   My father and my brethren, and their flocks, and their herds, and all that they have, are come out of the land of Canaan; and, behold, they are in the land of Goshen.

Narrator   2 And he took some of his brethren, even five men, and presented them unto Pharaoh. 3 And Pharaoh said unto his brethren,

Pharaoh   What is your occupation?

Narrator   And they said unto Pharaoh,

Brethren   Thy servants are shepherds, both we, and also our fathers.

Narrator   4 They said moreover unto Pharaoh,

Brethren   For to sojourn in the land are we come; for thy servants have no pasture for their flocks; for the famine is sore in the land of Canaan: now therefore, we pray thee, let thy servants dwell in the land of Goshen.

Narrator   5 And Pharaoh spake unto Joseph, saying,

Pharaoh   Thy father and thy brethren are come unto thee: 6 The land of Egypt is before thee; in the best of the land make thy father and brethren to dwell; in the land of Goshen let them dwell: and if thou knowest any men of activity among them, then make them rulers over my cattle.

Reference: Gen. 47:1-6

JACOB MEETS PHARAOH AND BLESSES HIM
[165]

Narrator	AND Joseph brought in Jacob his father, and set him before Pharaoh: and Jacob blessed Pharaoh. 8 And Pharaoh said unto Jacob,

Gen. 47:7-12

Egypt

Pharaoh   How old art thou?

Narrator   9 And Jacob said unto Pharaoh,

Jacob   The days of the years of my pilgrimage are an hundred and thirty years: few and evil [unpleasant] have the days of the years of my life been, and have not attained unto the days of the years of the life of my fathers in the days of their pilgrimage.

Narrator   10 And Jacob blessed Pharaoh, and went out from before Pharaoh.

11 And Joseph placed his father and his brethren, and gave them a possession in the land of Egypt, in the best of the land, in the land of Rameses, as Pharaoh had commanded. 12 And Joseph nourished his father, and his brethren, and all his father's household, with bread, according to their families.

Reference: Gen. 47:7-12

JOSEPH CHALLENGED BY FAMINE
[166]

Narrator   AND there was no bread in all the land; for the famine was   Gen. 47:13-26
very sore, so that the land of Egypt and all the land of   Egypt
Canaan fainted by reason of the famine. 14 And Joseph
gathered up all the money that was found in the land of
Egypt, and in the land of Canaan, for the corn which they
bought: and Joseph brought the money into Pharaoh's house.
15 And when money failed in the land of Egypt, and in the
land of Canaan, all the Egyptians came unto Joseph, and
said,

Egyptians   Give us bread: for why should we die in thy presence? for the
money faileth.

Narrator   16 And Joseph said,

Joseph   Give your cattle; and I will give you for your cattle, if money fail.

Narrator   17 And they brought their cattle unto Joseph: and Joseph
gave them bread in exchange for horses, and for the flocks,
and for the cattle of the herds, and for the asses: and he fed
them with bread for all their cattle for that year. 18 When that
year was ended, they came unto him the second year, and
said unto him,

Egyptians   We will not hide it from my lord, how that our money is spent; my
lord also hath our herds of cattle; there is not ought left in the sight
of my lord, but our bodies, and our lands: 19 Wherefore shall we
die before thine eyes, both we and our land? buy us and our land
for bread, and we and our land will be servants unto Pharaoh: and
give us seed, that we may live, and not die, that the land be not
desolate.

Narrator   20 And Joseph bought all the land of Egypt for Pharaoh; for
the Egyptians sold every man his field, because the famine
prevailed over them: so the land became Pharaoh's. 21 And
as for the people, he removed them to cities from one end of
the borders of Egypt even to the other end thereof. 22 Only
the land of the priests bought he not; for the priests had a
portion assigned them of Pharaoh, and did eat their portion
which Pharaoh gave them: wherefore they sold not their
lands. 23 Then Joseph said unto the people,

Joseph   Behold, I have bought you this day and your land for Pharaoh: lo,
here is seed for you, and ye shall sow the land. 24 And it shall
come to pass in the increase [at the harvests], that ye shall give the
fifth part unto Pharaoh, and four parts shall be your own, for seed
of the field, and for your food, and for them of your households,
and for food for your little ones.

Narrator   25 And they said,

Egyptians	Thou hast saved our lives: let us find grace in the sight of my lord, and we will be Pharaoh's servants.	Gen. 47:13-26 Egypt
Narrator	26 And Joseph made it a law over the land of Egypt unto this day, that Pharaoh should have the fifth part; except the land of the priests only, which became not Pharaoh's.	

Reference: Gen. 47:13-26

JACOB REQUESTS BURIAL IN CANAAN
[167]

Narrator	AND Israel dwelt in the land of Egypt, in the country of Goshen; and they had possessions therein, and grew, and multiplied exceedingly. 28 And Jacob lived in the land of Egypt seventeen years: so the whole age of Jacob was an hundred forty and seven years. 29 And the time drew nigh that Israel must die: and he called his son Joseph, and said unto him,

Gen. 47:27-31
Land of Goshen

Jacob   If now I have found grace in thy sight, put, I pray thee, thy hand under my *hand*, and deal kindly and truly with me; bury me not, I pray thee, in Egypt: 30 But I will lie with my fathers, and thou shalt carry me out of Egypt, and bury me in their buryingplace.

Narrator   And he said,

Joseph   I will do as thou hast said.

Narrator   31 And he said,

Jacob   Swear unto me.

Narrator   And he sware unto him. And Israel bowed himself upon the bed's head [at the head of the bed].

Reference: Gen. 47:27-31

JACOB CLAIMS JOSEPH'S TWO SONS AS HIS
[168]

Narrator	AND it came to pass after these things, that one told Joseph,	Gen. 48:1-7
Person	Behold, thy father is sick:	Egypt

Narrator and he took with him his two sons, Manasseh and Ephraim.

2 And one told Jacob, and said,   Land of Goshen

Person Behold, thy son Joseph cometh unto thee:

Narrator and Israel strengthened himself, and sat upon the bed. 3 And Jacob said unto Joseph,

Jacob God Almighty appeared unto me at Luz [Beth-el] in the land of Canaan, and blessed me, 4 And said unto me,

God Behold, I will make thee fruitful, and multiply thee, and I will make of thee a multitude of people; and will give this land to thy seed after thee for an everlasting possession.

Jacob 5 And now, *of* thy two sons, Ephraim and Manasseh, which were born unto thee in the land of Egypt before I came unto thee into Egypt; *behold, they* are mine, *and the God of my fathers shall bless them; even* as Reuben and Simeon, they shall be *blessed, for they are* mine; *wherefore they shall be called after my name. (Therefore they were called Israel.)*

6 And thy issue which thou begettest after them, shall be thine, and shall be called after the name of their brethren in their inheritance, *in the tribes;*

Narrator *therefore they were called the tribes of Manasseh and of Ephraim. And Jacob said unto Joseph,*

Jacob *When the God of my fathers appeared unto me in Luz, in the land of Canaan; he sware unto me, that he would give unto me, and unto my seed, the land for an everlasting possession.*

Therefore, O my son, he hath blessed me in raising thee up to be a servant unto me, in saving my house from death; In delivering my people, thy brethren, from famine which was sore in the land; wherefore the God of thy fathers shall bless thee, and the fruit of thy loins, that they shall be blessed above thy brethren, and above thy father's house;

For thou hast prevailed, and thy father's house hath bowed down unto thee, even as it was shown unto thee, before thou wast sold into Egypt by the hands of thy brethren; wherefore thy brethren shall bow down unto thee, from generation to generation, unto the fruit of thy loins forever;

For thou shalt be a light unto my people, to deliver them in the days of their captivity, from bondage; and to bring salvation unto them, when they are altogether bowed down under sin.

Jacob   7 And as for me, when I came from Padan, Rachel died by me in   Gen. 48:1-7
the land of Canaan in the way, when yet there was but a little way   Land of Goshen
to come unto Ephrath: and I buried her there in the way of Ephrath;
the same is Beth-lehem.

Reference: Gen. 48:1-7

JACOB SETS EPHRAIM BEFORE MANASSEH
[169]

Narrator	AND Israel beheld Joseph's sons, and said,	Gen. 48:8-22
Jacob	Who are these?	Land of Goshen

Narrator 9 And Joseph said unto his father,

Joseph They are my sons, whom God hath given me in this place.

Narrator And he said,

Jacob Bring them, I pray thee, unto me, and I will bless them.

Narrator 10 Now the eyes of Israel were dim for age, so that he could not see. And he brought them near unto him; and he kissed them, and embraced them. 11 And Israel said unto Joseph,

Jacob I had not thought to see thy face: and, lo, God hath shewed me also thy seed.

Narrator 12 And Joseph brought them out from between his knees, and he bowed himself with his face to the earth. 13 And Joseph took them both, Ephraim in his right hand toward Israel's left hand, and Manasseh in his left hand toward Israel's right hand, and brought them near unto him. 14 And Israel stretched out his right hand, and laid it upon Ephraim's head, who was the younger, and his left hand upon Manasseh's head, guiding [crossing] his hands wittingly; for Manasseh was the firstborn. 15 And he blessed Joseph [them], and said,

Jacob God, before whom my fathers Abraham and Isaac did walk, the God which fed [shepherded] me all my life long unto this day, 16 The Angel which redeemed me from all evil, bless the lads; and let my name be named on them, and the name of my fathers Abraham and Isaac; and let them grow into a multitude in the midst of the earth.

Narrator 17 And when Joseph saw that his father laid his right hand upon the head of Ephraim, it displeased him [it was wrong in his eyes]: and he held up his father's hand, to remove it from Ephraim's head unto Manasseh's head. 18 And Joseph said unto his father,

Joseph Not so, my father: for this is the firstborn; put thy right hand upon his head.

Narrator 19 And his father refused, and said,

Jacob I know it, my son, I know it: he also shall become a people, and he also shall be great: but truly his younger brother shall be greater than he, and his seed shall become a multitude of nations.

Narrator 20 And he blessed them that day, saying,

Jacob	In [through] thee shall Israel bless [be blessed],	Gen. 48:8-22
Narrator	saying,	Land of Goshen
Jacob	God make thee as Ephraim and as Manasseh:	

Narrator   and he set Ephraim before Manasseh. 21 And Israel said unto Joseph,

Jacob   Behold, I die: but God shall be with you, and bring you again unto the land of your fathers. 22 Moreover I have given to thee one portion above thy brethren, which I took out of the hand of the Amorite with my sword and with my bow.

Reference: Gen. 48:8-22

JACOB BLESSES SONS AND PREDICTS FUTURE
[170]

Narrator AND Jacob called unto his sons, and said,

Gen. 49:1-28

Land of Goshen

Jacob Gather yourselves together, that I may tell you that which shall befall you in the last days. 2 Gather yourselves together, and hear, ye sons of Jacob; and hearken unto Israel your father.

3 Reuben, thou art my firstborn, my might, and the beginning of my strength, the excellency of dignity, and the excellency of power: 4 Unstable as water, thou shalt not excel; because thou wentest up to thy father's bed; then defiledst thou it: he went up to my couch.

5 Simeon and Levi are brethren; instruments of cruelty are in their habitations. 6 O my soul, come not thou into their secret; unto their assembly, mine honour, be not thou united: for in their anger they slew a man, and in their selfwill they digged down a wall. 7 Cursed be their anger, for it was fierce; and their wrath, for it was cruel: I will divide them in Jacob, and scatter them in Israel.

8 Judah, thou art he whom thy brethren shall praise: thy hand shall be in the neck of thine enemies; thy father's children shall bow down before thee. 9 Judah is a lion's whelp: from the prey, my son, thou art gone up: he stooped down, he couched as a lion, and as an old lion; who shall rouse him up? 10 The sceptre shall not depart from Judah, nor a lawgiver from between his feet, until Shiloh* come; and unto him shall the gathering of the people be. 11 Binding his foal unto the vine, and his ass's colt unto the choice vine; he washed his garments in wine, and his clothes in the blood of grapes: 12 His eyes shall be red with wine, and his teeth white with milk.

13 Zebulun shall dwell at the haven of the sea; and he shall be for an haven of ships; and his border shall be unto Zidon.

14 Isaachar is a strong ass couching down between two burdens: 15 And he saw that rest was good, and the land that it was pleasant; and bowed his shoulder to bear, and became a servant unto tribute.

16 Dan shall judge his people, as one of the tribes of Israel. 17 Dan shall be a serpent by the way, an adder in the path, that biteth the horse heels, so that his rider shall fall backward. 18 I have waited for thy salvation, O LORD.

19 Gad, a troop shall overcome him: but he shall overcome at the last.

20 Out of Asher his bread shall be fat, and he shall yield royal dainties.

21 Naphtali is a hind let loose: he giveth goodly words.

22 Joseph is a fruitful bough, even a fruitful bough by a well; whose branches run over the wall: 23 The archers have sorely grieved him, and shot at him, and hated him: 24 But his bow abode in strength, and the arms of his hands were made strong by the hands of the mighty God of Jacob; (from thence is the shepherd**,

Jacob

the stone of Israel:) 25 Even by the God of thy father, who shall help thee; and by the Almighty, who shall bless thee with blessings of heaven above, blessings of the deep that lieth under, blessings of the breasts, and of the womb: 26 The blessings of thy father have prevailed above the blessings of my progenitors unto the utmost bound of the everlasting hills: they shall be on the head of Joseph, and on the crown of the head of him that was separate from his brethren.

27 Benjamin shall ravin as a wolf: in the morning he shall devour the prey, and at night he shall divide the spoil.

Gen. 49:1-28

Land of Goshen

Narrator

28 All these are the twelve tribes of Israel: and this is it that their father spake unto them, and blessed them; every one according to his blessing he blessed them.

Reference: Gen. 49:1-28

* The Hebrew word shiloh may be a short form of asher-lo, which can be rendered "whose right it is."

** It is from the lineage of Jacob that the Messiah comes.

JACOB DIES IN EGYPT
[171]

Narrator | AND he [Jacob] charged them, and said unto them,

Gen. 49:29-33

Land of Goshen

Jacob | I am to be gathered unto my people: bury me with my fathers in the cave that is in the field of Ephron the Hittite, 30 In the cave that is in the field of Machpelah, which is before Mamre, in the land of Canaan, which Abraham bought with the field of Ephron the Hittite for a possession of a buryingplace. 31 There they buried Abraham and Sarah his wife; there they buried Isaac and Rebekah his wife; and there I buried Leah. 32 The purchase of the field and of the cave that is therein was from the children of Heth.

Narrator | 33 And when Jacob had made an end of commanding his sons, he gathered up his feet into the bed, and yielded up the ghost, and was gathered unto his people.

Reference: Gen. 49:29-33

MANY RETURN TO CANAAN TO BURY JACOB
[172]

Narrator   AND Joseph fell upon his father's face, and wept upon him,   Gen. 50:1-13
and kissed him. 2 And Joseph commanded his servants the   Land of Goshen
physicians to embalm his father: and the physicians
embalmed Israel. 3 And forty days were fulfilled for him; for
so are fulfilled the days of those which are embalmed: and
the Egyptians mourned for him threescore and ten days.
4 And when the days of his mourning were past, Joseph
spake unto the house of Pharaoh, saying,

Joseph   If now I have found grace in your eyes, speak, I pray you, in the
ears of Pharaoh, saying, 5 My father made me swear, saying,

Jacob   Lo, I die: in my grave which I have digged for me in the land of
Canaan, there shalt thou bury me.

Joseph   Now therefore let me go up, I pray thee, and bury my father, and I
will come again.

Narrator   6 And Pharaoh said,

Pharaoh   Go up, and bury thy father, according as he made thee swear.

Narrator   7 And Joseph went up to bury his father: and with him went
up all the servants of Pharaoh, the elders of his house, and
all the elders of the land of Egypt, 8 And all the house of
Joseph, and his brethren, and his father's house: only their
little ones, and their flocks, and their herds, they left in the
land of Goshen. 9 And there went up with him both chariots
and horsemen: and it was a very great company.

10 And they came to the threshingfloor of Atad, which is   Land of Canaan
beyond Jordan, and there they mourned with a great and
very sore lamentation: and he made a mourning for his
father seven days. 11 And when the inhabitants of the land,
the Canaanites, saw the mourning in the floor of Atad, they
said,

Inhabitants   This is a grievous mourning to the Egyptians:

Narrator   wherefore the name of it was called Abel-mizraim [The
mourning of the Egyptians], which is beyond Jordan. 12 And
his sons did unto him according as he commanded them:

13 For his sons carried him into the land of Canaan, and   Hebron
buried him in the cave of the field of Machpelah, which
Abraham bought with the field for a possession of a
buryingplace of Ephron the Hittite, before Mamre.

Reference: Gen. 50:1-13

JOSEPH FORGIVES HIS BROTHERS
[173]

Narrator	AND Joseph returned into Egypt, he, and his brethren, and all that went up with him to bury his father, after he had buried his father. 15 And when Joseph's brethren saw that their father was dead, they said,

Gen. 50:14-21

Egypt

Brethren

> Joseph will peradventure hate us, and will certainly requite us all the evil which we did unto him [If Joseph bears a grudge against us he will certainly repay us].

Narrator

16 And they sent a messenger unto Joseph, saying,

Messenger

> Thy father did command before he died, saying, 17 So shall ye say unto Joseph,

Jacob

>> Forgive, I pray thee now, the trespass of thy brethren, and their sin; for they did unto thee evil:

Brethren

> and now, we pray thee, forgive the trespass of the servants of the God of thy father.

Narrator

And Joseph wept when they spake unto him. 18 And his brethren also went and fell down before his face; and they said,

Brethren

> Behold, we be thy servants.

Narrator

19 And Joseph said unto them,

Joseph

> Fear not: for am I in the place of God? 20 But as for you, ye thought evil against me; but God meant it unto good, to bring to pass, as it is this day, to save much people alive. 21 Now therefore fear ye not: I will nourish you, and your little ones.

Narrator

And he comforted them, and spake kindly unto them.

Reference: Gen. 50:14-21

JOSEPH FORESEES MOSES AND JOSEPH SMITH
[174]

Narrator AND Joseph dwelt in Egypt, he, and his father's house: and   Gen. 50:22-26
Joseph lived an hundred and ten years. 23 And Joseph saw   Egypt
Ephraim's children of the third generation: the children also
of Machir the son of Manasseh were brought up upon
Joseph's knees. 24 And Joseph said unto his brethren,

Joseph I die, *and go unto my fathers; and I go down to my grave with joy.*
The God of my father Jacob be with you, to deliver you out of
affliction in the days of your bondage; for the Lord hath visited me,
and I have obtained a promise of the Lord, that out of the fruit of
my loins, the Lord God will raise up a righteous branch out of my
loins; and unto thee, whom my father Jacob hath named Israel, a
prophet [Moses]; (not the Messiah who is called Shilo;) and this
prophet shall deliver my people out of Egypt in the days of thy
bondage.

And it shall come to pass that they shall be scattered again; and a
branch shall be broken off, and shall be carried into a far country;
nevertheless they shall be remembered in the covenants of the
Lord, when the Messiah cometh; for he shall be made manifest
unto them in the latter days, in the Spirit of power; and shall bring
them out of darkness into light; out of hidden darkness, and out of
captivity unto freedom.

A seer [Joseph Smith] shall the Lord my God raise up, who shall
be a choice seer unto the fruit of my loins. Thus saith the Lord God
of my fathers unto me,

God *A choice seer [Joseph Smith] will I raise up out of the fruit of*
thy loins, and he shall be esteemed highly among the fruit of thy
loins; and unto him will I give commandment that he shall do a
work for the fruit of thy loins, his brethren. And he shall bring
them to the knowledge of the covenants which I have made with
thy fathers; and he shall do whatsoever work I shall command
him.

And I will make him great in mine eyes, for he shall do my
work; and he shall be great like unto him [Moses] whom I have
said I would raise up unto you, to deliver my people, O house of
Israel, out of the land of Egypt; for a seer will I raise up to
deliver my people out of the land of Egypt; and he shall be
called Moses. And by this name he shall know that he is of thy
house; for he shall be nursed by the king's daughter, and shall
be called her son.

And again, a seer [Joseph Smith] will I raise up out of the fruit
of thy loins, and unto him will I give power to bring forth my
word unto the seed of thy loins; and not to the bringing forth of
my word only, saith the Lord, but to the convincing them of my
word, which shall have already gone forth among them in the
last days;

Wherefore the fruit of thy loins shall write, and the fruit of the
loins of Judah shall write; and that which shall be written by the

God   *fruit of thy loins, and also that which shall be written by the*   Gen. 50:22-26
fruit of the loins of Judah, shall grow together unto the   Egypt
confounding of false doctrines, and laying down of contentions,
and establishing peace among the fruit of thy loins, and
bringing them to a knowledge of their fathers in the latter days;
and also to the knowledge of my covenants, saith the Lord. And
out of weakness shall he [Joseph Smith] be made strong, in that
day when my work shall go forth among all my people, which
shall restore them, who are of the house of Israel, in the last
days.

And that seer [Joseph Smith] will I bless, and they that seek to
destroy him shall be confounded; for this promise I give unto
you; for I will remember you from generation to generation;
and his name shall be called Joseph, and it shall be after the
name of his father; and he shall be like unto you; for the thing
which the Lord shall bring forth by his hand shall bring my
people unto salvation.

Narrator   *And the Lord sware unto Joseph that he would preserve his*
seed forever, saying,

The Lord   *I will raise up Moses, and a rod shall be in his hand, and he shall*
gather together my people, and he shall lead them as a flock, and
he shall smite the waters of the Red Sea with his rod. And he shall
have judgment, and shall write the word of the Lord. And he shall
not speak many words, for I will write unto him my law by the
finger of mine own hand. And I will make a spokesman for him,
and his name shall be called Aaron.

And it shall be done unto thee in the last days also, even as I have
sworn.

Narrator   *Therefore, Joseph said unto his brethren,*

Joseph   God will surely visit you, and bring you out of this land unto the
land which he sware to Abraham, to Isaac, and to Jacob.

Narrator   25 And Joseph *confirmed many other things unto his*
brethren, and took an oath of the children of Israel, saying,

Joseph   God will surely visit you, and ye shall carry up my bones from
hence.

Narrator   26 So Joseph died *when he was* an hundred and ten years   Shechem
old; *and they embalmed him, and they put him in a coffin in*
Egypt; and he was kept from burial by the children of Israel,
that he might be carried up and laid in the sepulchre with
his father*. And thus they remembered the oath which they
sware unto him.

Reference: Gen. 50:22-26

* The Book of Joshua states that Joseph's remains were buried in
Shechem (Josh. 24:32). According to some traditions, Ephraim and
Manasseh, Joseph's sons, were buried with him.

MOSES

GOD remembered his covenant with Abraham, with Isaac, and with Jacob. Saying: I am the Lord God Almighty, and Endless is my name; for I am without beginning of days or end of years; and is not this endless? And, behold, thou art my son [Moses]; wherefore look, and I will show thee the workmanship of mine hands; but not all, for my works are without end, and also my words, for they never cease.

EXODUS 2:24; MOSES 1:3-4

CHILDREN OF ISRAEL MULTIPLY IN EGYPT
[175]

Narrator NOW these are the names of the children of Israel, which   Ex. 1:1-7
came into Egypt [with Jacob]; every man and his household   Egypt
came with Jacob.

2 Reuben, Simeon, Levi, and Judah, 3 Isaachar, Zebulun, and
Benjamin, 4 Dan, and Naphtali, Gad, and Asher.

5 And all the souls that came out of the loins of Jacob were
seventy souls: for Joseph was in Egypt already. 6 And
Joseph died, and all his brethren, and all that generation.

7 And the children of Israel were fruitful, and increased
abundantly, and multiplied, and waxed [grew] exceeding
mighty; and the land was filled with them.

Reference: Ex. 1:1-7

TASKMASTERS AFFLICT ISRAELITES
[176]

Narrator NOW there arose up a new king over Egypt, which knew not Joseph. 9 And he said unto his people,

Ex. 1:8-14

Egypt

King of Egypt (Pharaoh) Behold, the people of the children of Israel are more and mightier than we: 10 Come on, let us deal wisely with them; lest they multiply, and it come to pass, that, when there falleth [breaks] out any war, they join also unto our enemies, and fight against us, and so get them up out of the land.

Narrator 11 Therefore they did set over them taskmasters to afflict them with their burdens. And they built for Pharaoh treasure [storage] cities, Pithom and Raamses. 12 But the more they afflicted them, the more they multiplied and grew. And they were grieved [apprehensive] because of the children of Israel. 13 And the Egyptians made the children of Israel to serve with rigour: 14 And they made their lives bitter with hard bondage [labor], in mortar, and in brick, and in all manner of service in the field: all their service, wherein they made them serve, was with rigour.

Reference: Ex. 1:8-14

PHARAOH SEEKS TO DESTROY ISRAELITE SONS
[177]

Narrator	AND the king of Egypt spake to the Hebrew midwives, of which the name of the one was Shiphrah, and the name of the other Puah: 16 And he said,	Ex. 1:15-22 Egypt

Pharaoh

When ye do [serve as] the office of a midwife to the Hebrew women, and see them upon the stools [birth-stools]; if it be a son, then ye shall kill him: but if it be a daughter, then she shall live.

Narrator

17 But the midwives feared God, and did not as the king of Egypt commanded them, but saved the men children alive. 18 And the king of Egypt called for the midwives, and said unto them,

Pharaoh

Why have ye done this thing, and have saved the men children alive?

Narrator

19 And the midwives said unto Pharaoh,

Midwives

Because the Hebrew women are not as the Egyptian women; for they are lively, and are delivered ere the midwives come in unto them.

Narrator

20 Therefore God dealt well with the midwives: and the people multiplied, and waxed very mighty.

21 And it came to pass, because the midwives feared [revered] God, that he made them houses [households (descendants)]. 22 And Pharaoh charged all his people, saying,

Pharaoh

Every son that is born [to the Hebrews] ye shall cast into the river, and every daughter ye shall save alive.

Reference: Ex. 1:15-22

MOSES BORN TO LEVITE FAMILY
[178]

Narrator	AND there went a man of the house of Levi, and took to wife a daughter of Levi. 2 And the woman conceived, and bare a son: and when she saw him that he was a goodly child, she hid him three months.

Ex. 2:1-10
Egypt

3 And when she could not longer hide him, she took for him an ark of bulrushes, and daubed it with slime and with pitch, and put the child therein; and she laid it in the flags [among the reeds] by the river's brink. 4 And his sister stood afar off, to wit [to know, or learn] what would be done to him.

5 And the daughter of Pharaoh came down to wash herself at the river; and her maidens walked along by the river's side; and when she saw the ark among the flags, she sent her maid to fetch it. 6 And when she had opened it, she saw the child: and, behold, the babe wept. And she had compassion on him, and said,

Daughter   This is one of the Hebrews' children.

Narrator   7 Then said his sister to Pharaoh's daughter,

Moses' Sister   Shall I go and call to thee a nurse of the Hebrew women, that she may nurse the child for thee?

Narrator   8 And Pharaoh's daughter said to her,

Daughter   Go.

Narrator   And the maid went and called the child's mother. 9 And Pharaoh's daughter said unto her,

Daughter   Take this child away, and nurse it for me, and I will give thee thy wages.

Narrator   And the woman took the child, and nursed it. 10 And the child grew, and she brought him unto Pharaoh's daughter, and he became her son. And she called his name Moses*: and she said,

Daughter   Because I drew him out of the water.

Reference: Ex. 2:1-10

* In Egyptian "To beget a child" and in Hebrew "To draw out."

MOSES MARRIES ZIPPORAH
[179]

Narrator	AND it came to pass in those days, when Moses was grown, that he went out unto his brethren, and looked on their burdens: and he spied an Egyptian smiting an Hebrew, one of his brethren. 12 And he looked this way and that way, and when he saw that there was no man, he slew the Egyptian, and hid him in the sand. 13 And when he went out the second day, behold, two men of the Hebrews strove together: and he said to him that did the wrong,	Ex. 2:11-22 Land of Goshen

Moses   Wherefore smitest thou thy fellow?

Narrator   14 And he said,

Hebrew Man   Who made thee a prince and a judge over us? intendest thou to kill me, as thou killedst the Egyptian?

Narrator   And Moses feared, and said,

Moses   Surely this thing is known.

Narrator   15 Now when Pharaoh heard this thing, he sought to slay Moses. But Moses fled from the face [presence] of Pharaoh, and dwelt in the land of Midian: and he sat down by a well.   Land of Midian

16 Now the priest of Midian had seven daughters: and they came and drew water, and filled the troughs to water their father's flock. 17 And the shepherds came and drove them away: but Moses stood up and helped them, and watered their flock. 18 And when they came to Reuel their father, he said,

Jethro (Reuel)   How is it that ye are come so soon to day?

Narrator   19 And they said,

Daughters   An Egyptian delivered us out of the hand of the shepherds, and also drew water enough for us, and watered the flock.

Narrator   20 And he said unto his daughters,

Jethro (Reuel)   And where is he? why is it that ye have left the man? call him, that he may eat bread.

Narrator   21 And Moses was content to dwell with the man: and he gave Moses Zipporah his daughter. 22 And she bare him a son, and he called his name Gershom [a sojourner there]: for he said,

Moses   I have been a stranger in a strange land.

Reference: Ex. 2:11-22

ISRAELITES PRAY FOR RELIEF
[180]

Narrator AND it came to pass in process of time, that the king of   Ex. 2:23-25
Egypt died: and the children of Israel sighed by reason of   Land of Goshen
the bondage, and they cried, and their cry came up unto God
by reason of the bondage. 24 And God heard their groaning,
and God remembered his covenant with Abraham, with
Isaac, and with Jacob. 25 And God looked upon the children
of Israel, and God had respect unto [knew] them.

Reference: Ex. 2:23-25

MOSES SEES AND TALKS WITH GOD
[181]

Narrator	NOW Moses kept the flock of Jethro his father in law, the priest of Midian: and he led the flock to the backside of the desert, and came to the mountain of God, even to Horeb.	Ex. 3:1-6 Near Land of Midian
	2 And the *presence* of the LORD appeared unto him in a flame of fire out of the midst of a bush: and he looked, and, behold, the bush burned with fire, and the bush was not consumed. 3 And Moses said,	Mountain
Moses	I will now turn aside, and see this great sight, why the bush is not burnt.	
Narrator	4 And when the LORD saw that he turned aside to see, God called unto him out of the midst of the bush, and said,	
God	Moses, Moses.	
Narrator	And he said,	
Moses	Here am I.	
Narrator	5 And he said,	
God	Draw not nigh hither: put off thy shoes from off thy feet, for the place whereon thou standest is holy ground.	
Narrator	6 Moreover he said,	
God	I am the God of thy father, the God of Abraham, the God of Isaac, and the God of Jacob.	
Narrator	And Moses hid his face; for he was afraid to look upon God.	

Reference: Ex. 3:1-6

MOSES SHOWN WORKS OF GOD
[182]

Narrator THE words of God, which he spake unto Moses at a time when Moses was caught up into an exceedingly high mountain, 2 And he saw God face to face, and he talked with him, and the glory of God was upon Moses; therefore Moses could endure his presence. 3 And God spake unto Moses, saying:

Moses 1:1-8
Mountain

God Behold, I am the Lord God Almighty, and Endless is my name; for I am without beginning of days or end of years; and is not this endless? 4 And, behold, thou art my son; wherefore look, and I will show thee the workmanship of mine hands; but not all, for my works are without end, and also my words, for they never cease. 5 Wherefore, no man can behold all my works, except he behold all my glory; and no man can behold all my glory, and afterwards remain in the flesh on the earth. 6 And I have a work for thee, Moses, my son; and thou art in the similitude of mine Only Begotten; and mine Only Begotten is and shall be the Savior, for he is full of grace and truth; but there is no God beside me, and all things are present with me, for I know them all.

7 And now, behold, this one thing I show unto thee, Moses, my son, for thou art in the world, and now I show it unto thee.

Narrator 8 And it came to pass that Moses looked, and beheld the world upon which he was created; and Moses beheld the world and the ends thereof, and all the children of men which are, and which were created; of the same he greatly marveled and wondered.

Reference: Moses 1:1-8

SATAN APPEARS AND TEMPTS MOSES
[183]

Narrator   AND the presence of God withdrew from Moses, that his   Moses 1:9-23
glory was not upon Moses; and Moses was left unto himself.   Mountain
And as he was left unto himself, he fell unto the earth.
10 And it came to pass that it was for the space of many
hours before Moses did again receive his natural strength
like unto man; and he said unto himself:

Moses   Now, for this cause I know that man is nothing, which thing I never
had supposed. 11 But now mine own eyes have beheld God; but not
my natural, but my spiritual eyes, for my natural eyes could not
have beheld; for I should have withered and died in his presence;
but his glory was upon me; and I beheld his face, for I was
transfigured before him.

Narrator   12 And it came to pass that when Moses had said these
words, behold, Satan came tempting him, saying:

Satan   Moses, son of man, worship me.

Narrator   13 And it came to pass that Moses looked upon Satan and
said:

Moses   Who art thou? For behold, I am a son of God, in the similitude of
his Only Begotten; and where is thy glory, that I should worship
thee? 14 For behold, I could not look upon God, except his glory
should come upon me, and I were transfigured before him. But I
can look upon thee in the natural man. Is it not so, surely?
15 Blessed be the name of my God, for his Spirit hath not
altogether withdrawn from me, or else where is thy glory, for it is
darkness unto me? And I can judge between thee and God; for God
said unto me:

God   Worship God, for him only shalt thou serve.

Moses   16 Get thee hence, Satan; deceive me not; for God said unto me:

God   Thou art after the similitude of mine Only Begotten.

Moses   17 And he also gave me commandments when he called unto me
out of the burning bush, saying:

God   Call upon God in the name of mine Only Begotten, and worship
me.

Narrator   18 And again Moses said:

Moses   I will not cease to call upon God, I have other things to inquire of
him: for his glory has been upon me, wherefore I can judge
between him and thee. Depart hence, Satan.

Narrator   19 And now, when Moses had said these words, Satan cried
with a loud voice, and ranted upon the earth, and
commanded, saying:

Satan	I am the Only Begotten, worship me.	Moses 1:9-23

Mountain

Narrator   20 And it came to pass that Moses began to fear exceedingly; and as he began to fear, he saw the bitterness of hell. Nevertheless, calling upon God, he received strength, and he commanded, saying:

Moses   Depart from me, Satan, for this one God only will I worship, which is the God of glory.

Narrator   21 And now Satan began to tremble, and the earth shook; and Moses received strength, and called upon God, saying:

Moses   In the name of the Only Begotten, depart hence, Satan.

Narrator   22 And it came to pass that Satan cried with a loud voice, with weeping, and wailing, and gnashing of teeth; and he departed hence, even from the presence of Moses, that he beheld him not.

23 And now of this thing Moses bore record; but because of wickedness it is not had among the children of men.

Reference: Moses 1:9-23

MOSES TO DELIVER ISRAEL FROM BONDAGE
[184]

Narrator AND it came to pass that when Satan had departed from the   Moses 1:24-26
presence of Moses, that Moses lifted up his eyes unto   Mountain
heaven, being filled with the Holy Ghost, which beareth
record of the Father and the Son; 25 And calling upon the
name of God, he beheld his glory again, for it was upon
him; and he heard a voice, saying:

God Blessed art thou, Moses, for I, the Almighty, have chosen thee, and
thou shalt be made stronger than many waters; for they shall obey
thy command as if thou wert God. 26 And lo, I am with thee, even
unto the end of thy days; for thou shalt deliver my people from
bondage, even Israel my chosen.

Reference: Moses 1:24-26

MOSES SHOWN IN VISION MANY EARTHS
[185]

Narrator AND it came to pass, as the voice [of God] was still *Moses 1:27-35*
speaking, Moses cast his eyes and beheld the earth, yea, *Mountain*
even all of it; and there was not a particle of it which he did
not behold, discerning it by the Spirit of God. 28 And he
beheld also the inhabitants thereof, and there was not a soul
which he beheld not; and he discerned them by the Spirit of
God; and their numbers were great, even numberless as the
sand upon the sea shore. 29 And he beheld many lands; and
each land was called earth, and there were inhabitants on the
face thereof. 30 And it came to pass that Moses called upon
God, saying:

Moses Tell me, I pray thee, why these things are so, and by what thou
madest them?

Narrator 31 And behold, the glory of the Lord was upon Moses, so
that Moses stood in the presence of God, and talked with
him face to face. And the Lord God said unto Moses:

God For mine own purpose have I made these things. Here is wisdom
and it remaineth in me. 32 And by the word of my power, have I
created them, which is mine Only Begotten Son, who is full of
grace and truth. 33 And worlds without number have I created; and
I also created them for mine own purpose; and by the Son I created
them, which is mine Only Begotten. 34 And the first man of all
men have I called Adam, which is many. 35 But only an account of
this earth, and the inhabitants thereof, give I unto you. For behold,
there are many worlds that have passed away by the word of my
power. And there are many that now stand, and innumerable are
they unto man; but all things are numbered unto me, for they are
mine and I know them.

Reference: Moses 1:27-35

MOSES SHOWN IN VISION THIS EARTH
[186]

Narrator	AND it came to pass that Moses spake unto the Lord, saying:	Moses 1:36-42 Mountain
Moses	Be merciful unto thy servant, O God, and tell me concerning this earth, and the inhabitants thereof, and also the heavens, and then thy servant will be content.	
Narrator	37 And the Lord God spake unto Moses, saying:	
God	The heavens, they are many, and they cannot be numbered unto man; but they are numbered unto me, for they are mine. 38 And as one earth shall pass away, and the heavens thereof even so shall another come; and there is no end to my works, neither to my words.	
	39 For behold, this is my work and my glory—to bring to pass the immortality and eternal life of man.	
	40 And now, Moses, my son, I will speak unto thee concerning this earth upon which thou standest; and thou shalt write the things which I shall speak. 41 And in a day when the children of men shall esteem my words as naught and take many of them from the book which thou shalt write, behold, I will raise up another like unto thee; and they shall be had again among the children of men —among as many as shall believe.	
Narrator	42 (These words were spoken unto Moses in the mount, the name of which shall not be known among the children of men. And now they are spoken unto you. Show them not unto any except them that believe. Even so. Amen.)	

Reference: Moses 1:36-42

EPILOGUE
THE COVENANTS OF OUR FATHERS

The historical events within this harmony end with the children of Israel preparing to escape bondage in Egypt under the charge of Moses (a Levite). But the story does not end there. After a 40-year sojourn in the wilderness, the Israelites settled within their covenant or promised land of Canaan (the Holy Land) under the command of Joshua (an Ephraimite). Throughout the remainder of the Old Testament, and within New Testament times, the promised covenants of the Fathers were made available to the House of Israel. Lamentably, the descendants of Jacob often fell into transgression and forfeited their promised blessings. As a result, the destiny of the Israelites became more uncertain as these descendants struggled to uphold their commitments within the everlasting covenant.

THE SCATTERING OF ISRAEL

The transgressions of ancient Israel provoked their scattering by the Lord to the far corners of the world.

> And the Lord shall scatter thee among all people, from the one end of the earth even unto the other; and there thou shalt serve other gods, which neither thou nor thy fathers have known, even wood and stone. (Deuteronomy 28:64)

In 721 B.C. the Assyrians subjugated 10 of the 12 tribes of Israel. They are known as the Northern Kingdom or the "ten lost tribes." This substantial group of wayward Israelites had been led by king Jeroboam (an Ephraimite). They were taken as captives into Assyria and later migrated into the north countries of Europe and Asia where their descendants eventually scattered to more distant locations. The remaining tribes— basically Judah and part of Benjamin and a few from other tribes, such as Ephraim and Manasseh—stayed behind in the covenant land of Canaan under the rule of king Rehoboam (a descendant of Judah).

Obedient to the Lord's command, Lehi and Ishmael's families fled the land of Jerusalem in 600 B.C. and were led to the North American continent where they established a righteous branch of Israel and inherited a new promised land. They were descendants of Joseph through Ephraim and Manasseh. At about the same time, other "natural branches" of the House of Israel were led to "nethermost" parts of the earth (Jacob 5:8-28, 38-46). This migration of the Book of Mormon people and others allowed them to escape Jerusalem before the pending destruction of the city and its Temple—which was brought about by the wickedness of the people.

Some 14 years later (586 B.C.), the Babylonians destroyed Jerusalem and annihilated most of its Jewish inhabitants. The surviving remnant of Judah was taken by their captors to Babylon in the lands we today call Iraq. After 70 years, these exiled Jews were allowed to return to Jerusalem and rebuild the city and the Temple. Their descendants were among those living in the land of Jerusalem during the Savior's ministry.

The Lord prophesied at the time of his ministry that within a few years, because of transgression and the breaking of the covenants, Jerusalem and its Temple once more would be destroyed and the inhabitants would suffer an "abomination of desolation" as spoken by Daniel the prophet (Matthew 24:15). In fulfillment of this prediction, the Romans in A.D. 70 seized Jerusalem and killed nearly all its Jewish inhabitants. The few Jews who escaped the carnage scattered into Europe and beyond. Over the last two thousand years their descendants have migrated to widespread locations in Russia, England, the United States and in nearly all countries. The scattering of these exiled Jews is called the "diaspora." Through many centuries, these scattered descendants of Judah never forgot their lineage nor their heritage, whereas the dispersed descendants of the banished 10 tribes of Israel (a goodly number were of Ephraim) soon forgot their storied past and covenanted lineage.

THE GATHERING OF ISRAEL

The restoration of the gospel beginning in 1830 ushered in the fulness of the gospel through the renewal of the new and everlasting covenant and the fulfillment of the Lord's promise to gather Israel in the last days. These pivotal events were set in motion by the restoration of the priesthood and its keys by John the Baptist, Peter James and John, Moses, Adam, Elijah, Elias and others representing past dispensations and covenants (Doctrine and Covenants 110:11-16; 128:18-21). Missionary work became the vehicle to reach out to the descendants of the House of Israel and others. Joseph Smith stated:

> "We believe in the literal gathering of Israel and in the restoration of the Ten Tribes; … . (Article of Faith 10)

The process of gathering continues to this day, primarily into the Stakes of Zion. The pronouncing of Patriarchal Blessings is the way we declare ones lineage within the tribes of Israel. The Lord affirmed:

> And for this cause, that men might be made partakers of the glories which were to be revealed, the Lord sent forth the fulness of his gospel, his everlasting covenant, reasoning in plainness and simplicity— (Doctrine and Covenants 133:57)

The scriptures, both modern and ancient, are the means for teaching the everlasting covenant and its role in the eternal salvation of mankind through the atonement of Jesus Christ. The scriptures—the Old Testament, the New Testament, the Book of Mormon: Another Testament of Jesus Christ and the Doctrine and Covenants—all carry the name "Covenant" or "Testament" in their titles. The word "Testament" represents a Hebrew word meaning covenant—the everlasting covenant. Indeed, a major purpose of the Book of Mormon,

> ... is to show unto the remnant of the House of Israel what great things the Lord hath done for their fathers; and that they may know the covenants of the Lord, that they are not cast off forever — (Title Page)

The prophet Jeremiah (a contemporary of Lehi) prophesied the eminent role of the gathering of Israel in our day and the all-important fulfillment of the covenants made to the fathers:

> Therefore, behold, the days come, saith the Lord, that it shall no more be said, The Lord liveth, that brought up the children of Israel out of the land of Egypt; But, The Lord liveth, that brought up the children of Israel from the land of the north, and from all the lands whither he had driven them: and I will bring them again into their land that I gave unto their fathers. (Jeremiah 16:14-15)

Today, the covenants and promises made to our fathers (the new and everlasting covenant) have been restored for the blessing of God's children. Temples around the world have been provided for the bestowal of these covenants through ordinances.

> And this shall be our covenant—that we will walk in all the ordinances of the Lord. (Doctrine and Covenants 136:4)

The study helps in the LDS scriptures—Bible Dictionary, Guide to the Scriptures, Topical Guide, Index to Triple Combination, Maps and Photographs—contain extensive information about "our fathers" and the restoration of the new and everlasting covenant. This information can be readily searched through electronic scriptures. We suggest this is best accomplished in the Classic electronic version of the LDS scriptures. The website can be found at:

http://classic.scriptures.lds.org

This site was developed with advanced search engines, including a powerful Topic Search system, as well as innovative formatting for printing. We suggest users consult the help files on the website. We use this site for our scripture projects including this book.

APPENDIX

THE LINEAGE OF OUR FATHERS

The following two-page chart shows the lineage of our fathers from Adam to Moses. The eight "fathers" represented by the major sections of this book are shown in bold: Adam, Enoch, Noah, Abraham, Isaac, Jacob, Joseph and Moses. Their wives and daughters are indicated with a gray background.

The Lord covenanted with Abraham that his posterity over time would became exceedingly numerous and bless the nations of the earth.

> That in blessing I will bless thee, and in multiplying I will multiply thy seed as the stars of the heaven, and as the sand which is upon the sea shore; and thy seed shall possess the gate of his enemies; And in thy seed shall all the nations of the earth be blessed; because thou hast obeyed my voice. (Genesis 22:17-18)

Today, the Lord has declared that we—His sons and daughters—are indeed literal descendants of Abraham, Isaac and Jacob with the sacred responsibility to continue the covenants made to our fathers and to bless all nations through His priesthood.

> Therefore, thus saith the Lord unto you, with whom the priesthood hath continued through the lineage of your fathers— For ye are lawful heirs, according to the flesh, and have been hid from the world with Christ in God— Therefore your life and the priesthood have remained, and must needs remain through you and your lineage until the restoration of all things spoken by the mouths of all the holy prophets since the world began. Therefore, blessed are ye if ye continue in my goodness, a light unto the Gentiles, and through this priesthood, a savior unto my people Israel. The Lord hath said it. Amen. (Doctrine and Covenants 86:8-11)

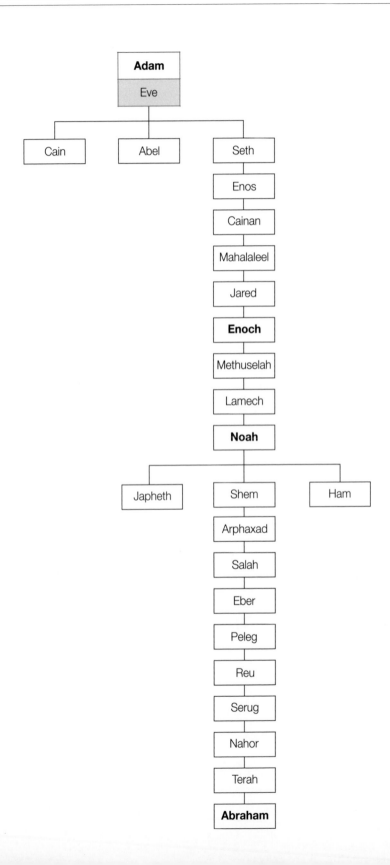

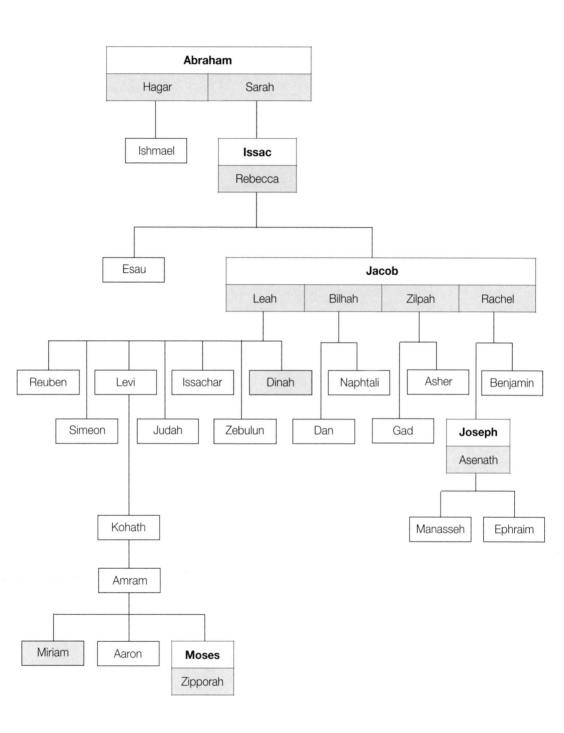

THE TRIBES OF ISRAEL

This chart shows the familial relationships of the 12 sons of Jacob (Israel). Jacob's name was changed by God to Israel and his descendants to this day are known as the House of Israel (see events 121 and 127). The left side lists Jacob's four wives (Leah, Bilhah, Zilpah and Rachel) and their sons. The numbers represent the order of their birth. Dinah is the only daughter of Jacob mentioned in the scriptures. Her mother was Leah. The right side lists the sons who became the 12 tribes of Israel with land inheritances in Canaan (the Holy Land). Note Levi is not listed. His priestly responsibilities under the Aaronic (Levitical) Priesthood precluded a land legacy. Joseph's two sons, Ephraim and Manasseh, were each given land inheritances thus bringing the number of the tribes of Israel to 12.

The names with a gray background are the 10 tribes who were taken by the Assyrians in 721 B.C. and eventually scattered into the northern countries of Europe and Asia. They were led by Jeroboam of the tribe of Ephraim. The tribes of Judah and Benjamin and a few from other tribes remained within the land of Canaan. These two tribes were led by Rehoboam a descendant of Judah (see Epilogue).

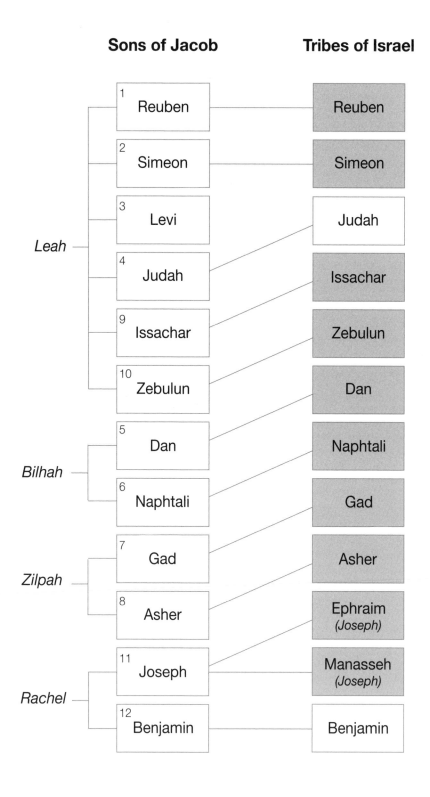

THE LANDS OF OUR FATHERS

This map focuses solely on places of residence prominent in the lives of Abraham, Isaac, Jacob, Joseph and Moses. Understandably, a map centered on Canaan (the Holy Land) does not show the residency locations of Adam, Enoch and Noah. According to scripture, these earlier "fathers" lived before the time of the flood in what is now North America (Doctrine and Covenants 117:8; 116:1; 107:53-57).

Haran—This is where Abraham settled after leaving Ur of the Chaldees. Abraham's family lived in Haran for some time before migrating to the land of Canaan. Issac's servant obtained a wife for Isaac from among Abraham's extended family in Nahor near Haran. Jacob received his four wives from among these same family members. Fully 11 of the 12 sons of Jacob were born in Haran. His twelfth son, Benjamin, was born near Bethlehem. Haran is located in the region of Padan-aram which extends between the Tigris and Euphrates rivers (Mesopotamia) in present-day Turkey.

Shechem—Here Abraham entered the promised land of Canaan and offered sacrifices. Shechem is located 35 miles north of Jerusalem in the plains of Moreh. Jacob acquired land here which he gave to Joseph. The region of Shechem later become part of the land inheritance of the Ephraimites. The physical remains of Joseph, Ephraim and Manasseh were brought from Egypt and buried in Shechem near Jacob's well.

Bethel—The name Bethel means "house of God." It is located 13 miles north of Jerusalem. Here Abraham built his altar after arriving in Canaan. Jacob's dream took place at this location. Abraham and Lot separated in Bethel.

Salem—This place was the home of Melchizedek to whom Abraham paid tithes. Salem was called the city of peace. Here Abraham was asked by God to sacrifice his son Isaac (land of Moriah). Years later, the site became the capital city of Jerusalem under the rule of David, king of Israel, and the location of Solomon's temple.

Hebron—This town is 20 miles south of Jerusalem. Abraham, Isaac and Jacob all lived in Hebron at some time. Abraham built an altar here. His son Ishmael was born in Hebron. Joseph left from Hebron to search for his brothers in Dothan, some 15 miles north of Shechem. Jacob was living in Hebron when his sons were sent to Egypt to buy grain. Later Jacob's entire family moved to Egypt from Hebron. The cave of Machpelah (the tomb of the Patriarchs) was purchased by Abraham in Hebron. Abraham, Isaac and Jacob and their wives were buried in this cave.

Beersheba—At times, Abraham, Isaac and Jacob lived in Beersheba, 50 miles south of Jerusalem. Here an angel appeared to Hagar and God spoke to Isaac. Jacob stopped in Beersheba to offer sacrifices on his journey from Hebron to be with Joseph in Egypt. Abraham and Isaac also resided for a time in Gerar, 20 miles to the west of Beersheba.

Egypt—Joseph was taken to Egypt after being sold by his brothers in Dothan. Here he rose to become Pharaoh's second in command. Jacob's extended family—at Pharaoh's invitation—moved to Egypt from Hebron and settled in the land of Goshen. From here Jacob's descendants, under Moses' direction, escaped the bondage of Pharaoh and wandered for 40 years before entering the land of Canaan to accept their land inheritances, as promised by the Lord.

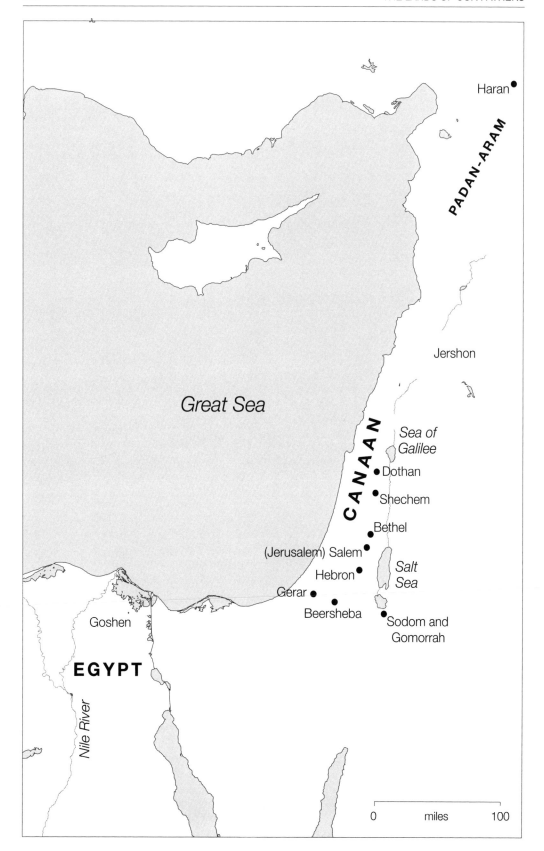

NOTES

NOTES

NOTES

NOTES

NOTES

NOTES

NOTES

A NEW APPROACH TO STUDYING THE SCRIPTURES

After the resurrection of Jesus Christ, the Apostle Peter declared to his people:

> Ye are the children of the prophets, and of the covenant which God made with our fathers, saying unto Abraham, And in thy seed shall all the kindreds of the earth be blessed. (Acts 3:25)

While considering ways of making the covenants of "our fathers" as recorded in the books of Genesis, Moses and Abraham easier to understand, a comprehensive harmony structure and a distinguishing format was devised. It was determined to include all the Joseph Smith Translation (JST) changes. The text formatting has been enhanced by adding wider margins for notes, two type sizes, and spaces between textual subdivisions. These contextual enhancements are designed to help the reader visualize the context, speaker and doctrine of the scripture narrative.

This harmony divides the text into 186 events or episodes. An event-based approach provides an alternate way to read the scripture text without the obvious intrusion of verse and chapter breaks which can obscure the narrative as it was originally written or even the continuity of doctrinal discourses. Short text headings in the margins indicate names of speakers, locational information and other scriptural references. These marginal annotations allow the reader to quickly and consistently place the narrative within "space" and "time."

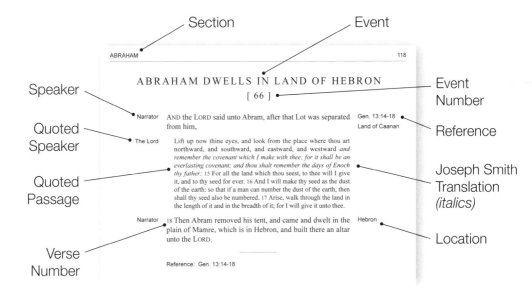

ABOUT THIS EDITION

Starting in the 1980s—as a father and son team—we developed and helped the Church publish the first online edition of the scriptures. Parallel to that project we considered ways to isolate doctrinal precepts by reformatting the scriptures for easier reading and pondering. We also investigated ways to go beyond merely searching electronically for words in the text. We quickly discovered these reformatted editions—emphasizing events rather than chapters—were our preferred way to study.

More than a decade in the making, "The Covenants of Our Fathers" has been a labor of love. We are ever mindful of the long line of record keepers from Adam to Abraham to Moses to Joseph Smith who have made this edition possible. We express appreciation to The Church of Jesus Christ of Latter-day Saints for providing a license to publish the text of the 2013 edition of the scriptures. For more information on other scripture-based publications see our website: www.StudyTheScriptures.com.

We add our testimony to the millions before us that the Old Testament is an account of God's dealing with His covenant people, and its preservation and translation came through the Lord's direction and power. We also testify the Bible, along with other scripture, is a witness of Jesus Christ and contains the gospel doctrines of salvation that lead to joy and happiness.

Lynn A. Rosenvall
David L. Rosenvall

THE OLIVE LEAF FOUNDATION
*An Organization Dedicated to the
Development of Innovative Scripture Study Resources*

www.StudyTheScriptures.com